OXFORD WORLD'S CLASSICS

THOMAS HARDY

Life's Little Ironies

Edited by
ALAN MANFORD

With an Introduction by
NORMAN PAGE

OXFORD
UNIVERSITY PRESS

OXFORD

UNIVERSITY PRESS

Great Clarendon Street, Oxford OX2 6DP

Oxford University Press is a department of the University of Oxford.
It furthers the University's objective of excellence in research, scholarship,
and education by publishing worldwide in

Oxford New York

Athens Auckland Bangkok Bogotá Buenos Aires Calcutta
Cape Town Chennai Dar es Salaam Delhi Florence Hong Kong Istanbul
Karachi Kuala Lumpur Madrid Melbourne Mexico City Mumbai
Nairobi Paris São Paulo Singapore Taipei Tokyo Toronto Warsaw

with associated companies in Berlin Ibadan

Oxford is a registered trade mark of Oxford University Press
in the UK and in certain other countries

Published in the United States
by Oxford University Press Inc., New York

Text, Note on the Text, Select Bibliography, Explanatory Notes
© Alan Manford 1996
Introduction © Norman Page 1996
Preface, Chronology © Simon Gatrell 1985
Appendix B manuscript material reproduced courtesy of Manchester Central Library
Appendix C manuscript material reproduced courtesy of Henry W. and Albert A. Berg
Collection, The New York Public Library, Astor, Lenox and Tilden Foundations

The moral rights of the author have been asserted

Database right Oxford University Press (maker)

First issued as a World's Classics paperback 1996
Reissued as an Oxford World's Classics paperback 1999
Reissued 2008

British Library Cataloguing in Publication Data

Data available

Library of Congress Cataloging in Publication Data
Hardy, Thomas, 1840–1928.
Life's little ironies/Thomas Hardy; edited by Alan Manford;
with an introduction by Norman Page.
p. cm.—(Oxford world's classics)
1. Wessex (England)—Social life and customs—Fiction.
I. Manford, Alan. II. Title. III. Series.
PR4570.L549 1996 823'.8—dc20 95–19679

ISBN 978–0–19–954969–6

4

Printed in Great Britain by
Clays Ltd, St Ives plc

OXFORD WORLD'S CLASSICS

LIFE'S LITTLE IRONIES

THOMAS HARDY was born in Higher Bockhampton, Dorset, on 2 June 1840; his father was a builder in a small way of business, and he was educated locally and in Dorchester before being articled to an architect. After sixteen years in that profession and the publication of his earliest novel *Desperate Remedies* (1871), he determined to make his career in literature; not, however, before his work as an architect had led to his meeting, at St Juliot in Cornwall, Emma Gifford, who became his first wife in 1874.

In the 1860s Hardy had written a substantial amount of unpublished verse, but during the next twenty years almost all his creative effort went into novels and short stories. *Jude the Obscure*, the last written of his novels, came out in 1895, closing a sequence of fiction that includes *Far from the Madding Crowd* (1874), *The Return of the Native* (1878), *Two on a Tower* (1882), *The Mayor of Casterbridge* (1886), and *Tess of the d'Urbervilles* (1891).

Hardy maintained in later life that only in poetry could he truly express his ideas; and the more than nine hundred poems in his collected verse (almost all published after 1898) possess great individuality and power.

In 1910 Hardy was awarded the Order of Merit; in 1912 Emma died and two years later he married Florence Dugdale. Thomas Hardy died in January 1928; the work he left behind—the novels, the poetry, and the epic drama *The Dynasts*—forms one of the supreme achievements in English imaginative literature.

ALAN MANFORD is Head of English at a Birmingham comprehensive school. For his Ph.D. he prepared a critical edition of *A Pair of Blue Eyes*, which novel he has also edited for the Oxford World's Classics. He has published articles and reviews concerning Thomas Hardy.

NORMAN PAGE is Emeritus Professor of Modern English Literature at the University of Nottingham. His books include *Thomas Hardy* (1977), *A. E. Housman: A Critical Biography* (1983), *A Dickens Companion* (1984), and *Tennyson: An Illustrated Life* (1992). He has edited the *Thomas Hardy Annual* and the *Thomas Hardy Journal*, he is a Vice-President of the Thomas Hardy Society, and he has recently edited *The Oxford Reader's Companion to Thomas Hardy*.

OXFORD WORLD'S CLASSICS

*For over 100 years Oxford World's Classics have brought
readers closer to the world's great literature. Now with over 700
titles—from the 4,000-year-old myths of Mesopotamia to the
twentieth century's greatest novels—the series makes available
lesser-known as well as celebrated writing.*

*The pocket-sized hardbacks of the early years contained
introductions by Virginia Woolf, T. S. Eliot, Graham Greene,
and other literary figures which enriched the experience of reading.
Today the series is recognized for its fine scholarship and
reliability in texts that span world literature, drama and poetry,
religion, philosophy and politics. Each edition includes perceptive
commentary and essential background information to meet the
changing needs of readers.*

CONTENTS

ACKNOWLEDGEMENTS

My thanks are due to staff at numerous institutions (most of which hold the primary material I have consulted), in particular: Colin A. McLaren and the staff of Aberdeen University Library ('An Imaginative Woman' MS); Dr Hans E. Braun, Director of the Fondation Martin Bodmer, Bibliotheca Bodmeriana, Geneva ('The Son's Veto' MS); Dr Peter McNiven, The John Rylands University Library, Manchester ('For Conscience' Sake' and 'A Tragedy of Two Ambitions' MSS); the staff of Manchester Central Public Library ('On the Western Circuit' MS); the staff of the Berg Collection, New York Public Library ('Wessex Folk' MS); R. N. R. Peers, Richard de Peyer, and the staff of the Dorset County Museum; the staff of the John Johnson Collection, the Bodleian Library; and the staff of the Department of Manuscripts, the British Library.

I am also indebted to the British Academy for a 'Small Personal Research Grant', which enabled me to travel to study those manuscripts now kept outside England.

This edition has been prepared using various technological aids. Certain editions of the stories have been transferred to computer files by using a Logitech 'ScanMan' and 'CatchWord' character recognition software. Collation of texts has been carried out by means of the CASE software developed by Peter Shillingsburg, to whom my grateful thanks are due.

I would like to dedicate this volume to Peter Davison, who encouraged my early interest in scholarly editing.

A. M.

GENERAL EDITOR'S PREFACE

THE first concern in The World's Classics editions of Hardy's works has been with the texts. Individual editors have compared every version of the novel or stories that Hardy might have revised, and have noted variant readings in words, punctuation, and styling in each of these substantive texts; they have thus been able to exclude much that their experience suggests that Hardy did not intend. In some cases, this is the first time that the work has appeared in a critical edition purged of errors and oversights; where possible Hardy's manuscript punctuation is used, rather than what his compositors thought he should have written.

Some account of the editor's discoveries will be found in the Note on the Text in each volume, while the most interesting revisions their work has revealed are included as an element of the Explanatory Notes. In some cases a Clarendon Press edition of the work provides a wealth of further material for the reader interested in the way Hardy's writing developed from manuscript to final collected edition.

SIMON GATRELL

HARDY'S WESSEX
OF THE NOVELS AND POEMS

0   10   20
Miles

River Thames

Christminster

Lumsdon·

N O R T H

·Alfredston

The Brown House
·Cresscombe
·Marygreen

M I D -

W E S S E X

River Thames

Castle
Royal

Marlbury Downs

Gaymead· ·Aldbrickham

·Kennetbridge

W E S S E X

·Inkpen Beacon

Stoke Barehills·

Quartershot

The Great
Plain

·Weydon
Priors

·Icenway
House

Stonehenge·

U P P E R

Stour Head

·Wintoncester

Leddenton

Melchester

·Fernel Hall

Shaston
Marlott·   ▲Wingreen

·Deansleigh
Park

W E S S E X

The Chase · The Slopes
Trantridge Cross Chaseborough

·Southampton

Stourcastle   Knollingwood Hall

Portsmouth

▲Bulbarrow Shottsford · Lornton
· Forum   Inn

The Great

·Bramshurst

Jintcombe
Ash

·Warborne   Forest
Yewsholt   ·Chene Manor

Solentsea

Weatherbury
·Kingsbere   ·Welland R. Stour

W E S S E X   Egdon Heath

Talbothays·Anglebury ·Kidnapool

·airies Wellbridge

·Sandbourne

The
Island

Nether Minton

well   Corvesgate ·Knollsea

mnd
Cove

Lightship

The   Channel

INTRODUCTION

*Since this Introduction includes references to the plots
of some of the stories, readers may prefer to turn to it
after reading the stories themselves.*

THE time is past, though not very long past, when it was
possible for distinguished critics on both sides of the Atlantic
to refer to Hardy's short stories as 'pot boilers' and 'not worth
salvaging'.[1] The work of scholars and critics in the last two
decades has demonstrated that, far from producing them
perfunctorily or even cynically for the quick profits offered by
magazine editors constantly in quest of material, Hardy took
considerable pains with his stories both before and after their
initial publication. A glance at one of the surviving manuscripts reveals not signs of haste or carelessness but numerous
and scrupulous revisions, and Hardy continued to take a close
interest in the texts of his stories as they passed through
various volume-editions. A case in point in the present volume is 'On the Western Circuit', which shows revisions, sometimes numerous, on every single page of its manuscript
and was again extensively revised after its magazine appearance in bowdlerized form (see Appendix B). He was concerned, moreover, to give shape and coherence to the
collections in which the stories appeared, and *Life's Little
Ironies* reached its final form only after two stories, originally
included, had been removed and another introduced from a
different collection.

None of this sounds like a writer indifferent to his substantial output of shorter fiction. The truth is that Hardy's short
stories deserve to take their place alongside his fourteen novels, nearly a thousand poems, and other works collectively

---

[1] J. I. M. Stewart, *Thomas Hardy: A Critical Biography* (London: Longmans,
1971), 147; Irving Howe, 'A Note on Hardy's Stories', *Hudson Review*, 19
(1966–7), 259.

constituting a massive achievement over nearly seventy years. 'Alongside', however, is not quite the word, for there often exists an intimate relationship, involving patterns of cross-reference, self-allusion, and even self-plagiarism, between Hardy's works in different genres. Hence, just as there are poems that closely parallel passages in the novels, certain themes, situations and characters in the full-length fiction are echoed or anticipated in some of the stories.

Those collected in *Life's Little Ironies* belong to one of the richest periods of the English short story, when major writers such as James, Stevenson, Kipling, and Wilde were publishing some of their best work and a strong supporting cast included such figures as Arthur Morrison, Hubert Crackanthorpe, and 'George Egerton'. It was also, arguably, Hardy's own most richly creative period as a writer of prose: the earliest story in this volume was written in 1888, not long after the appearance of *The Mayor of Casterbridge* and *The Woodlanders*; the larger part of the material first appeared in 1891, the year that saw the publication of *Tess of the d'Urbervilles*; and the last story to be written belongs to 1893, the year in which *Jude the Obscure* was begun. It was a period when Hardy, habitually self-deprecatory concerning his fiction, showed a new-found confidence in his own powers. As he told a correspondent in June 1891, 'Much of my work hitherto has been of a tentative kind, & it is but lately that I have felt any sureness of method'.[2]

At the same time, many of the finest stories are not simply offshoots of the full-length fiction but explore an alternative fictional world to that of the Wessex Novels. In the latter, a stable rural community is characteristically disturbed by the arrival of one or more strangers from a wider, more sophisticated (and often more corrupt) world. In many of the stories, however, this situation is reversed: the outsiders, usually middle-class and moneyed, now occupy the centre of the stage, pushing into the background the smaller communities in which their status is that of visitor or temporary resident. The world of rural occupations, including traditional crafts, is

[2] Richard Little Purdy and Michael Millgate (eds.), *Collected Letters of Thomas Hardy*, i (Oxford: Clarendon Press, 1978), 239.

replaced by that of metropolitan or urban professional or commercial lives; the social order represented by church, manor-house, farm, cottage, and village inn gives way to the seaside lodgings, the railway hotel, the suburban villa. And whereas the Wessex Novels are often set back in time—the main action of *The Mayor of Casterbridge*, for instance, takes place around the mid-century—the stories often sound a distinctly *fin-de-siècle* note.

A good example of this type of story is the one that stands first in the present collection, 'An Imaginative Woman'. Hardy had his own good reasons for placing it at the head of the list, but they were not chronological reasons, since it was probably the last of these stories to be written and certainly the last to achieve magazine publication. Originally included in another volume, it was transferred to *Life's Little Ironies* as late as 1912. The decision to transfer it from the 1896 edition of *Wessex Tales*, where it had also stood first, reflects Hardy's concern to increase the thematic coherence of his collections, but to explain the prominent position granted it in both volumes we must look for more personal motives.

Though the idea for 'An Imaginative Woman' appears to have been derived from his scientific reading, and specifically from August Weismann's *Essays on Heredity*, which he is known to have read in 1890, its emotional power reflects his infatuation with Florence Henniker. He had met her on 19 May 1893 while a guest at the Vice-Regal Lodge in Phoenix Park, Dublin, where she was acting as hostess for her brother, the Lord-Lieutenant of Ireland. The daughter of Lord Houghton, she was herself a writer of fiction and before the end of the year had collaborated with Hardy on a short story, 'The Spectre of the Real'. Several details in 'An Imaginative Woman' are thinly coded allusions to Mrs Henniker: the fictional seaside town of 'Solentsea' is based on Southsea, where she lived for a time; her husband was a professional soldier, and in the story the heroine's husband is a 'small-arms manufacturer' called Marchmill, a name with military (and even military-march) echoes; 'Crewe', the name given to the poet in Hardy's manuscript (later prudentially changed to 'Trewe'), was that of Florence Henniker's mother. The poet's philosophical outlook and extreme sensitivity to hostile criticism reflect those of Hardy himself, while his 'erotic and passionate' poems are perhaps those that Hardy might, in a less intolerant world, have wished to write. Hardy is known to have had a high opinion of this story, but it seems likely that his judgement was not exclusively literary.

Written between Hardy's two greatest marriage novels, *Tess* and *Jude*, 'An Imaginative Woman' concerns a wife trapped in a loveless marriage. The situation resists melodrama in favour of a severe, rather bleak realism: Marchmill is not cruel or brutal, just insensitively unaware of his wife's emotional frustration. She, on the other hand, is of 'nervous' temperament—an epithet anticipating the phrase 'bundle of nerves' that Hardy was to apply to Sue Bridehead and her kind in the 1912 preface to *Jude*—and is poetic and 'imaginative'. (After meeting Florence Henniker, Hardy had described her in his diary as 'a charming, *intuitive* woman'.[3]) Her husband's business as 'gunmaker' seems almost calculated to give offence to her delicate sensibilities, and their home in an affluent suburb of a Midlands city (presumably Hardy has Birmingham in mind) is a painfully incongruous setting for her artistic nature. Another roll of the dice of fate might have cast her lot in London literary circles, like Mrs Henniker herself, but such provincial heartache is, in Hardy's observation, a common enough instance of life's ironies. If we are reminded of Ibsen's heroines eating their hearts out in a comparable social setting, that is no accident, for Hardy had seen *Hedda Gabler* on the London stage in 1891 and saw it again, along with *Rosmersholm* and *The Master Builder*, in June 1893, precisely at the time this story was taking shape in his mind.

From their home in 'a thriving city northwards' the Marchmills visit Wessex—not, however, the relatively isolated and self-contained communities of Hardy's novels, but the crowded seaside resort of Solentsea. There, by what the narrator admits to be 'an odd conjunction' (p. 12), her life intersects with that of a poet whose work she admires and has even

---

[3] Thomas Hardy, *The Life and Work of Thomas Hardy*, ed. Michael Millgate (London: Macmillan, 1984), 270.

imitated. For she has not only written but published poems—though, like many women in her time, under a male pseudonym. What ensues is an unusual variation on the eternal triangle and a kind of spiritual adultery. For the 'conjunction' never becomes physical and, despite several near-misses, the two never meet, though Ella comes as close to physical contact as is possible with a man she has never seen by wearing his clothes (anticipating the scene where Sue puts on Jude's suit) and sleeping in his bed.

This bizarrely but touchingly spiritualized affair has some interesting affinities with the story of another artist, the sculptor Jocelyn Pierston, in Hardy's *The Well-Beloved*, the novel whose first version had been serialized in the closing months of 1892. Terms such as 'dream' and 'reverie', so prominent in the language of that novel, also find a place in 'An Imaginative Woman'. *The Well-Beloved* is a full-length exploration of intense, obsessive but physically unexpressed passion and its relationship to artistic creativity, and the story written a few months later seems to represent a return on Hardy's part to a subject that had deep personal implications.

Like Jocelyn Pierston, and to some extent like Hardy himself, Ella Marchmill projects her intense feelings on an idealized rather than a real object. Robert Langbaum has suggested, indeed, that both she and the poet Robert Trewe 'pursued ideal figures comparable to Jocelyn's Well-Beloved'.[4] Her 'living ardour' reaches its climax when she discovers that the poet has scribbled scraps of verse on the wallpaper as he lay in bed, and she lies where he has rested, her head on his pillow, seeming to feel 'his very breath, warm and loving'. It is a highly erotic scene that this English Emma Bovary—and 'Ella' is not a great distance from 'Emma'—has created out of her own imaginings: 'And now her hair was dragging where his arm had lain when he secured the fugitive fancies; she was sleeping on a poet's lips, immersed in the very essence of him, permeated by his spirit as by an ether' (p. 20). Hardy gives the scene a daring and effective twist when he

[4] Robert Langbaum, *Thomas Hardy in Our Time* (London: Macmillan, 1994), 144.

makes her husband shatter this idyll by returning home unexpectedly and demanding sexual intercourse (a point missed by some of the story's commentators, so tactfully is it hinted by Hardy). Her ensuing pregnancy and childbirth, and the fate of the son she bears, bring this fine story to a compelling ironic conclusion.

'On the Western Circuit' also deals with the obsessive but unfulfilled passion of a woman trapped in a marriage that has become a mockery. Here, however, the sexuality is more explicit—so much so that Hardy was compelled to make extensive and damaging changes before a magazine editor would print it. Also prominent is the effect of social and educational differences on romantic relationships: in this story, written soon after *Tess of the d'Urbervilles*, the situation of the village girl, a 'fascinating child of nature' (p. 102) who has '"hardly ever seen a black-coated man"' (p. 100) but who marries the young London barrister, recalls that of Tess and Angel Clare. Anna's mistress, Edith Harnham, resembles Ella Marchmill in being a sensitive woman married to a dull commercial husband. Hardy's epithets for Edith, 'lonely' and 'impressionable', could equally well have been applied to the later Ella, although Edith differs in not only meeting the young man she comes to idealize but, through a misunderstanding, feeling an erotic thrill from the touch of his hand.

Just as Ella builds her romantic dreams on the poems of Trewe, Edith's contact with the absent man is through texts, the letters he sends to the servant and those Edith herself writes and largely composes on the girl's behalf. (Hardy may have been recalling that in his youth he had similarly acted as amanuensis for the amatory correspondence of illiterate village maidens, possibly his first steps as a writer of romantic fiction.) This curious long-distance flirtation takes on the complexion of a kind of epistolary adultery, and Hardy makes it quite clear that though her feelings are 'subtle and imaginative truly' they are also 'strong and absorbing' (p. 110), and indeed distinctly sexual. A strong factor in the attraction he possesses for Edith is Raye's success in seducing the girl, and when Anna becomes pregnant Edith wishes the child had been her own. Again, there is a link with 'An Imaginative

Woman', in which Ella's child is spiritually if not biologically fathered by the poet.

But Raye, as much as Edith herself, is now trapped in a marriage he bitterly regrets, and in one of the story's many ironic phrases he acknowledges that they are '"devoted lovers—by correspondence"' (p. 116). For each of them, a disastrous marriage amounts to a life-sentence—a theme already debated in *The Woodlanders* and to be further explored in *Jude the Obscure*. While insisting that '"in soul and spirit"' he has married Edith, Raye knows that law, religion, and social convention all insist on his marriage to another. Hardy, whose own marriage had come to grief by this time, seems to be defining two kinds of 'marriage': one a matter of outward forms and sanctions, the other ideal or spiritual. At the same time he recognizes in the story's uncompromising conclusion that in nineteenth-century England only one of these kinds was tolerated.

The sensitive issues of sexual transgression and marriage are approached somewhat differently in 'For Conscience' Sake', a story written a few months earlier than 'On the Western Circuit'. Instead of marrying the girl he has made pregnant, Millborne has abandoned her, as Alec did Tess. Now, twenty years later, he wishes to make amends. It would seem to be a case of sin repented and better late than never, but Hardy makes it mercilessly plain that Millborne's motives are wholly selfish: he re-enters the life of his lost love not because he still cares for her, and not even out of remorse, but '"to recover my sense of being a man of honour"' (p. 52).

So, from London, where he has long been living the self-indulgent life of a bachelor of independent means, he goes to Exonbury, woos and wins the 'widow' who has struggled hard to retrieve her respectability and has become one of the pillars of society in the prim cathedral city, and takes her back to London. Again, one has the sense of Wessex being not the centre of action but on its periphery, a place people visit and return from. The marriage, to which she has consented through a kind of moral blackmail ('"we ought as honest persons to marry"' (p. 57)), and also to facilitate the match between their daughter and a clerical suitor, is, inevitably, a failure. The episode in which the curate discovers the truth about his intended's birth is an example both of Hardy's keen interest in scientific aspects of heredity and of his sometimes underrated comic sense.

Eventually the story, which might easily have taken a tragic turn, moves towards a resolution of everyone's problems and restores the status quo. It makes the serious point, however, that marriage for socially approved reasons is more likely to create problems than to resolve them. It also subjects to severe ironic scrutiny the Victorian stock phrase that provides the story with its title, and questions, even subverts, such moral shibboleths as 'conscience', 'honour', and 'respectability', just as *Tess* had recently and challengingly questioned orthodox notions of sexual purity. Millborne's attempt to satisfy his belatedly nagging conscience has come close to wreaking havoc with four lives: the marriage that makes the couple respectable makes everyone unhappy. Like the other two stories discussed so far, 'For Conscience' Sake' forms part of the extended critique of the institution of marriage that Hardy undertook during his later years as a novelist.

These are also stories that are explicitly of their time: rather than the patient and loving re-creation of a largely remembered but vanished past, they have very much the feel of the Nineties. In 'For Conscience' Sake' the curate's sensibility is described as 'fastidious—distinctly tempered with the alloys of the century's decadence' (p. 61), a comment paralleled in 'On the Western Circuit', where the young barrister is presented as typical of 'the end-of-the-age young man' (p. 101). The latter is also described as fashionably pessimistic, 'full of vague latter-day glooms and popular melancholies' (p. 95). Hardy was to treat *fin de siècle* cosmic pessimism of the kind associated with Schopenhauer less lightly in *Jude*, with its portentous reference to ' "the coming universal wish not to live" '.

'A Tragedy of Two Ambitions', 'The Son's Veto', and 'To Please His Wife' are all stories in which social ambitions and class-divisions—subjects on which Hardy was an expert—play a prominent role. The first of these stories looks forward to *Jude* in its presentation of young men who are prevented by poverty from going to university. However, Joshua differs from the idealistic Jude in his hard-headed view of the teaching profession and the Church as ladders to socio-economic advancement—to what he describes as ' "moving onwards and upwards"' (p. 72). Again, this is a late-nineteenth-century world of board schools, training colleges, and theological colleges as well as ancient universities. Opening in a world of traditional rural craftsmen, where the brothers are incongruously studying the Greek Testament (as the young Jude also does, and the young Hardy had done), the story quickly moves to urban settings.

Another subject on which painful personal experience had made Hardy an expert was the embarrassment that humble relatives could cause a successful man. Some three years before this story was written, he had settled in Dorchester, not far from his childhood home, and his sense of the social awkwardness of having his family so close at hand may be reflected (and, of course, exaggerated) in the disreputable, drunken father. This engagingly Dionysiac figure is dispatched to the colonies by his socially ambitious children in a desperate bid to safeguard their threatened respectability, only to return at the most inconvenient moment. He not only promises to wreck the socially advantageous marriage planned for the young men's sister, but maliciously reveals that his son had been born out of wedlock. Hardy himself, though not born thus, had certainly been conceived before his parents' marriage, though naturally enough he did not advertise the fact and his autobiography endeavours to conceal it.

The father represents a spirit of disorder and misrule in stark contrast to the well-planned lives of his sons, and possibly it is not going too far to see him as standing for a kind of Lawrencian spontaneity that constitutes a dramatic protest against the repression that is the price of their ambitions, and had been the price of Hardy's. At any rate this seems to be implied by the unexpected and surely symbolic detail of the old man's walking-stick, thrust carelessly into a hedge after his death, putting forth leaves as a growing tree. (Hardy was to turn a walking-stick into a symbol again near the end of *The*

Well-Beloved.) Events in the latter part of the story have the flavour of black comedy, and the tableau of Joshua conducting his father's burial service in his professional capacity is, like much else in this story, rich in irony.

'The Son's Veto' also involves a parent–child relationship soured by social ambitions. As in 'On the Western Circuit', a village girl has married above her station, with results that hardly conduce to her happiness. Her clergyman husband has been unable to eradicate the tell-tale evidence of her social origins in her ungrammatical speech, and her Etonian son is deeply ashamed of her. Like Anna in 'On the Western Circuit', and like Tess Durbeyfield, she is a 'child of nature' (p. 40) from Wessex but has been uprooted and replanted in the dusty soil of a London suburb, where she lives a life of paralysing loneliness after her husband's death. Her existence, confined and 'insupportably dreary', recalls that of Tennyson's Mariana or Lady of Shalott, but Hardy's realism grants the picture no redeeming colour. Her chance of escape and happiness is vetoed by her snobbish and monstrously egotistical son, who has become a priest.

Like 'A Tragedy of Two Ambitions', this is a study of the heartache, even disaster, that can attend attempts to leave behind one's social origins and the physical environment that goes with them. And again, it is impossible not to detect urgent personal anxieties and self-recriminations behind the fiction when we recall that Hardy, now a professional writer in comfortable circumstances and living in a gentleman's residence, was very far from having achieved happiness. His deep interest in the transforming power of education, which reaches a climax in *Jude the Obscure*, is evident here, and the behaviour that results from the son's desire to be regarded as a 'gentleman' implies a sardonic questioning of that crucial Victorian concept.

'To Please His Wife' introduces two marriages that have very different social results for the women involved. Emily, cheated of her lover by Joanna, turns out to be the lucky one, while Joanna's envy and resentment lead her to urge her husband to make his fortune at all costs, with tragic results. Once again, education is perceived as a potent instrument of social advancement for those who can afford to purchase it: Joanna wants money not for herself but to send her sons to university, where they can be turned into 'gentlemen'.

This is another story that moves relentlessly towards an uncompromisingly tragic conclusion, but it differs in setting and structure from those previously discussed. It takes place in the little port of Havenpool, based on Poole in Dorset, with none of the movement from Wessex to the centres of urban civilization that have been noted elsewhere, and it is set in the past ('there were guineas on the earth in those days' (pp. 129–30)). There is, too, something of the ballad or the folktale in its simple but strongly-patterned plot, with the two women living in two houses facing each other, and Shadrach's successive departures to seek his fortune at sea. When he returns from a long voyage and empties a bag of gold coins only to be told that it is not enough, we seem almost to be in the world of fairy-tale, and in the lonely woman's vigil we are not far from the world of traditional ballads such as 'The Wife of Usher's Well'.

Some of the same non-realistic qualities are shared by 'The Fiddler of the Reels', one of the finest of all Hardy's short stories, and one of the boldest in its depiction of sexual attraction and sexual desire. This too is set in the past, around the mid-century—that is, at the time of Hardy's childhood, when his literary nourishment included the local and orally transmitted ballads and tales and he was immersed in the music-making traditions of his family. It resembles some of the more severely realistic stories in portraying a humdrum marriage invaded by a romantic outsider, but the intruder is now a figure with a touch of the exotic, even of the supernatural: almost, perhaps, the demon lover of another variety of traditional ballad. Mop Ollamoor, like Emily Brontë's Heathcliff, has 'un-English' looks and has 'never in all likelihood entered a church' (p. 139). 'Impish' and 'elfin', 'weird and wizardly', are among the epithets applied to Mop and his music, for he is a kind of provincial Paganini whose fiddling exerts an almost hypnotic power. Unlike the Mellstock musicians, who played in the church band (as did members of Hardy's own family), he plays only 'the devil's tunes'.

Mop's music-making is seductive in its effects, and he himself one of the most unashamedly sexual figures in all Hardy's fiction: as the narrator discreetly puts it, 'Many a worthy villager envied him his power over unsophisticated maidenhood' (p. 138). The effects of his music-making resemble those of sexual pleasure, for he can 'draw your soul out of your body like a spider's thread . . . till you felt as limp as withywind and yearned for something to cling to' (p. 141). In his sexual magnetism and his power to dominate a woman, Mop anticipates Lawrencian figures in such tales as *The Fox* and *The Virgin and the Gipsy*. Mop, a nominal horse-doctor, is close to Lawrence's gipsies, grooms, and gamekeepers, while Ned, who moves to London and takes up the trade of mechanic, is firmly assigned to an industrial and urbanized society.

Yet Hardy, or at least his narrator, is more deeply conditioned than Lawrence by Victorian scientific rationalism, and hints at explicable causes even while he is evoking a quasi-magical, semi-diabolical power. It would, the narrator observes, 'require a neurologist to fully explain' why Car'line suffers a sensation comparable to 'a galvanic shock' (p. 140) and bursts into tears at the mere sound of Mop's distant footsteps, and the language of such a statement is unmistakably that of nineteenth-century science.

By the same token, for all its echoes of ballad and folk-tale, this is a story set in a precise period of the past: Ned walks from Wessex to London in 1847, and Car'line follows him by one of the new excursion trains in 1851. (The *OED* dates the appearance of the term 'excursion train' as 1850.) She arrives in time to visit the Great Exhibition in Hyde Park on her wedding day and to have an uncanny and unsettling glimpse of Mop—or is it his fetch or *Doppelgänger*, or just a hallucination?—reflected in a mirror. (The reference to the Exhibition is a gesture towards the story's first appearance in a special issue of an American magazine to mark the Chicago World Fair.) The 1851 Exhibition celebrated the newly emerged technological civilization of Victorian Britain, and in invoking the mysterious figure of Mop Hardy, who made no secret of his longing to see a ghost, may be asserting the persistence of the irrational even in a scientific age. Mop's climactic abduction of the child (another folkloric motif), after reducing Car'line to convulsions and a paroxysm of weeping, is a final demonstration of his aggressive masculine power, and one of its results is the destruction of her marriage to Ned.

The final item in this collection is a group of nine stories linked in a manner that recalls Chaucer's *Canterbury Tales*. A group of country-folk, returning to their village from Casterbridge market at the leisurely pace of a carrier's van, pass the time by recounting the history of local individuals to a returned emigrant, Lackland, who has been absent for thirty-five years. As with Chaucer, the various narrators speak of what they know and in formal or demotic styles that reflect their education and status. Similarly Chaucerian is the contrast between the stories, which range from a humorous tale of a young man who could not decide which of three girls to marry ('Tony Kytes, the Arch-Deceiver') to a grim story of revenge ('The Winters and the Palmleys'), and from a slight anecdote about the indecorous behaviour of a church band ('Absent-Mindedness in a Parish Choir') to a dramatic story concerning a young woman's resolution in outwitting a harsh law ('Netty Sargent's Copyhold').

Topographically and chronologically, this is the world of the Wessex novels—in 'The History of the Hardcomes', for instance, there is a reference to the recent opening of the Casterbridge–Budmouth (Dorchester–Weymouth) railway— and there is even a side-glance at one of the earliest of them, *Under the Greenwood Tree* (p. 195). Lackland's return after a long absence provides the occasion for drawing attention to some of the profound changes that have taken place. In 'The Winters and the Palmleys', for instance, the audience are reminded that ' "burglary was . . . a capital offence in those days" ' (p. 205).

Many of the themes and motifs recall or anticipate Hardy's novels and short stories. The dramatic potential of a lapsing copyhold, for instance, had already been exploited in *The Woodlanders*. Music is a particularly prominent theme: 'Absent-Mindedness in a Parish Choir' recalls *Under the Greenwood Tree*, itself partly based on Hardy's childhood memories; rural music-making also appears in 'Old Andrey's Experience

as a Musician'; while 'The History of the Hardcomes' anticipates 'The Fiddler of the Reels' in its dramatic use of 'the
whirl and wildness of a dance' (p. 172), during which two
cousins exchange fiancées in the heat and excitement of
physical contact. In their evocation of a vanished past, the
stories comprising 'A Few Crusted Characters' contrast with
most of the others in this collection, which have a more
distinctly contemporary flavour; there is, however, a return to
modern sensibility in Lackland's abandoning of his sentimental quest for an ideal that he comes to perceive no longer
exists, if it has ever existed. His symbolic name anticipates the
rootlessness of the central characters in *Jude the Obscure*, and
like Jude he learns that the reality does not measure up to his
imaginings.

'Irony' has been a term impossible to avoid in the discussion of these stories, and this is a collection in which
ironies operate on several levels. Hardy's style of narratorial
commentary is often ironic, especially in relation to love and
marriage. In the brilliant opening scene of 'On the Western
Circuit', for example, as the young barrister watches the
servant-girl revolving on the 'pleasure-machine' at the
fairground,

Each time that she approached the half of her orbit that lay nearest
him they gazed at each other with smiles, and with that unmistakable
expression which means so little at the moment, yet so often leads up
to passion, heart-ache, union, disunion, devotion, overpopulation,
drudgery, discontent, resignation, despair.   (p. 97)

The Established Church is also a target of Hardy's irony, and
in 'A Tragedy of Two Ambitions' a young man reflects that 'in
old-fashioned country places, the Church conferred social
prestige up to a certain point at a cheaper price than any
other profession or pursuit . . .' (p. 82). Since Hardy had
once entertained serious thoughts of entering the Church,
but had come to recognize, according to Michael Millgate,
that 'he had been clinging to the prospect of a clerical career
for essentially selfish and non-religious reasons',[5] this may
well be a self-directed irony.

[5] Michael Millgate, *Thomas Hardy: A Biography* (New York: Random House,
1982), 96.

More pervasive than these local and narratorial ironies, however, are the ironies of situation to be found, sometimes plentifully, in nearly every story in the collection. As the purposeful volume-title warns us, these are not a writer's but *life*'s ironies, manifested in situations to be lived through and suffered by those concerned. At their most intense, these can recall the 'dramatic irony' of the Greek tragic dramatists whom Hardy had painstakingly studied in his youth. On a more mundane level, he had always had a taste, half-fascinated, half-appalled, for the tricks or bad jokes inflicted by fate on real individuals, and often recorded such oral anecdotes or newspaper reports in his notebooks. In 1870, for instance, he noted the case of a man who 'used his wife roughly, left her, & went to America. She pined for him. At last he sent for her to come with the children. She died of joy at the news.'[6]

Any newspaper, and anyone's experience, will provide analogous stories, but in *Life's Little Ironies* they are transformed into significant narrative devices. These are not the verbal ironies of an observer but ironies of endured experience, inflicted either through some freak of chance or through the unwitting agency of the victims themselves. In an important passage in chapter 11 of *Middlemarch*, George Eliot (a significant influence on Hardy's style and thought) had written of the 'calculated irony' of such experiences, and had commented: 'Destiny stands by sarcastic with our *dramatis personae* in her hand'.

Often these ironies are central to the action of one of Hardy's stories. In 'An Imaginative Woman' the implication is that the two who never meet, though they repeatedly come close to doing so, might have found happiness together; as it turns out, the poet kills himself after a hostile review of 'Lyrics to a Woman Unknown', confessing in his suicide note that he has ' "long dreamt of such an unattainable creature" ' (p. 27). The ' "imaginary woman" ' he has failed to find, however, is a role that Ella, the 'imaginative woman' of the title, has longed to fill: only circumstances—what Hardy in a very early poem

---

[6] *The Personal Notebooks of Thomas Hardy*, ed. Richard H. Taylor (London: Macmillan, 1979), 7.

('Hap') refers to as 'Crass Casualty'—have kept them apart. The question that Hardy does not confront, of course, is whether their idealized longings would have been satisfied by contact—but then it was a question he did not always care to confront in his own life and infatuations. At the centre of 'On the Western Circuit' is a similar irony of the opportunity for a real love, and a marriage based on it, being forfeited, partly on account of a deception promoted by Edith herself.

In Hardy's fiction, human endeavours are frequently counter-productive, and 'For Conscience' Sake' demonstrates that the attempt to make amends can leave matters worse than they were. Again, in 'A Tragedy of Two Ambitions', the brothers discover that what they have longed for so intensely, and behaved so reprehensibly to achieve, is simply not worth having when they once possess it. (A near-parallel that comes to mind is the great scene near the end of Thackeray's *Vanity Fair*, when Dobbin comes to understand that his long devotion to Amelia has been misplaced.) Netty, in the last story of 'A Few Crusted Characters', is another who makes great sacrifices to secure an end that brings her no happiness. The doubtful blessing of a 'good' marriage, in the sense of one that confers social and economic advancement, is also one of the themes of 'The Son's Veto', and Sophie's hard-won discovery that she would have been happier if she had remained in her own class is one with which Hardy had, at any rate intermittently, considerable personal sympathy. 'To Please His Wife' turns on a double irony, with marriage, as so often, a prominent issue: after behaving badly towards her friend, Joanna finds that she has after all got the worse of the matrimonial deal, and her desperate anxiety to compete with her rival makes her the agent of the disaster that wrecks her life.

Reflecting on such plots and situations, with their far-reaching and sometimes tragic effects on human lives, we may be inclined to question the epithet 'little' in Hardy's title, but not the centrality of irony to his narrative art. Conceivably, however, the smallness of scale is that of the short-story form adopted here, and the excellence of many of these stories confirms the view of Hardy as a writer who was in full control of both larger and smaller fictional canvases. A narrative poem such as 'A Trampwoman's Tragedy' is an outstanding example of its genre, and the full-length novels often work through episodes that, while forming part of a complex structure, could also stand alone: chapters such as the sword-drill scene in *Far from the Madding Crowd* and the pig-killing scene in *Jude the Obscure* possess such a self-contained, self-sustaining power, and two scenes from *Tess of the d'Urbervilles* were, by one of the little ironies of an author's life, actually published as separate sketches before being reunited to the mangled text of the novel's serial version. Hardy must be acknowledged as a master of the short narrative, and some of the stories in this remarkably coherent volume could hardly be bettered as examples of his art.

NOTE ON THE TEXT

ALTHOUGH the stories in *Life's Little Ironies* share much of their textual history (and have a unity supplied by their collective title and the themes they share), they are nevertheless from a textual editor's point of view a collection of independent units (written as individual pieces with their own prepublication and early publication histories), and must be edited with this in mind. This is particularly the case because no one manuscript that might be called *Life's Little Ironies* exists nor ever has existed and the manuscripts that are extant are not homogeneous in nature. The stories in the collection were originally written as separate entities, initially for publication in magazines, some of which were American and no two stories appeared in the same magazine. Even when the stories were collected together in one volume, they were not entirely the same arrangement of stories that Hardy finally settled upon. These circumstances have a direct bearing upon editorial decisions as to arrangement of the stories, the choice of copy-text and emendation to the texts of the individual stories.

A preliminary editorial decision concerns what exactly is to be edited. *Life's Little Ironies* has had two different arrangements, that of the first edition (Osgood, McIlvaine, 1894) and that of the Wessex Edition (Macmillan, 1912). In line with Hardy's final intentions (and to be consistent with the World's Classics edition of *Wessex Tales*) the stories in this volume (and their order within the volume) are as in the 1912 edition. Thus 'An Imaginative Woman' is included, but not 'The Melancholy Hussar of the German Legion' and 'A Tradition of Eighteen Hundred and Four'.

Copy-text for this edition has been chosen on the basis of the authority of the styling of the extant texts for each individual story, and emendations to the substantives have been accepted where the wording of later texts appears to be authorial. The general principle adopted has been that the holograph manuscript which served as printer's copy will be

copy-text when this is extant, otherwise the printed text nearest to the lost manuscript will be used (unless that has American house-styling, which Hardy was specifically against).
Of the eight units that make up the collection of stories in
Hardy's final arrangement, three have complete extant
manuscripts that served as printer's copy for that story's first
appearance in print and thus serve as copy-text for this edition—namely, 'An Imaginative Woman', 'For Conscience'
Sake', and 'A Tragedy of Two Ambitions'. However, of the
other stories 'To Please his Wife' and 'The Fiddler of the
Reels' have no extant manuscript; that of 'The Son's Veto' has
a section (of approximately one leaf) missing; that of 'A Few
Crusted Characters' is a very early draft that could not serve as
copy-text; and that of 'On the Western Circuit', although a
perfect manuscript, did not serve as printer's copy for any of
the printed texts (the printer's copy for magazine publication
being a typescript).

The case of 'On the Western Circuit' is particularly prob-
lematical because, although the extant manuscript is itself a
fair-copy, Hardy prepared separate copy (a bowdlerized version of the story) to be used for magazine publication. For
this purpose a typescript of the manuscript was produced
(presumably not by Hardy), on which Hardy wrote his revisions. Unfortunately this typescript is not yet available for
study.[1] But it seems clear that Hardy subsequently not only

---

[1] The typescript of 'On the Western Circuit' was sold abroad at Sotheby's in
1988, and the facsimile in the British Library is not yet available for study.
From the evidence of the small extract printed in the Sotheby's sale catalogue
(15 December 1988, p. 55), it would appear that the typescript was a direct
copy of the holograph manuscript. The typescript was then revised by Hardy
and some at least of these revisions were copied into the manuscript in pencil.
Thus, for example, the marginal insertion shown in the facsimile in the
Sotheby's catalogue is an earlier draft of the material in pencil on fo. 9 verso
of the manuscript. The two additions quoted in the catalogue as being 'not
deemed suitable for the original publication' are both in *The English Illustrated
Magazine* and the former is also in the manuscript in pencil. The typescript has
the deleted title 'The Writer of the Letters' and its description in the catalogue
continues: 'occasional autograph revisions, deletions and insertions throughout, some extending to several lines and one whole page (numbered 27–8)
autograph, the typescript bearing printer's cast-off marks and the names of
various compositors, with inky finger marks also indicating use as printer's

amended the manuscript with at least some of the additions made in the typescript, but also produced for the first edition fresh versions for most of the passages bowdlerized for the magazines, instead of returning to the original text (for examples of this see Appendix B).

Nevertheless, the holograph manuscript has great authority in the matter of styling (particularly spelling and hyphenation) and is the direct ancestor of the printed texts. It therefore seems reasonable (without having access to the typescript) to accept the manuscript as copy-text. The editorial problems for this story are more concerned with substantives. The later revisions (in that they are so near in time to the earlier drafts that they may be seen as an extension of the process of composition) have generally been accepted into the present edition. Also re-admitted to the text are several readings that represent revisions made by Hardy in the proofs of *The English Illustrated Magazine*, but which were omitted in later texts (because it would seem that the text Hardy used to prepare copy for the first edition was not the finally printed text of *The English Illustrated Magazine*).

The extant manuscript of 'The Son's Veto' has a brief lacuna. It should contain 17 leaves, but the bottom of fo. 15 has been removed, as has all of fo. 16 except the last three lines, which have been glued to the top of fo. 17. The reason for this is not apparent, but Hardy may have removed this section because it had been written in his wife's hand. It does not cause too great an editorial problem in that, as the missing section is relatively small, the magazine text for that section (having been printed from the manuscript) serves as copy-text.

The extant manuscript of 'A Few Crusted Characters', originally entitled 'Wessex Folk', is in Hardy's own words a 'First Rough Draft', and, although of great interest in terms of the insight it provides into Hardy's creative process (for an analysis of which, see *Hardy the Creator* by Simon Gatrell, pp. 110–17; see also Appendix C), is not as useful to the textual

copy, 43 pages, 4to, one page trimmed to half-size'. It would seem almost certain that the autograph page contains one of the lengthier bowdlerized passages.

editor as would be the manuscript that was printer's copy for the first printed text. Its spellings and hyphenations, however, need to be taken into account. The problem of a lack of fair-copy manuscript is compounded by the fact that the first printed text appeared in an American periodical and Hardy is on record as disapproving of the Americanization of his texts. There are instances of American spellings (for example, 'favorite'; 'parlor') and spellings contrary to Hardy's usual practice (for example, 'wagon'), which are easily enough rectified, but may be symptomatic of the amount of Americanization—if a compositor adopts American spellings, may he not also follow personal habit or house-style for pointing, rather than the author's practice in the manuscript? If the spelling 'jail' survives in the text unnoticed by Hardy, is not compositorial styling also likely to slip past? There must in any case be serious reservations about choosing for copy-text a text that deliberately deviates in any way from authorial practice. The English first edition thus serves as copy-text for 'A Few Crusted Characters'.

Likewise, copy-text for 'The Fiddler of the Reels' is also the English first edition, because there is no extant manuscript and the story first appeared in an American magazine with Americanized styling. For 'To Please his Wife', however, the first appearance in print in *Black and White* will serve as copy-text, being the text nearest to the non-extant manuscript and not subject to Americanized styling.

Little emendation to the styling of the various copy-texts has been made other than where copy-text is palpably inadequate (for example, missing speech marks or closing punctuation, as sometimes happens in Hardy's manuscripts), or where there is evidence of revision to styling by Hardy, particularly in the first-edition galley proofs.

Emendation to substantives, on the other hand, has been made where it is probable that Hardy revised the text. The substantives of the Wessex Edition in most cases represent Hardy's final intentions, but all substantive readings that differ from the copy-text have been subject to careful consideration as to whether they should be admitted as emendations to the text. Emendation to the prefatory note is made in the light of Hardy's study copy of the 1912 Wessex Edition (in Dorset County Museum), and the revisions of the 1920 Wessex Edition and the Mellstock Edition.

Details of the whereabouts of extant manuscripts are given at the beginning of the Explanatory Notes. Brief descriptions of the composition and first publication of each story also appear in the Explanatory Notes, together with some indication of manuscript revisions. For more detail of the revisions within the manuscripts of 'For Conscience' Sake', 'A Tragedy of Two Ambitions', and 'On the Western Circuit', see '*Life's Little Ironies*: The Manchester manuscripts', by Alan Manford, *Bulletin of the John Rylands University Library of Manchester*, 72 (1990), 89–100.

From the first edition in 1894 the stories (with one exception: the text of 'An Imaginative Woman' needs tracing independently up to 1912) share their textual history and can in general be treated as one text. Hardy gathered together the stories of *Life's Little Ironies* for publication in a single volume in 1893. There was considerable revision to the texts of all stories at this stage, the most significant of which are mentioned in the Explanatory Notes. Copy was sent to the publisher in October 1893, and Hardy was dealing with galley proofs in December. The extant set of marked galley proofs for the first edition (dated December 1893 and located now in the Dorset County Museum) is an important textual witness. The proofs contain numerous instances of revision to both substantives and styling in all the stories: of the 301 Osgood, McIlvaine printed pages 76 per cent contain a revision of some kind, 27 per cent have revisions to both substantives and styling, 22 per cent have revisions to substantives alone, and 26 per cent to styling alone. Furthermore (excluding the two stories later transferred to *Wessex Tales*) there are some 15 instances spread across six stories where the first edition text does not reproduce exactly what is marked in the galley proofs: several of these are probably later authorial revisions, made with others at the page-proof stage.

The first edition was published in London by Osgood,

McIlvaine on 22 February 1894. The stereotype plates produced for this edition were used in all successive Osgood, McIlvaine impressions (Purdy reckons '5 large editions' before the end of May 1894). In 1896 the collection appeared as volume XIV of Hardy's works published by Osgood, McIlvaine as 'The Wessex Novels', for which a preface was added, dated June 1896 (see Appendix A). When Macmillan took over the publication in Britain of Hardy's works, they used the Osgood, McIlvaine plates of *Life's Little Ironies*, but without the 1896 preface, for their Uniform Edition (The Wessex Novels, vol. XIV, 1903, 1910, 1917, and 1923) and Pocket Edition (1907, with nine reprintings between 1910 and 1927).

The American first edition was published by Harper and Brothers in March 1894. It is a different setting of the text, and it seems probable from Harper and Brothers' letter to Osgood, McIlvaine, 28 December 1893, that it was set from proofs of the English first edition: 'We have received a few slips of this collection of Mr. Hardy's short stories and are preparing to formally publish the volume at the close of next month. . . . We have no doubt that Mr. Hardy wishes us to publish the volume, as the proofs are marked by him with our name.' (Harper Brothers Contract Books, vol. 6, p. 544) These proofs evidently contained Hardy's galley revisions but not page-proof revisions: the American first edition contains readings marked by Hardy in the galley proofs of the English first edition which do not appear in the actual English first edition, but it lacks some readings of the English first edition which Hardy made in page proofs. Other variants are certainly compositorial (including American spellings).

A European edition (Leipzig: Bernhard Tauchnitz) appeared in 1894, a resetting based on the Osgood, McIlvaine text; whilst the Macmillan Colonial Library Edition (1895) was printed from the Osgood, McIlvaine plates.

The first appearance of 'An Imaginative Woman' in book form was in the 1896 Osgood, McIlvaine edition of *Wessex Tales* (The Wessex Novels, vol. XIII). The same plates were used for Macmillan's Uniform Edition (1903; four reprints before 1928) and Pocket Edition (1907; nine reprints before

1926). The story was transferred to *Life's Little Ironies* for the 1912 Macmillan Wessex Edition (vol. VIII).

The printer's copy for this edition was probably a composite of dismembered copies of Uniform Editions of *Life's Little Ironies* (with 'The Melancholy Hussar of the German Legion' and 'A Tradition of Eighteen Hundred and Four' removed) and *Wessex Tales* (for 'An Imaginative Woman'), into which Hardy had written revisions. The 1896 preface is replaced by a brief Prefatory Note. There are slight revisions to all stories. These are few and relatively unimportant (including slight revisions to dialect and a couple of alterations to place names); the more noteworthy are mentioned in the Explanatory Notes. The Wessex Edition marks the last stage of authorial revision to the text: the only changes in the plates for the 1920 reprint are (apart from type-wear) to the Prefatory Note. Most later editions derive directly from the Wessex Edition.

The Autograph Edition was published in America by Harpers in 1915. Although paginated the same as the Wessex Edition, it is actually a resetting (for copyright reasons). It contains all the Wessex Edition revisions to the text and has English spellings. Its variants appear to be entirely compositorial (occasionally where the Wessex Edition compositor had erred, but more often where the compositor of the American edition has deviated from his copy). Most of these variants are of punctuation or word-division, although there are odd substantives (such as the phrase 'black hair', an error for 'back hair' belonging to Sophy Twycott, the nut-brown colour of whose hair is emphasized in the story). The text of the Autograph Edition was reissued in 1920 as the Anniversary Edition, which contains four illustrations whose copy may have originated with Hardy.

Life's Little Ironies appeared as volume XIV of the 1920 Macmillan Mellstock Edition. This was a new typesetting, with the Wessex Edition as printer's copy; but Hardy made no revisions to the stories nor did he read proofs. There are no revisions marked in Hardy's study copy (in Colby College).

Two further resettings of the title appeared in 1928. It was included in *The Short Stories of Thomas Hardy*, which was posthumous (Macmillan, March 1928). This was set from the Wessex Edition text, according to Hardy's instructions. As late as 27 Sept 1927 Hardy wrote: 'the text of the Wessex Edition is the most correct to print from, and I hope the printers will be able to use that'. It is doubtful, however, if any of its variants are authorial, being almost exclusively variants to punctuation, capitalization, or word-division. The plates of the Uniform Edition were also reset (to bring them in line with the 1912 arrangement and text); these were used thereafter for reprintings of Uniform and Pocket Editions.

SELECT BIBLIOGRAPHY

ALTHOUGH slightly inaccurate now because of the passage of time, the standard bibliographical work is still R. L. Purdy's *Thomas Hardy: A Bibliographical Study* (Oxford: Clarendon Press, 1954, rev. 1968). More up-to-date information is given in the *Index of English Literary Manuscripts*, vol. iv: 1800–1900, part 2 Hardy–Lamb, by Barbara Rosenbaum (Mansell: London and New York, 1990). Valuable insights into Hardy's writing methods and a great deal of information about the publication of his works are contained in Simon Gatrell's *Hardy the Creator: A Textual Biography* (Oxford: Clarendon Press, 1988); ch. 6 includes a detailed account of the manuscript of 'Wessex Folk' ('A Few Crusted Characters'). The fullest collection of Hardy's correspondence is the seven volumes of *The Collected Letters of Thomas Hardy*, ed. R. L. Purdy and Michael Millgate (Oxford: Clarendon Press, 1978–88). Hardy's personal notebooks have been edited by Richard Taylor (London: Macmillan, 1978), and his literary notebooks by Lennart Björk (London: Macmillan, 1985). Useful general reference works are F. B. Pinion's *A Hardy Companion* (London: Macmillan, 1968, rev. 1976) and *A Thomas Hardy Dictionary* (London and Basingstoke: Macmillan, 1989).

Hardy's autobiography (published originally under the name of his second wife, Florence Emily Hardy) exists now in various versions. It was first published in two volumes as *The Early Life of Thomas Hardy 1840–1891* (London: Macmillan, 1928) and *The Later Years of Thomas Hardy 1892–1928* (London: Macmillan, 1930). These were brought together in one volume, *The Life of Thomas Hardy 1840–1928* (London: Macmillan, 1962). Michael Millgate has edited the text in an attempt to bring it nearer to what Hardy wrote: *The Life and Work of Thomas Hardy* (London and Basingstoke: Macmillan, 1985). Millgate has also written the most reliable biography of Hardy, *Thomas Hardy: A Biography* (Oxford: Clarendon Press, 1982), as well as *Thomas Hardy: His Career as a Novelist* (London: The Bodley Head, 1971). Also to be recommended, particularly for its visual impact, is Timothy O'Sullivan's *Thomas Hardy: An Illustrated Biography* (London: Macmillan, 1975). Readers interested in topographical matters should refer to Denys Kay-Robinson's *Hardy's Wessex Reappraised* (Newton Abbot: David & Charles, 1972).

Critical works concerning *Life's Little Ironies* are not overabundant, but *The Short Stories of Thomas Hardy* by Kristin Brady (London and Basingstoke: Macmillan, 1982) is to be highly recommended. There is a brief but worthwhile treatment of Hardy's short stories in Norman Page's *Thomas Hardy* (London: Routledge & Kegan Paul, 1977). Studies dealing with one or two stories include: Michael Benazon, 'Dark and Fair: Character Contrast in Hardy's "Fiddler of the Reels"', in *Ariel: A Review of International English Literature*, 9: 2 (April 1978), 75–82; Richard C. Carpenter, 'How to Read A Few Crusted Characters', in Dale Kramer (ed.), *Critical Approaches to the Fiction of Thomas Hardy* (London: Macmillan, 1979), 155–71; Roger Ebbatson Hardy, *The Margin of the Unexpressed* (Sheffield: Sheffield Academic Press, 1993) (ch. 4 discusses 'On the Western Circuit' and 'An Imaginative Woman'); and Frank R. Giordano, 'Characterization and Conflict in Hardy's "The Fiddler of the Reels"', *Texas Studies in Literature and Language*, 17 (1975–6), 617–33.

A CHRONOLOGY OF THOMAS HARDY

1840   2 June: Thomas Hardy born, first child of Thomas and Jemima (Hand) Hardy, five and a half months after their marriage. His father was a builder in a small but slowly developing way of business, thus setting the family apart socially from the 'work-folk' whom they closely resembled in financial circumstances.

1848   Entered the newly opened Stinsford National School.

1849   Sent to Dorchester British School kept by Isaac Last.

1853   Last established an independent 'commercial academy', and Hardy became a pupil there. His education was practical and effective, including Latin, some French, theoretical and applied mathematics, and commercial studies.

1856   11 July: articled to Dorchester architect John Hicks. Soon after this he became friendly with Horace Moule, an important influence on his life.

1860   Summer: Hardy's articles, having been extended for a year, completed. Employed by Hicks as an assistant.

1862   17 April: Without a position, travelled to London, but soon employed by Arthur Blomfield as a 'Gothic draughtsman'. November: Elected to the Architectural Association; began to find his feet in London.

1863   Won architectural prizes; began to consider some form of writing as a means of support.

1863–7 Possibly became engaged to Eliza Nicholls.

1865   March: 'How I Built Myself a House' published in *Chambers's Journal.* Began to write poetry.

1866   Hardy's commitment to the Church and his religious belief seem to have declined though he probably experienced no dramatic loss of faith.

1867   Returned to Dorset. Began his never-published first novel.

1868   Sent MS of *The Poor Man and the Lady* to four publishers, where it was read by Morley and Meredith, amongst others, but finally rejected.

1869   Worked in Weymouth for the Architect Crickmay; began writing *Desperate Remedies*.

1870   In order to take 'a plan and particulars' of the church, Hardy journeyed to St Juliot, near Boscastle in North Cornwall; there he met Emma Lavinia Gifford, who became his wife four years later.

1871   *Desperate Remedies* published after Hardy had advanced £75.

1872   *Under the Greenwood Tree* published; the copyright sold to Tinsley for £30. Hardy moved temporarily to London to work in the offices of T. Roger Smith. Contracted to provide serial for *Tinsley's Magazine* for £200 (to include first edition rights). *A Pair of Blue Eyes* began to appear in September. Hardy decided to relinquish architecture and concentrate on writing. Leslie Stephen requested a serial for the *Cornhill Magazine*.

1873   *A Pair of Blue Eyes* published in three volumes; Horace Moule, his close adviser and friend, committed suicide in Cambridge.

1874   *Far From the Madding Crowd* begun as a serial in *Cornhill* under Leslie Stephen's editorship and published later in the year in two volumes. Hardy married Emma Gifford on 17 September; they honeymooned in Paris and returned to live in London.

1875   *Cornhill* serialized *The Hand of Ethelberta*. The Hardys moved from London to Swanage in Dorset.

1876   Further moves to Yeovil and Sturminster Newton, where Hardy began writing *The Return of the Native*.

1878   Return to London (Tooting). *The Return of the Native* serialized in *Belgravia* and published in three volumes, to which Hardy affixed a map of the novel's environment. Made researches in the British Museum for the background of *The Trumpet-Major*.

1879   With 'The Distracted Young Preacher', began regularly to publish short stories.

1880   *Good Words* serialized *The Trumpet-Major*, which was also published in three volumes with covers designed by Hardy. In October he became seriously ill and believed himself close to death; the cause of his illness uncertain, but led to five months' total inactivity.

1881   *A Laodicean*, mostly written from his bed, published as a serial in *Harper's New Monthly Magazine* (the first in the new European edition), and in three volumes. The Hardys returned to Dorset, living at Wimborne Minster.

1882   Controversy with Pinero over Hardy's adaptation of *Far From the Madding Crowd* and Pinero's use of the same material. Hardy's third novel in three years, *Two on a Tower*, serialized in the *Atlantic Monthly* and issued in three volumes.

1883		The final move of his life—from Wimborne to Dorchester, though into temporary accommodation while his own house was being built.

1884		Made a Justice of the Peace and began to receive invitations from aristocracy. Began writing *The Mayor of Casterbridge.*

1885		Max Gate, designed by Hardy and built by his brother Henry, completed; on the outskirts of Dorchester, it remained his home for the rest of his life.

1886		*The Mayor of Casterbridge* serialized in the *Graphic* and brought out in two volumes; in the same year *The Woodlanders* began its run in *Macmillan's Magazine.* William Barnes, the Dorset poet and friend of Hardy, died.

1887		*The Woodlanders* issued in three volumes. The Hardys visited France and Italy. Began work on *Tess of the d'Urbervilles.*

1888		Hardy's first collection of short stories, *Wessex Tales*, published in two volumes. Also published the first of three significant essays on the theory of fiction, *The Profitable Reading of Fiction.*

1889		The novel that was to become *Tess* rejected by Tillotson's Fiction Bureau, which had commissioned it; subsequent further rejections fuelled the bitterness behind a second essay, *Candour in English Fiction*, published in January of the following year.

1890		*A Group of Noble Dames* appeared in the *Graphic.*

1891		*Tess of the d'Urbervilles* serialized in the *Graphic* and published in three volumes; *A Group of Noble Dames* brought out in one volume. The third important essay, *The Science of Fiction*, appeared. A Copyright Bill passed through the United States Congress in time for *Tess* to benefit from its provisions, a factor of considerable financial significance in Hardy's career.

1892		Father died 20 July. *The Pursuit of the Well-Beloved* serialized in the *Illustrated London News.*

1893		Met Florence Henniker, object of the intensest of his romantic attachments to artistic women. Wrote *The Spectre of the Real* in collaboration with her. Began writing *Jude the Obscure.*

1894		Third collection of short stories, *Life's Little Ironies*, published in one volume.

1895   First collected edition of Hardy's work begun; published
        by Osgood, McIlvaine, it included the first edition of *Jude
        the Obscure*, previously serialized in *Harper's New Monthly
        Magazine*. Some reviews of *Jude* quite savage, a contributory
        factor in Hardy's writing no further novels. Hardy drama-
        tized *Tess*.

1896   The first group of major poems with identifiable dates
        written since the 1860s; they included the three *In Tenebris*
        poems and *Wessex Heights*.

1897   *The Well-Beloved*, substantially revised from the 1892 se-
        rialization, published as part of the Osgood, McIlvaine
        edition. Visited Switzerland.

1898   Hardy's first collection of verse published, *Wessex Poems*,
        comprising mainly poems written in the 1860s and 1890s;
        and illustrated by himself.

1899   Boer War began, to which Hardy responded in verse. The
        gradual physical separation between Hardy and Emma in-
        tensified, following the mental separation that set in after
        the publication of *Jude the Obscure*.

1901   *Poems of the Past and the Present* published.

1902   Changed publishers for the last time, to Macmillan.

1904   First part of *The Dynasts* appeared. 3 April: Hardy's mother
        died, leaving a tremendous gap in his life.

1905   Met Florence Dugdale. Received LLD from Aberdeen
        University.

1906   *The Dynasts* completed with the publication of the third
        part; it embodied Hardy's most complete statement of his
        philosophical outlook. Also published his *Select Poems of
        William Barnes*, undertaken as a memorial to his great pre-
        decessor. The first Dorchester dramatization of a Hardy
        novel, *The Trumpet-Major*. Meredith and Swinburne died,
        leaving Hardy as the greatest living English writer.

1909   Relationship with Florence Dugdale deepened. *Time's
        Laughingstocks*, Hardy's third volume of poems, published.

1910   Awarded the Order of Merit, having previously refused a
        knighthood. Received the freedom of Dorchester.

1912   Second collected edition of Hardy's works begun, the
        Wessex Edition. Received the gold medal of the Royal
        Society of Literature. 27 November: Emma Hardy died; as
        a direct result Hardy began writing the poems of 1912–13.

1913   Visited Cornwall in search of his and Emma's youth.
        Awarded Litt.D. at Cambridge and became an Honorary

Fellow of Magdalene College—a partial fulfilment of an early aspiration. His final collection of short stories published, *A Changed Man.*

1914   10 February: married Florence Dugdale.*Satires of Circumstance* published. First World War began; Hardy's attitude to the future of humanity coloured by it in a profound way.

1915   At the age of 75 Hardy began to become reclusive. Frank George, his chosen heir, killed at Gallipoli. Hardy's sister Mary died 24 November.

1916   *Selected Poems of Thomas Hardy* published.

1917   Hardy's fifth collection of verse published, *Moments of Vision.* He and Florence began work on what was eventually to become *The Life of Thomas Hardy.*

1919–20 The de luxe edition of Hardy's work issued, the Mellstock Edition.

1922   *Late Lyrics and Earlier,* with its important Preface, published.

1923   Florence Henniker died. The Prince of Wales visited Max Gate. Friendship with T. E. Lawrence dveloped. *The Queen of Cornwall* published.

1924   Hardy's adaptation of *Tess* acted in Dorchester with the last of his romantic attachments, Gertrude Bugler, in the title role.

1925   *Tess* acted in London, but not by Miss Bugler. *Human Shows, Far Phantasies, Songs, and Trifles,* Hardy's seventh volume of verse, published.

1928   11 January: Hardy died. His final book of poems, *Winter Words,* published posthumously.

Life's Little Ironies

A SET OF TALES
WITH SOME COLLOQUIAL SKETCHES
ENTITLED
A FEW CRUSTED CHARACTERS

AUTHOR'S PREFATORY NOTE

OF the following collection the first story, "An Imaginative Woman", originally stood in *Wessex Tales*, but was brought into this volume as being more nearly its place, turning as it does upon a trick of Nature, so to speak, a physical possibility that may attach to a wife of vivid imaginings, as is well known to medical practitioners and other observers of such manifestations.

The two stories named "A Tradition of Eighteen Hundred and Four" and "The Melancholy Hussar of the German Legion", which were formerly printed in this series, have been transferred to *Wessex Tales*, where they more naturally belong.

The present narratives and sketches, though separately published at various antecedent dates, were first collected and issued in a volume in 1894.

T. H.

May 1912

CONTENTS

AN IMAGINATIVE WOMAN

WHEN William Marchmill had finished his inquiries for lodgings at the well-known watering-place of Solentsea in Upper Wessex, he returned to the hotel to find his wife. She, with the children, had rambled along the shore, and Marchmill followed in the direction indicated by the military-looking hall-porter.

"By Jove—how far you've gone—I am quite out of breath!" Marchmill said rather impatiently, when he came up with his wife, who was reading as she walked, the three children being considerably further ahead with the nurse.

Mrs Marchmill started out of the reverie into which the book had thrown her. "Yes," she said. "You've been such a long time. I was tired of staying in that dreary hotel. But I am sorry if you have wanted me, Will?"

"Well—I have had trouble to suit myself. When you see the airy and comfortable rooms heard of you find they are stuffy and uncomfortable. Will you come and see if what I've fixed on will do? There isn't much room, I am afraid: but I can light on nothing better. The town is rather full."

The pair left the children and nurse to continue their ramble, and went back together.

In age well-balanced, in personal appearance fairly matched, and in domestic requirements conformable, in temper this couple differed, though even here they did not often clash, he being equable, if not lymphatic, and she decidedly nervous and sanguine. It was to their tastes and fancies—those smallest, greatest particulars—that no common denominator could be applied. Marchmill considered his wife's likes and inclinations somewhat silly; she considered his sordid and material. The husband's business was that of a gunmaker in a thriving city northwards, and his soul was in that business always. The lady was best characterized by that superannuated phrase of elegance, "a votary of the muse." An impressionable palpitating creature was Ella, shrinking humanely from detailed knowledge of her husband's trade, whenever she reflected that everything he manufactured had for its purpose the destruction of life. She could only recover her equanimity by assuring herself that some, at least, of his weapons were sooner or later used for the extermination of horrid vermin, and animals almost as cruel to their inferiors in species as human beings were to theirs.

She had never antecedently regarded this occupation of his as any objection to having him for a husband. Indeed, the necessity of getting life-leased at all cost, a cardinal virtue which all good mothers teach, kept her from thinking of it at all till she had closed with William, had passed the honeymoon, and reached the reflecting stage. Then, like a person who has stumbled upon some object in the dark, she wondered what she had got; mentally walked round it, estimated it; whether it was rare or common; contained gold, silver, or lead; was a clog or a pedestal; everything to her, or nothing.

She came to some vague conclusions, and since then had kept her heart alive by pitying her proprietor's obtuseness and want of refinement, pitying herself, and letting off her delicate and ethereal emotions in imaginative occupations, day-dreams, and night-sighs. Which perhaps would not much have disturbed William if he had known of them.

Her figure was small, elegant, and slight in build; tripping, or rather bounding, in movement. She was dark-eyed, and had that marvellously bright and liquid sparkle in each pupil which characterizes persons of Ella's cast of soul, and is too often a cause of heart-ache to the possessor's male friends; ultimately, sometimes, to herself. Her husband was a tall long-featured man with a brown beard; he had a pondering regard; and was, it must be added, usually kind and tolerant to her. He spoke in squarely shaped sentences, and was supremely satisfied with a condition of sublunary things which made weapons a necessity.

Husband and wife walked till they had reached the house they were in search of, which stood in a terrace facing the sea, and was fronted by a small garden of wind-proof and salt-proof evergreens, stone steps leading up to the porch. It had its number in the row, but being rather larger than the rest,

was in addition sedulously distinguished as Coburg House by
its landlady, though everybody else called it Thirteen New
Parade. The spot was bright and lively now; but in winter it
became necessary to place sandbags against the door, and to
stuff up the key-hole against the wind and rain, which had
worn the paint so thin that the priming and knotting showed
through.

The householder who had been watching for the gentleman's return met them in the passage, and showed the
rooms. She informed them that she was a professional man's
widow left in needy circumstances by the rather sudden death
of her husband, and she spoke anxiously of the conveniences
of the establishment.

Mrs Marchmill said that she liked the situation and the
house; but it being small there would not be accommodation
enough, unless she could have all the rooms.

The landlady mused with an air of disappointment.
She wanted the visitors to be her tenants very badly, she said,
with obvious honesty. But unfortunately two of the rooms
were occupied permanently by a bachelor gentleman. He did
not pay season-prices, it was true; but as he kept on his apart-
ments all the year round, and was an extremely nice and
interesting young man, who gave no trouble, she did not like
to turn him out for a month's "let", even at a high figure.
"Perhaps, however," she added, "he might offer to go for a
time."

They would not hear of this, and went back to the hotel,
intending to proceed to the agent's to inquire further. Hardly
had they sat down to tea when the landlady called. Her gentleman, she said, had been so obliging as to offer to give up his
rooms for three or four weeks rather than drive the new-
comers away.

"It is very kind. But we won't inconvenience him in that
way," said the Marchmills.

"O it won't inconvenience him, I assure you," said the
landlady eloquently. "You see he's a different sort of young
man from most—dreamy, solitary, rather melancholy—and
he cares more to be here when the Southwesterly gales are
beating against the door, and the sea washes over the Parade,

and there's not a soul in the place, than he does now in the season. He'd just as soon be where in fact he's going temporarily, to a little cottage on the Island opposite, for a change." She hoped therefore that they would come.

The Marchmill family accordingly took possession of the house next day, and it seemed to suit them very well. After luncheon Mr Marchmill strolled out towards the pier, and Mrs Marchmill, having despatched the children to their outdoor amusements on the sands, settled herself in more completely, examining this and that article, and testing the reflecting powers of the mirror in the wardrobe door.

In the small back sitting-room, which had been the young bachelor's, she found furniture of a more personal nature than in the rest. Shabby books, of correct rather than rare editions, were piled up in a queerly reserved manner in corners, as if the previous occupant had not conceived the possibility that any incoming person of the season's bringing could care to look inside them. The landlady hovered on the threshold to rectify anything that Mrs Marchmill might not find to her satisfaction.

"I'll make this my own little room," said the latter, "because the books are here. By the way, the person who has left seems to have a good many? He won't mind my reading some of them, Mrs Hooper, I hope?"

"O dear no, ma'am. Yes, he has a good many. You see he is in the literary line himself, somewhat. He is a poet—yes, really a poet—and he has a little income of his own, which is enough to write verses on, but not enough for cutting a figure, even if he cared to."

"A poet. Oh. I did not know that."

Mrs Marchmill opened one of the books, and saw the owner's name written on the title-page. "Dear me," she continued, "I know his name very well—Robert Trewe—of course I do; and his writings! And it is *his* rooms we have taken, and *him* we have turned out of his home."

Ella Marchmill, sitting down alone a few minutes later, thought with interested surprise of Robert Trewe. Her own latter history will best explain that interest. Herself the only daughter of a struggling man of letters, she had during the last year or two taken to writing poems, in an endeavour to find a congenial channel in which to let flow her painfully embayed emotions, whose former limpidity and sparkle seemed departing in the stagnation caused by the routine of a practical household and the gloom of bearing children to a commonplace father. These poems, subscribed with a masculine pseudonym, had appeared in various obscure magazines, and in two cases in rather prominent ones. In the second of the latter the page which bore her effusion at the bottom, in smallish print, bore at the top in large print a few verses on the same subject by this very man Robert Trewe. Both of them had, in fact, been struck by a tragic incident reported in the daily papers, and had used it simultaneously as an inspiration, the editor remarking in a note upon the coincidence, and that the excellence of both poems prompted him to give them together.

After that event Ella, otherwise "John Ivy," had watched with much attention the appearance anywhere in print of verse bearing the signature of Robert Trewe, who, with a man's unsusceptibility on the question of sex, had never once thought of passing himself off as a woman. To be sure, Mrs Marchmill had satisfied herself with a sort of reason for doing the contrary in her case—that nobody might believe in her inspiration if they found that the sentiments came from a pushing tradesman's wife—from the mother of three children by a matter-of-fact small-arms manufacturer.

Trewe's verse contrasted with that of the rank and file of recent minor poets in being impassioned rather than ingenious, luxuriant rather than finished. Neither *symboliste* nor *décadent*, he was a pessimist in so far as that character applies to a man who looks at the worst contingencies as well as the best in the human condition. Being little attracted by excellencies of form and rhythm apart from content, he sometimes, when feeling outran his artistic speed, perpetrated sonnets in the loosely-rhymed Elizabethan fashion, which every right-minded reviewer said he ought not to have done.

With sad and hopeless envy Ella Marchmill had often and often scanned the rival poet's work, so much stronger as it always was than her own feeble lines. She had imitated him, and her inability to touch his level would send her into fits of despondency. Months passed away thus till she observed from the publishers list that Trewe had collected his fugitive pieces into a volume, which was duly issued, and was much or little praised according to chance, and had a sale quite sufficient to pay for the printing.

This step onward had suggested to John Ivy the idea of collecting her pieces also, or at any rate of making up a book of her rhymes by adding many in manuscript to the few that had seen the light, for she had been able to get no great number into print. A ruinous charge was made for costs of publication: a few reviews noticed her poor little volume; but nobody talked of it, nobody bought it, and it fell dead in a fortnight—if it had ever been alive.

The author's thoughts were diverted to another groove just then by the discovery that she was going to have a third child, and the collapse of her poetical venture had perhaps less effect upon her mind than it might have done if she had been domestically unoccupied. Her husband had paid the publisher's bill with the doctor's, and there it all had ended for the time. But though less than a poet of her century, Ella was more than a mere multiplier of her kind, and latterly she had begun to feel the old *afflatus* once more. And now by an odd conjunction she found herself in the rooms of Robert Trewe.

She thoughtfully rose from her chair and searched the apartment with the interest of a fellow-tradesman. Yes, the volume of his own verse was among the rest. Though quite familiar with its contents she read it here as if it spoke aloud to her; then called up Mrs Hooper the landlady for some trivial service, and inquired again about the young man.

"Well, I'm sure you'd be interested in him, ma'am, if you could see him; only he's so shy that I don't suppose you will." Mrs Hooper seemed nothing loth to administer to her tenant's curiosity about her predecessor. "Lived here long? Yes, nearly two years. He keeps on his rooms even when he's not here: the soft air of this place suits his chest, and he likes to be able to come back at any time. He is mostly writing or reading, and doesn't see many people. Though for the matter of that he is such a good kind young fellow that folks would only be too glad to be friendly with him if they knew him. You don't meet kind-hearted people every day."

"Ah—he's kind-hearted, . . . and good."

"Yes—he'll oblige me in anything if I ask him. 'Mr Trewe,' I say to him sometimes, 'you are rather out of spirits.'—'Well, I am Mrs Hooper,' he'll say; 'though I don't know how you should find it out.'—'Why not take a little change?' I ask. Then in a day or two he'll say that he will take a trip to Paris, or Norway, or somewhere; and I assure you he comes back all the better for it."

"Ah, indeed. His is a sensitive nature, no doubt."

"Yes. Still, he's odd in some things. Once when he had finished a poem of his composition late at night he walked up and down the room rehearsing it; and the floors being so thin—jerry-built houses, you know, though I say it myself—he kept me awake up above him till I wished him further. . . . But we get on very well."

This was but the beginning of a series of conversations about the rising poet as the days went on. On one of these occasions Mrs Hooper drew Ella's attention to what she had not noticed before—minute scribblings in pencil on the wall-paper behind the curtains at the head of the bed.

"Oh—let me look," said Mrs Marchmill, unable to conceal a rush of tender curiosity as she bent her pretty face close to the wall.

"These," said Mrs Hooper with the manner of a woman who knew things, "are the very beginnings and first thoughts of his verses. He has tried to rub most of them out, but you can read them still. My belief is that he wakes up in the night, you know, with some rhyme in his head, and jots it down there on the wall lest he should forget it by the morning. Some of these very lines you see here I have seen afterwards in print in the magazines. Some are newer: indeed I have not seen that one before. It must have been done only a few days ago."

"O yes. . . ." Ella flushed without knowing why, and suddenly wished her companion would go away, now that the information was imparted. An indescribable consciousness of personal interest rather than literary made her anxious to read the inscriptions alone; and she accordingly waited till she could do so, with a sense that a great store of emotion would be enjoyed in the act.

Perhaps because the sea was choppy outside the Island, Ella's husband found it much pleasanter to go sailing and steaming about without his wife—who was a bad sailor—than with her. He did not disdain to go thus alone on board the steam-boats of the cheap-trippers, where there was dancing by moonlight, and where the couples would come suddenly down with a lurch into each other's arms—for as he blandly told her, the company was too mixed for him to take her amid such scenes. Thus while this thriving manufacturer got a great deal of change and sea-air out of his sojourn here, the life, external at least, of Ella was monotonous enough, and mainly consisted in passing a certain number of hours each day in bathing and walking up and down a stretch of shore. But the poetic impulse having again waxed strong, she was possessed by an inner flame which left her hardly conscious of what was proceeding around her.

She had read till she knew by heart Trewe's last little volume of verses, and spent a great deal of time in vainly attempting to rival some of them; till in her failure she burst into tears. The personal element in the magnetic attraction exercised by this circumambient, unapproachable master of hers was so much stronger than the intellectual and abstract that she could not understand it. To be sure, she was surrounded noon and night by his customary environment, which literally whispered of him to her at every moment; but he was a man she had never seen: and that all that moved her was the instinct to specialize a waiting emotion on the first fit thing that came to hand, did not, of course, suggest itself to Ella.

In the natural way of passion under the too practical conditions which civilization has devised for its fruition, her husband's love for her had not survived, except in the form of fitful friendship, any more than or even so much as her own for him. And being a woman of very living ardours that required sustenance of some sort, they were beginning to feed on this chancing material, which was, indeed, of a quality far better than Chance usually offers.

One day the children had been playing hide-and-seek in a closet, whence in their excitement they pulled out some clothing. Mrs Hooper explained that it belonged to Mr Trewe, and hung it up in the closet again. Possessed of her fantasy Ella went later in the afternoon, when nobody was in that part of the house, opened the closet, unhitched one of the articles, a mackintosh, and put it on, with the waterproof cap belonging to it.

"The mantle of Elijah," she said. "Would it might inspire me to rival him, glorious genius that he is!"

Her eyes always grew wet when she thought like that, and she turned to look at herself in the glass. *His* heart had beat inside that coat, and *his* brain had worked under that hat at levels of thought she would never reach. The consciousness of her weakness beside him made her feel quite sick. Before she had got the things off her the door opened and her husband entered the room.

"What the devil—"

She blushed, and removed them: "I found them in the closet here," she said, "and put them on in a freak. What have I else to do? You are always away!"

"Always away. Well. . . ."

That evening she had a further talk with the landlady, who might herself have nourished a half-tender regard for the poet, so ready was she to discourse ardently about him. "You are interested in Mr Trewe I know, ma'am," she said. "And he has just sent to say that he is going to call to-morrow afternoon to look up some books of his that he wants, if I'll be in, and he may select them from your room?"

"O yes."

"You could very well meet Mr Trewe then, if you'd like to be in the way?"

She promised with secret delight, and went to bed musing of him.

Next morning her husband observed: "I've been thinking of what you said, Ell; that I have gone about a good deal and left you without much to amuse you. Perhaps it's true. To-day, as there's not much sea I'll take you with me on board the yacht."

For the first time in her experience of such an offer Ella was not glad. But she accepted it for the moment. The time for setting out drew near, and she went to get ready. She stood reflecting; the longing to see the poet she was now distinctly in love with overpowered all other considerations.

"I don't want to go!" she said to herself. "I can't bear to be away. And I won't go."

She told her husband that she had changed her mind about wishing to sail. He was indifferent, and went his way. For the rest of the day the house was quiet, the children having gone out upon the sands. The blinds waved in the sunshine to the soft steady stroke of the sea beyond the wall, and the notes of the Green Silesian band, a troop of foreign gentlemen hired for the season, had drawn almost all the residents and promenaders away from the vicinity of Coburg House. A knock was audible at the door.

Mrs Marchmill did not hear any servant go to answer it, and she became impatient. The books were in the room where she sat: but nobody came up. She rang the bell. "There is some person waiting at the door?" she said.

"O no, ma'am. He's gone long ago. I answered it."

Mrs Hooper came in herself. "So disappointing," she said; "Mr Trewe not coming after all."

"But I heard him knock, I fancy?"

"No—that was somebody inquiring for lodgings who came to the wrong house. I forgot to tell you that Mr Trewe sent a note just before lunch to say I needn't get any tea for him, as he should not require the books, and wouldn't come to select them."

Ella was miserable, and for a long time could not even re-read his mournful ballad on "Severed Lives", so aching was her erratic little heart, and so tearful her eyes. When the children came in with wet stockings and ran up to her to tell her of their adventures she could not feel that she cared about them half as much as usual.

.   .   .   .

"Mrs Hooper; have you a photograph of—the gentleman who lived here?" She was getting to be curiously shy in mentioning his name.

"Why yes. It's in the ornamental frame on the mantel-piece in your own bedroom, ma'am."

"No, the Royal Duke and Duchess are in that."

"Yes, so they are. But he's behind them. He belongs rightly to that frame, which I bought on purpose; but as he went away he said: 'Cover me up from those strangers that are coming, for God's sake. I don't want them staring at me, and I am sure they won't want me staring at them.' So I slipped in the Duke and Duchess temporarily in front of him, as they had no frame, and Royalties are more suitable for letting furnished than a private young man. If you take 'em out you'll see him under. Lord, ma'am; he wouldn't mind if he knew it! He didn't think the next tenant would be such an attractive lady as you, or he wouldn't have thought of hiding himself perhaps."

"Is he handsome?" she asked timidly.

"*I* call him so. Some perhaps wouldn't."

"Should I?" she asked with eagerness.

"I think you would. Though some would say he's more striking than handsome. A large-eyed thoughtful fellow, you know, with a very electric flash in his eye when he looks round quickly. Such as you'd expect a poet to be who doesn't get his living by it."

"How old is he?"

"Several years older than yourself, ma'am. About thirty-one or two I think."

Ella was, as a matter of fact, a few months over thirty herself, but she did not look nearly so much. Though so immature in nature, she was entering on that tract of life in which emotional women begin to suspect that last love may be stronger than first love; and she would soon, alas, enter on the still more melancholy tract, when at least the vainer ones of her sex shrink from receiving a male visitor otherwise than

with their backs to the window or the blinds half down. She
reflected on Mrs Hooper's remark, and said no more about
age.

Just then a telegram was brought up. It came from her
husband, who had gone down the Channel as far as
Budmouth with his friends in the yacht, and would not be
able to get back till next day.

After her light dinner Ella idled about the shore with the
children till dusk, thinking of the yet uncovered photograph
in her room, with a serene sense of something ecstatic to
come. For, with the subtle luxuriousness of fancy in which this
young woman was an adept, on learning that her husband was
to be absent that night she had refrained from incontinently
rushing upstairs and opening the picture-frame; preferring to
reserve the inspection till she could be alone, and a more
romantic tinge be imparted to the occasion by silence,
candles, solemn sea and stars outside, than was afforded by
the garish afternoon sunlight.

The children had been sent to bed, and Ella soon followed,
though it was not yet ten o'clock. To gratify her passionate
curiosity she now made her preparations, first getting rid of
superfluous garments and putting on her dressing-gown,
then arranging a chair in front of the table and reading
several pages of Trewe's tenderest utterances. Next she
fetched the portrait-frame to the light, opened the back, took
out the likeness, and set it up before her.

It was a striking countenance to look upon. The poet wore
a luxuriant black moustache and imperial, and a slouched hat
which shaded the forehead. The large dark eyes described by
the landlady showed an unlimited capacity for misery: they
looked out from beneath well-shaped brows as if they were
reading the universe in the microcosm of the confronter's
face, and were not altogether overjoyed at what the spectacle
portended.

Ella murmured in her lowest, richest, tenderest tone: "And
it's *you* who've so cruelly eclipsed me these many times!"

As she gazed long at the portrait she fell into thought, till
her eyes filled with tears, and she touched the cardboard with

her lips. Then she laughed with a nervous lightness, and wiped her eyes.

She thought how wicked she was, a woman having a husband and three children, to let her mind stray to a stranger in this unconscionable manner. No: he was not a stranger! She knew his thoughts and feelings as well as she knew her own; they were, in fact, the selfsame thoughts and feelings as hers; which her husband distinctly lacked; perhaps luckily for himself, considering that he had to provide for family expenses.

"He's nearer my real self, he's more intimate with the real me than Will is, after all, even though I've never seen him!" she said.

She laid his book and picture on the table at the bedside, and when she was reclining on the pillow she re-read those of Robert Trewe's verses which she had marked from time to time as most touching and true. Putting these aside she set up the photograph on its edge upon the coverlet, and contemplated it as she lay. Then she scanned again by the light of the candle the half-obliterated pencillings on the wall-paper beside her head. There they were—phrases, couplets, *bouts-rimés*, beginnings and middles of lines, ideas in the rough, like Shelley's scraps; yet the least of them so intense, so sweet, so palpitating, that it seemed as if his very breath, warm and loving, fanned her cheeks from those walls; walls that had surrounded his head times and times as they surrounded her own now. He must often have put up his hand, so—with the pencil in it;—yes, the writing was sideways, as it would be if executed by one who extended his arm thus.

These inscribed shapes of the poet's world,

> "Forms more real than living man,
> Nurslings of immortality,"

were, no doubt, the thoughts and spirit-stirrings which had come to him in the dead of night when he could let himself go, and have no fear of the frost of criticism. No doubt they had often been written up hastily by the light of the moon, the rays of the lamp, in the blue-grey dawn—in full daylight perhaps never. And now her hair was dragging where his arm had lain when he secured the fugitive fancies: she was sleeping on a poet's lips, immersed in the very essence of him, permeated by his spirit as by an ether.

While she was dreaming the minutes away thus a footstep came upon the stairs, and in a moment she heard her husband's heavy step on the landing immediately without.

"Ell! where are you?"

What possessed her she could not have described, but with an instinctive objection to let her husband know what she had been doing, she slipped the photograph under the pillow just as he flung open the door with the air of a man who had dined not badly.

"O—I beg pardon," said William Marchmill. "Have you a headache? I am afraid I have disturbed you."

"No—I've not got a headache," said she. "How is it you've come?"

"Well—we found we could get back in very good time after all, and I didn't want to make another day of it, because of going somewhere else to-morrow."

"Shall I come down again?"

"O no. I'm as tired as a dog. I've had a good feed, and I shall turn in straight off. I want to get out at six o'clock to-morrow if I can. . . . I shan't disturb you by my getting up: it will be long before you are awake." And he came forward into the room.

While her eyes followed his movements, Ella softly pushed the photograph further out of sight.

"Sure you're not ill?" he asked, bending over her.

"No—only wicked!"

"Never mind that." And he stooped and kissed her. "I wanted to be with you to-night."

Next morning Marchmill was called at six o'clock; and in waking and yawning she heard him muttering to himself: "What the devil's this that's been crackling under me so!" Imagining her asleep he searched round him and withdrew something. Through her half-opened eyes she perceived it to be Mr Trewe.

"Well I'm damned!" her husband exclaimed.

"What, dear?" said she.

"Oh—you are awake.—Ha-ha!"

"What *do* you mean?"

"Some bloke's photograph—a friend of our landlady's, I suppose. I wonder how it came here: whisked off the mantel-piece by accident perhaps when they were making the bed."

"I was looking at it yesterday, and it must have dropped in then."

"Oh, he's a friend of yours. Bless his picturesque heart!"

Ella's loyalty to the object of her admiration could not endure to hear him ridiculed. "He's a clever man!" she said with a tremor in her gentle voice which she herself felt to be absurdly uncalled for. "He is a rising poet—the gentleman who occupied two of these rooms before we came—though I've never seen him."

"How do you know, if you've never seen him?"

"Mrs Hooper told me when she showed me the photo-graph."

"Oh, well—I must up and be off. I shall be home rather early. Sorry I can't take you to-day, dear. Mind the children don't go getting drowned."

That day Mrs Marchmill inquired if Mr Trewe were likely to call at any other time.

"Yes," said Mrs Hooper. "He's coming this day week to stay with a friend near here till you leave. He'll be sure to call."

Marchmill did return quite early in the afternoon; and opening some letters which had arrived in his absence de-clared suddenly that he and his family would have to leave a week earlier than they had expected to do—in short, in three days.

"Surely we can stay a week longer?" she pleaded. "I like it here!"

"I don't. It is getting rather slow."

"Then you might leave me and the children?"

"How perverse you are, Ell! What's the use? And have to come to fetch you. No: we'll all return together; and we'll make out our time in North Wales, or Brighton a little later on. Besides, you've three days longer yet."

It seemed to be her doom not to meet the man for whose

rival talent she had a despairing admiration, and to whose person she was now absolutely attached. Yet she determined to make a last effort, and having gathered from her land-lady that Trewe was living in a lonely spot not far from the fashionable town on the Island opposite, she crossed over in the packet from the neighbouring pier the following afternoon.

What a useless journey it was! Ella knew but vaguely where the house stood, and when she fancied she had found it, and ventured to inquire of a pedestrian if he lived there, the answer returned by the man was that he did not know. And if he did live there, how could she call upon him? Some women might have the assurance to do it, but she had not. How crazy he would think her. She might have asked him to call upon her, perhaps; but she had not the courage for that, either. She lingered mournfully about the picturesque sea-side eminence till it was time to return to the town and enter the steamer for recrossing, reaching home for dinner without having been greatly missed.

At the last moment, unexpectedly enough, her husband said that he should have no objection to letting her and the children stay on till the end of the week, since she wished to do so, if she felt herself able to get home without him. She concealed the pleasure this extension of time gave her; and Marchmill went off the next morning alone.

But the week passed, and Trewe did not call.

On Saturday morning the remaining members of the Marchmill family departed from the place which had been productive of so much fervour in her. The dreary, dreary train; the sun shining in moted beams upon the hot cushions; the dusty permanent way; the mean rows of wire—these things were her accompaniment: while out of the window the deep blue sea-levels disappeared from her gaze, and with them her poet's home. Heavy-hearted, she tried to read; and wept instead.

Mr Marchmill was in a thriving way of business, and he and his family lived in a large new house which stood in rather extensive grounds a few miles outside the midland city wherein he carried on his trade. Ella's life was lonely here, as the suburban life is apt to be, particularly at certain seasons; and she had ample time to indulge her taste for lyric and elegiac composition. She had hardly got back when she encountered a piece by Robert Trewe in the new number of her favourite magazine, which must have been written almost immediately before her visit to Solentsea, for it contained the very couplet she had seen pencilled on the wall-paper by the bed, and Mrs Hooper had declared to be recent. Ella could resist no longer, but seizing a pen impulsively wrote to him as a brother-poet—using the name of John Ivy— congratulating him in her letter on his triumphant execu- tions in metre and rhythm of thoughts that moved his soul, as compared with her own brow-beaten efforts in the same pathetic trade.

To this address there came a response in a few days, little as she had dared to hope for it: a civil and brief note, in which the young poet stated that though he was not well-acquainted with Mr Ivy's verse he recalled the name as being one he had seen attached to some very promising pieces; that he was glad to gain Mr Ivy's acquaintance by letter, and should cer- tainly look with much interest for his productions in the future.

There must have been something juvenile or timid in her own epistle, as one ostensibly coming from a man, she de- clared to herself; for Trewe quite adopted the tone of an elder and superior in this reply. But what did it matter? He had replied; he had written to her with his own hand from that very room she knew so well, for he was now back again in his quarters.

The correspondence thus begun was continued for two months or more, Ella Marchmill sending him from time to time some that she considered to be the best of her pieces, which he very kindly accepted, though he did not say he sedulously read them; nor did he send her any of his own in return. Ella would have been more hurt at this than she was if she had not known that Trewe laboured under the im- pression that she was one of his own sex.

Yet the situation was unsatisfactory. A flattering little voice told her that, were he only to see her, matters would be otherwise. No doubt she would have helped on this by making a frank confession of womanhood to begin with, if something had not happened, to her delight, to render it unnecessary. A friend of her husband's, the editor of the most important newspaper in their city and county, who was dining with them one day, observed during their conversation about the poet that his (the editor's) brother the landscape-painter was a friend of Mr Trewe's, and that the two men were, at that very moment, in Wales together.

Ella was slightly acquainted with the editor's brother. The next morning down she sat and wrote, inviting him to stay at her house for a short time on his way back, and requesting him to bring with him if practicable his companion Mr Trewe, whose acquaintance she was anxious to make. The answer arrived after some few days. Her correspondent and his friend Trewe would have much satisfaction in accepting her invitation on their way southward, which would be on such and such a day in the following week.

Ella was blithe and buoyant. Her scheme had succeeded: her beloved unseen one was coming.—"Behold he standeth behind our wall, he looketh forth at the windows, shewing himself through the lattice," she thought ecstatically. "And, lo, the winter is past, the rain is over and gone; the flowers appear on the earth, the time of the singing of birds is come, and the voice of the turtle is heard in our land."

But it was necessary to consider the details of lodging and feeding him. This she did most solicitously, and awaited the pregnant day and hour.

It was about five in the afternoon when she heard a ring at the door and the editor's brother's voice in the hall. Poetess as she was, or as she thought herself, she had not been too sublime that day to dress with infinite trouble in a fashionable robe of rich material, having a faint resemblance to the *chiton* of the Greeks, a style just then in vogue among ladies of an artistic and romantic turn, which had been obtained by Ella of her Bond Street dressmaker when she was last in London. Her visitor entered the drawing-room: she looked towards his rear; nobody else came through the door. Where in the name of the God of Love was Robert Trewe?

"O, I'm sorry," said the painter after their introductory words had been spoken. "Trewe is a curious fellow, you know, Mrs Marchmill. He said he'd come; then he said he couldn't. He's rather dusty. We've been doing a few miles with knap-sacks, you know; and he wanted to get on home."

"He—he's not coming!"

"He's not. And he asked me to make his apologies."

"When did you p-p-part from him?" she asked, her nether lip starting off quivering so much that it was like a *tremolo* stop opened in her speech. She longed to run away from this dreadful bore, and cry her eyes out.

"Just now—in the turnpike-road yonder there."

"What—he has actually gone past my gates?"

"Yes: when we got to them—handsome gates they are, too; the finest bit of modern wrought-iron work I have seen—when we came to them we stopped, talking there a little while, and then he wished me good-bye and went on. The truth is he's a little bit depressed just now, and doesn't want to see anybody. He's a very good fellow, and a warm friend, but a little uncertain and gloomy sometimes—he thinks too much of things. His poetry is rather too erotic and passionate, you know, for some tastes; and he has just come in for a terrible slating from the ———— *Review* that was published yester-day; he saw a copy of it at the station by accident. Perhaps you've read it?"

"No."

"So much the better. O, it is not worth thinking of—just one of those articles written to order, to please the narrow-minded set of subscribers upon which the circulation de-pends. But he's upset by it. He says it is the misrepresentation that hurts him so: that though he can stand a fair attack he can't stand lies that he's powerless to refute and stop from spreading. That's just Trewe's weak point. He lives so much by himself that these things affect him much more than they would if he were in the bustle of fashionable or commercial life.—So he wouldn't come here, making the excuse that it all looked so new and monied if you'll pardon——"

"But—he must have known—there was sympathy here? Has he never said anything about getting letters from this address?"

"Yes; yes he has. From John Ivy—perhaps a relative of yours, he thought, visiting here at the time."

"Did he—like Ivy, did he say?"

"Well, I don't know that he took any great interest in Ivy."

"Or in his poems?"

"Or in his poems—so far as I know, that is."

Robert Trewe took no interest in her house, in her poems, or in their writer. As soon as she could get away she went into the nursery and tried to let off her emotion by unnecessarily kissing the children—till she had a sudden sense of disgust at being reminded how plain-looking they were—like their father.

The obtuse and single-minded landscape-painter never once perceived from her conversation that it was only Trewe she wanted, and not himself. He made the best of his visit, seeming to enjoy the society of Ella's husband, who also took a great fancy to him, and showed him everywhere about the neighbourhood, neither of them noticing Ella's mood.

The painter had been gone only a day or two when, while sitting upstairs alone one morning, she glanced over the London paper just arrived, and read the following paragraph:

["SUICIDE OF A POET."]

"Mr Robert Trewe, who has been favourably known for some years as one of our rising lyrists, committed suicide at his lodgings at Solentsea on Saturday evening last by shooting himself in the right temple with a revolver. Readers hardly need to be reminded that Mr Trewe has recently attracted the attention of a much wider public than had hitherto known him, by his new volume of verse, mostly of an impassioned kind, entitled 'Lyrics to a Woman Unknown,' which has been already favourably noticed in these pages for the extraordinary gamut of feeling it traverses, and which has been made the subject of a severe if not ferocious criticism in the ———— *Review.* It is supposed, though not certainly known, that the article may have partially conduced to the sad act, as a copy of the review in question was found on his writing-table; and he has been observed to be in a somewhat depressed state of mind since the *critique* appeared."

Then came the report of the inquest, at which the following letter was read; it having been addressed to a friend at a distance.

"Dear————. Before these lines reach your hands I shall be delivered from the inconveniences of seeing, hearing, and knowing more of the things around me. I will not trouble you by giving my reasons for the step I have taken, though I can assure you they were sound and logical. Perhaps had I been blessed with a mother, or a sister, or a female friend of another sort tenderly devoted to me, I might have thought it worth while to continue my present existence. I have long dreamt of such an unattainable creature, as you know; and she, this undiscoverable, elusive one, inspired my last volume; the imaginary woman alone; for in spite of what has been said in some quarters there is no real woman behind the title. She has continued to the last unrevealed, unmet, unwon. I think it desirable to mention this in order that no blame may attach to any real woman as having been the cause of my decease by cruel or cavalier treatment of me. Tell my landlady that I am sorry to have caused her this unpleasantness; but my occupancy of the rooms will soon be forgotten. There are ample funds in my name at the bank to pay all expenses.

"R. Trewe."

Ella sat for a while as if stunned: then rushed into the adjoining chamber and flung herself upon her face on the bed.

Her grief and distraction shook her to pieces; and she lay in this frenzy of sorrow for more than an hour. Broken words came every now and then from her quivering lips: "O if he had only known of me—known of me—me! . . . O if I had only once met him—only once; and put my hand upon his hot forehead—kissed him—let him know how I loved him—that I would have suffered shame and scorn, would have lived and died for him! Perhaps it would have saved his dear life!. . . But no—it was not allowed! God is a jealous God; and that happiness was not for him and me!"

All possibilities were over; the meeting was stultified. Yet it was almost visible to her in her fantasy even now, though it could never be substantiated:

> "The hour which might have been yet might not be,
> Which man's and woman's heart conceived and bore
> Yet whereof life was barren."

.   .   .   .

She wrote to the landlady at Solentsea in the third person, in as subdued a style as she could command, enclosing a postal order for a sovereign, and informing Mrs Hooper that Mrs Marchmill had seen in the papers the sad account of the poet's death, and having been, as Mrs Hooper was aware, much interested in Mr Trewe during her stay at Coburg House, she would be obliged if Mrs Hooper could obtain a small portion of his hair before his coffin was closed down, and send it her as a memorial of him; as also the photograph that was in the frame.

By the return post a letter arrived containing what had been requested. Ella wept over the portrait and secured it in her private drawer; the lock of hair she tied with white ribbon and put in her bosom, whence she drew it and kissed it every now and then in some unobserved nook.

"What's the matter?" said her husband looking up from his newspaper on one of these occasions. "Crying over something? A lock of hair? Whose is it?"

"He's dead," she murmured.

"Who?"

"I don't want to tell you, Will, just now, unless you insist!" she said, a sob hanging heavy in her voice.

"O, all right."

"Do you mind my refusing? I will tell you some day."

"It doesn't matter in the least, of course."

He walked away whistling a few bars of no tune in particular; and when he had got down to his factory in the city the subject came into Marchmill's head again.

He, too, was aware that a suicide had taken place recently at the house they had occupied at Solentsea. Having seen the volume of poems in his wife's hand of late, and heard fragments of the landlady's conversation about Trewe when they were her tenants, he all at once said to himself, "Why, of course it's he.... How the devil did she get to know him? ... What sly animals women are!"

Then he placidly dismissed the matter, and went on with his daily affairs. By this time Ella at home had come to a determination. Mrs Hooper, in sending the hair and photograph, had informed her of the day of the funeral; and as the morning and noon wore on an overpowering wish to know where they were laying him took possession of the sympathetic woman. Caring very little now what her husband or any one else might think of her eccentricities she wrote Marchmill a brief note, stating that she was called away for the afternoon and evening, but would return on the following morning. This she left on his desk, and having given the same information to the servants went out of the house on foot.

When Mr Marchmill reached home early in the afternoon the servants looked anxious. The nurse took him privately aside, and hinted that her mistress's sadness during the past few days had been such that she feared she had gone out to drown herself. Marchmill reflected. Upon the whole he thought that she had not done that. Without saying whither he was bound he also started off, telling them not to sit up for him. He drove to the railway-station and took a ticket for Solentsea.

It was dark when he reached the place, though he had come by a fast train, and he knew that if his wife had preceded him thither it could only have been by a slower train, arriving not a great while before his own. The season at Solentsea was now past; the parade was gloomy, and the flys were few and cheap. He asked the way to the cemetery, and soon reached it. The gate was locked, but the keeper let him in, declaring however that there was nobody within the precincts. Although it was not late the autumnal darkness had now become intense, and he found some difficulty in keeping to the serpentine path which led to the quarter where, as the man had told him, the one or two interments for the day had taken place. He stepped upon the grass, and, stumbling over some pegs, stooped now and then to discern if possible a figure against the sky. He could see none; but lighting on a spot where the soil was trodden, beheld a crouching object beside a newly made grave. She heard him, and sprang up.

"Ell—how silly this is!" he said indignantly. "Running away from home—I never heard such a thing! Of course I am not jealous of this unfortunate man; but it is too ridiculous that you, a married woman with three children and a fourth coming, should go losing your head like this over a dead lover! . . . Do you know you were locked in? You might not have been able to get out all night."

She did not answer.

"I hope it didn't go far between you and him, for your own sake."

"Don't insult me, Will."

"Mind, I won't have any more of this sort of thing; do you hear?"

"Very well," she said.

He drew her arm within his own and conducted her out of the cemetery. It was impossible to get back that night; and not wishing to be recognized in their present sorry condition he took her to a miserable little coffee-house close to the station, whence they departed early in the morning, travelling almost without speaking, under the sense that it was one of those dreary situations occurring in married life which words could not mend, and reaching their own door at noon.

The months passed, and neither of the twain ever ventured to start a conversation upon this episode. Ella seemed to be only too frequently in a sad and listless mood which might almost have been called pining. The time was approaching when she would have to undergo the stress of childbirth for a fourth time, and that apparently did not tend to raise her spirits.

"I don't think I shall get over it this time!" she said one day.

"Pooh: what childish foreboding! Why shouldn't it be as well now as ever?"

She shook her head. "I feel almost sure I am going to die.

And I should be glad, if it were not for Nelly and Frank and Tiny."

"And me?"

"You'll soon find somebody to fill my place," she murmured with a sad smile. "And you'll have a perfect right to—I assure you of that."

"Ell—you are not thinking still about that—poetical friend of yours?"

She neither admitted nor denied the charge. "I am not going to get over my illness this time," she reiterated. "Something tells me I shan't."

This view of things was rather a bad beginning, as it usually is. And in fact six weeks later, in the month of May, she was lying in her room, pulseless and bloodless, with hardly strength enough left to follow up one feeble breath with another, the infant for whose unnecessary life she was slowly parting with her own being fat and well. Just before her death she spoke to Marchmill softly:

"Will—I want to confess to you the entire circumstances of that—about you know what—that time we visited Solentsea. I can't tell what possessed me—how I could forget you so, my husband. But I had got into a morbid state—I thought you had been unkind—that you had neglected me—that you weren't up to my intellectual level; while he was, and far above it. I wanted a fuller appreciator, perhaps, rather than another lover. . . ."

She could get no further then, for very exhaustion. And she went off in sudden collapse a few hours later, without having said anything more to her husband on the subject of her love for the poet; William Marchmill, in truth, like most husbands of several years' standing, was little disturbed by retrospective jealousies, and had not shown the least anxiety to press her for confessions concerning a man dead and gone beyond any power of inconveniencing him more.

But when she had been buried a couple of years it chanced one day that, in turning over some forgotten papers that he wished to destroy before his second wife entered the house, he lighted on a lock of hair in an envelope, with the photograph of the deceased poet; a date being written on the back in his late wife's hand. It was that of the time they spent at Solentsea.

Marchmill looked long and musingly at the hair and portrait, for something struck him. Fetching the little boy who had been the death of his mother—now a noisy toddler—he took him on his knee, held the lock of hair against the child's head, and set up the photograph on the table behind, so that he could closely compare the features each countenance presented. By a known but inexplicable trick of Nature there were undoubtedly strong traces of resemblance to the man Ella had never seen; the dreamy and peculiar expression of the poet's face sat, as the transmitted idea, upon the child's, and the hair was of the same hue.

"I'm damned if I didn't think so!" murmured Marchmill. "Then she *did* play me false with that fellow at the lodgings! Let me see: the dates—the second week in August. . . . the third week in May. . . . Yes. . . . yes. . . . Get away, you poor little brat! You are nothing to me!"

1893.

THE SON'S VETO

I

To the eye of a man viewing it from behind, the nut-brown hair was a wonder and a mystery. Under the black beaver hat, surmounted by its tuft of black feathers, the long locks, braided and twisted and coiled like the rushes of a basket, composed a rare, if somewhat barbaric, example of ingenious art. One could understand such weavings and coilings being wrought to last intact for a year, or even a calendar month; but that they should be all demolished regularly at bedtime, after a single day of permanence, seemed a reckless waste of successful fabrication.

And she had done it all herself, poor thing. She had no maid, and it was almost the only accomplishment she could boast of. Hence the unstinted pains.

She was a young invalid lady—not so very much of an invalid—sitting in a wheeled chair which had been pulled up in the front part of a green enclosure, close to a band-stand, where a concert was going on during a warm June afternoon. It had place in one of the minor parks or private gardens that are to be found in the suburbs of London, and was the effort of a local association to raise money for some charity. There are worlds within worlds in the great city, and though nobody outside the immediate district had ever heard of the charity, or the band, or the gardens, the enclosure was filled with an interested audience sufficiently informed on all these.

As the strains proceeded many of the listeners observed the chaired lady whose back-hair, by reason of her prominent position, so challenged inspection. Her face was not easily discernible, but the aforesaid cunning tress-weavings, the white ear and poll, and the curve of a cheek which was neither flaccid nor sallow, were signals that led to the expectation of good beauty in front. Such expectations are not infrequently disappointed as soon as the disclosure comes; and, in the present case, when the lady, by a turn of the head, at length revealed herself, she was not so handsome as the people behind her had supposed, and even hoped—they did not know why.

For one thing (alas, the commonness of this complaint), she was less young than they had fancied her to be. Yet attractive her face unquestionably was; and not at all sickly. The revelation of its details came each time she turned to talk to a boy of twelve or thirteen who stood beside her, and the shape of whose hat and jacket implied that he belonged to a well-known public school. The immediate bystanders could hear that he called her Mother.

When the end of the recital was reached and the audience withdrew, many chose to find their way out by passing at her elbow. Almost all turned their heads to take a full and near look at the interesting woman, who remained stationary in the chair till the way should be clear enough for her to be wheeled out without obstruction. As if she expected their glances, and did not mind gratifying their curiosity, she met the eyes of several of her observers by lifting her own, showing these to be soft, brown, and affectionate orbs, a little plaintive in their regard.

She was conducted out of the gardens, and passed along the pavement till she disappeared from view, the schoolboy walking beside her. To inquiries made by some persons who watched her away the answer came that she was the second wife of the incumbent of a neighbouring parish, and that she was lame. She was generally believed to be a woman with a story; an innocent one; but a story of some sort or other.

In conversing with her on their way home the boy who walked at her elbow said that he hoped his father had not missed them.

"He have been so comfortable these last few hours that I am sure he cannot have missed us," she replied.

"*Has* dear mother; not *have*!" exclaimed the public-school-boy with an impatient fastidiousness that was almost harsh. "Surely you know that by this time!"

His mother hastily adopted the correction; and did not resent his making it, or retaliate, as she might well have done, by bidding him to wipe that crumby mouth of his, whose condition had been caused by surreptitious attempts to eat a piece of cake without taking it out of the pocket wherein it lay concealed. After this the pretty woman and the boy went onward in silence.

That question of grammar bore upon her history, and she fell into reverie of a somewhat sad kind, to all appearance. It might have been assumed that she was wondering if she had done wisely in shaping her life as she had shaped it, to bring out such a result as this.

In a remote nook in North Wessex forty miles from London, near the thriving county-town of Aldbrickham, there stood a pretty village with its church and parsonage, which she knew well enough, but her son had never seen. It was her native village, Gaymead, and the first event bearing upon her present situation had occurred at that place when she was only a girl of nineteen.

How well she remembered it, that first act in her little tragi-comedy; the death of her reverend husband's first wife. It happened on a spring evening, and she who now and for many years had filled that first wife's place was then parlourmaid in the parson's house.

When everything had been done that could be done, and the death was announced, she had gone out in the dusk to visit her parents who were living in the same village, to tell them the sad news. As she opened the white swing-gate and looked towards the trees which rose westward, shutting out the pale light of the evening sky, she discerned, without much surprise, the figure of a man standing in the hedge, though she roguishly exclaimed as a matter of form: "O Sam; how you frightened me!"

He was a young gardener of her acquaintance. She told him particulars of the late event, and they stood silent, these two young people, in that elevated philosophic mood which is engendered when a tragedy has happened close at hand, and has not happened to the philosophers themselves. But it had its bearing upon their relations.

"And will you stay on now at the vicarage just the same?" asked he.

She had hardly thought of that. "O yes—I suppose," she said. "Everything will be just as usual, I imagine."

He walked beside her towards her mother's. Presently his arm stole round her waist. She gently removed it; but he placed it there again, and she yielded the point. "You see, dear Sophy, you don't know that you'll stay on; you may want a home; and I shall be ready to offer one some day, though I may not be ready just yet."

"Why, Sam; how can you be so fast! I've never even said I liked 'ee; and it is all your own doing, coming after me!"

"Still—it is nonsense to say I am not to have a try at you, like the rest." He stooped to kiss her a farewell, for they had reached her mother's door.

"No, Sam—you shan't!" she cried, putting her hand over his mouth. "You ought to be more serious on such a night as this!" And she bade him adieu without allowing him to kiss her or to come indoors.

The vicar, just left a widower, was at this time a man about forty years of age, of good family, and childless. He had led a secluded existence in this college living, partly because there were no resident landowners; and his loss now intensified his habit of withdrawal from outward observation. He was seen still less than heretofore; kept himself still less in time with the rhythm and racket of the movements called progress in the world without. For many months after his wife's decease the economy of his household remained as before; the cook, the housemaid, the parlourmaid, and the man out of doors, performed their duties or left them undone, just as Nature prompted them—the vicar knew not which. It was then represented to him that his servants seemed to have nothing to do in his small family of one. He was struck with the truth of this representation, and decided to cut down his establishment. But he was forestalled by Sophy the parlourmaid, who said one evening that she wished to leave him.

"And why?" said the parson.

"Sam Hobson has asked me to marry him, sir."

"Well—do you want to marry?"

"Not much. But it would be a home for me. And we have heard that one of us will have to leave."

A day or two after she said: "I don't want to leave just yet, sir, if you don't wish it. Sam and I have quarrelled."

He looked up at her. He had hardly ever observed her before, though he had been frequently conscious of her soft presence in the room. What a kitten-like, flexuous, tender creature she was. She was the only one of the servants with whom he came into immediate and continuous relations. What should he do if Sophy were gone?

Sophy did not go; but one of the others did; and things went on quietly again.

When Mr Twycott, the vicar, was ill, Sophy brought up his meals to him; and she had no sooner left the room one day than he heard a noise on the stairs. She had slipped down with the tray, and so twisted her foot that she could not stand. The village surgeon was called in; the vicar got better, but Sophy was incapacitated for a long time; and she was informed that she must never again walk much or engage in any occupation which required her to stand long on her feet. As soon as she was comparatively well she spoke to him alone. Since she was forbidden to walk and bustle about, and indeed, could not do so, it became her duty to leave. She could very well work at something sitting down, and she had an aunt a seamstress.

The parson had been very greatly moved by what she had suffered on his account, and he exclaimed, "No, Sophy, lame or not lame, I cannot let you go. You must never leave me again!"

He came close to her, and, though she could never exactly tell how it happened, she became conscious of his lips upon her cheek. He then asked her to marry him.

Sophy did not exactly love him, but she had a respect for him which almost amounted to veneration. Even if she had wished to get away from him she hardly dared refuse a personage so reverend and august in her eyes; and she assented forthwith to be his wife.

Thus it happened that one fine morning when the doors of the church were naturally open for ventilation, and the singing birds fluttered in and alighted on the tie-beams of the roof, there was a marriage-service at the communion-rails, which hardly a soul knew of. The parson and a neighbouring curate had entered at one door, and Sophy at another, followed by two necessary persons; whereupon in a short time there emerged a newly-made husband and wife.

Mr Twycott knew perfectly well that he had committed social suicide by this step, despite Sòphy's spotless character; and he had taken his measures accordingly. An exchange of livings had been arranged with an acquaintance who was incumbent of a church in the south of London, and as soon as possible the couple removed thither, abandoning their pretty country home with trees and shrubs and glebe for a narrow dusty house in a long straight street, and their fine peal of bells for the wretchedest one-tongued clangour that ever tortured mortal ears. It was all on her account. They were, however, away from every one who had known her former position; and also under less observation from without than they would have had to put up with in any country parish.

Sophy the woman was as charming a partner as a man could possess, though Sophy the lady had her deficiencies. She showed a natural aptitude for little domestic refinements, so far as related to things and manners; but in what is called culture she was less intuitive. She had now been married more than fourteen years, and her husband had taken much trouble with her education; but she still held confused ideas on the use of "was" and "were", which did not beget a respect for her among the few acquaintances she made. Her great grief in this relation was that her only child, on whose education no expense had been and would be spared, was now old enough to perceive these deficiencies in his mother; and not only to see them but to feel irritated at their existence.

Thus she lived on in the city, and wasted hours in braiding her beautiful hair, till her once apple cheeks waned to pink of the very faintest. Her foot had never regained its natural strength after the accident, and she was mostly obliged to avoid walking altogether. Her husband had grown to like London for its freedom and its domestic privacy; but he was twenty years his Sophy's senior and had latterly been seized with a serious illness. On this day, however, he had seemed to be well enough to justify her accompanying her son Randolph to the concert.

II

THE next time we get a glimpse of her is when she appears in the mournful attire of a widow.

Mr Twycott had never rallied, and now lay in a well-packed cemetery to the South of the Great City, where, if all the dead it contained had stood erect and alive, not one would have known him or recognized his name. The boy had dutifully followed him to the grave, and was now again at school.

Throughout these changes Sophy had been treated like the child she was in nature though not in years. She was left with no control over anything that had been her husband's beyond her modest personal income. In his anxiety lest her inexperience should be overreached he had safeguarded with trustees all he possibly could. The completion of the boy's course at the public school, to be followed in due time by Oxford and ordination, had been all previsioned and arranged, and she really had nothing to occupy her in the world but to eat and drink, and make a business of indolence, and go on weaving and coiling the nut-brown hair; merely keeping a home open for the son whenever he came to her during vacations.

Foreseeing his probable decease long years before her, her husband in his lifetime had purchased for her use a semi-detached villa in the same long straight road whereon the church and parsonage faced, which was to be hers as long as she chose to live in it. Here she now resided, looking out upon the fragment of lawn in front, and through the railings at the ever-flowing traffic; or, bending forward over the window-sill on the first floor, stretching her eyes far up and down the vista of sooty trees, hazy air, and drab house-façades, along which echoed the noises common to a suburban main thoroughfare.

Somehow her boy, with his aristocratic school knowledge, his grammars, and his aversions, was losing those wide infantine sympathies, extending as far as to the sun and moon themselves, with which he, like other children, had been born, and which his mother, a child of nature herself, had loved in him; he was reducing their compass to a population of a few thousand wealthy and titled people, the mere veneer of a thousand million or so of others who did not interest him at all. He drifted further and further away from her. Sophy's *milieu* being a suburb of minor tradesmen and under-clerks, and her almost only companions the two servants of her own house, it was not surprising that after her husband's death she soon lost the little artificial tastes she had acquired from him, and became in her son's eyes a mother whose mistakes and origin it was his painful lot as a gentleman to blush for. As yet he was far from being man enough—if he ever would be—to rate these sins of hers at their true infinitesimal value beside the yearning fondness that welled up and remained penned in her heart till it should be more fully accepted by him, or by some other person or thing. If he had lived at home with her he would have had all of it; but he seemed to require so very little in present circumstances, and it remained stored.

Her life became unsupportably dreary; she could not take walks, and had no interest in going for drives, or indeed in travelling anywhere. Nearly two years passed without an event, and still she looked on that suburban road, thinking of the village in which she had been born, and whither she would have gone back—O how gladly!—even to work in the fields.

Taking no exercise she often could not sleep, and would rise in the night or early morning to look out upon the then vacant thoroughfare, where the lamps stood like sentinels waiting for some procession to go by. An approximation to such a procession was indeed made early every morning about one o'clock when the country vehicles passed up with loads of vegetables for Covent Garden market. She often saw them creeping along at this silent and dusky hour—waggon after waggon, bearing green bastions of cabbages nodding to their fall, yet never falling, walls of baskets enclosing masses of beans and peas, pyramids of snow-white turnips, swaying howdahs of mixed produce—creeping along behind aged night-horses, who seemed ever patiently wondering between their hollow coughs why they had always to work at that still hour when all other sentient creatures were privileged to rest. Wrapped in a cloak, it was soothing to watch and sympathize with them when depression and nervousness hindered sleep, and to see how the fresh green-stuff brightened to life as it came opposite the lamp, and how the sweating animals steamed and shone with their miles of travel.

They had an interest, almost a charm, for Sophy, these semi-rural people and vehicles moving in an urban atmosphere, leading a life quite distinct from that of the daytime toilers on the same road. One morning a man who accompanied a waggon-load of potatoes gazed rather hard at the house-fronts as he passed, and with a curious emotion she thought his form was familiar to her. She looked out for him again. His being an old-fashioned conveyance with a yellow front it was easily recognizable, and on the third night after she saw it a second time. The man alongside was, as she had fancied, Sam Hobson, formerly gardener at Gaymead, who would at one time have married her.

She had occasionally thought of him, and wondered if life in a cottage with him would not have been a happier lot than the life she had accepted. She had not thought of him passionately; but her now dismal situation lent an interest to his resurrection—a tender interest which it is impossible to exaggerate. She went back to bed, and began thinking. When did these market gardeners, who travelled up to town so regularly at one or two in the morning, come back? She dimly recollected seeing their empty waggons, hardly noticeable amid the ordinary day-traffic, passing down at some hour before noon.

It was only April, but that morning after breakfast she had the window opened, and sat looking out, the feeble sun shining full upon her. She affected to sew, but her eyes never left the street. Between ten and eleven the desired waggon, now unladen, reappeared on its return journey. But Sam was not looking round him then, and drove on in a reverie.

"Sam!" cried she.

Turning with a start, his face lighted up. He called to him a little boy to hold the horse, alighted, and came and stood under her window.

"I can't come down easily, Sam, or I would," she said. "Did you know I lived here?"

"Well, Mrs Twycott, I knew you lived along here somewhere. I have often looked out for 'ee."

He briefly explained his own presence on the scene. He had long since given up his gardening in the village near Aldbrickham, and was now manager at a market gardener's on the south side of London, it being part of his duty to go up to Covent Garden with waggonloads of produce two or three times a week. In answer to her curious inquiry he admitted that he had come to this particular district because he had seen in the Aldbrickham paper, a year or two before, the announcement of the death in South London of the aforetime vicar of Gaymead, which had revived an interest in her dwelling-place that he could not extinguish, leading him to hover about the locality till his present post had been secured.

They spoke of their native village in dear old North Wessex, the spots in which they had played together as children. She tried to feel that she was a dignified personage now, that she must not be too confidential with Sam. But she could not keep it up, and the tears hanging in her eyes were indicated in her voice.

"You are not happy, Mrs Twycott, I'm afraid?" he said.

"O, of course not. I lost my husband only the year before last."

"Ah—I meant in another way. You'd like to be home again."

"This is my home—for life. The house belongs to me. But I understand." She let it out then. "Yes, Sam. I long for home—*our* home! I *should* like to be there; and never leave it, and die there." But she remembered herself. "That's only a momentary feeling. I have a son you know—a dear boy. He's at school now."

"Somewhere handy I suppose? I see there's lots on 'em along this road."

"O no. Not in one of these wretched holes! At a public school—one of the most distinguished in England."

"Chok' it all, of course! I forget ma'am, that you've been a lady for so many years."

"No—I am not a lady," she said sadly. "I never shall be. But he's a gentleman; and that—makes it—O how difficult for me!"

III

THE acquaintance thus oddly reopened proceeded apace. She often looked out to get a few words with him, by night or by day. Her sorrow was that she could not accompany her one old friend on foot a little way, and talk more freely than she could do whilst he paused before the house. One night at the beginning of June, when she was again on the watch after an absence of some days from the window, he entered the gate and said softly: "Now wouldn't some air do you good? I've only half a load this morning. Why not ride up to Covent Garden with me? There's a nice seat on the cabbages, where I've spread a sack. You can be home again in a cab before anybody is up?"

She refused at first, and then, trembling with excitement, hastily finished her dressing, and wrapped herself up in cloak and veil, afterwards sliding downstairs by the aid of the hand-rail, in a way she could adopt on an emergency. When she had opened the door she found Sam on the step, and he lifted her bodily on his strong arm across the little fore-court into his vehicle. Not a soul was visible or audible in the infinite length of the straight flat highway, with its ever-waiting lamps converging to points in each direction. The air was fresh as country air at this hour, and the stars shone, except to the north-eastward, where there was a whitish light—the dawn. Sam carefully placed her in the seat, and drove on.

They talked as they had talked in old days, Sam pulling himself up now and then, when he thought himself too familiar. More than once she said with misgiving that she wondered if she ought to have indulged in the freak. "But I am so lonely in my house," she added; "and this makes me so happy!"

"You must come again, dear Mrs Twycott. There is no time o' day for taking the air like this."

It grew lighter and lighter. The sparrows became busy in the streets, and the city waxed denser around them. When they approached the river it was day, and on the bridge they beheld the full blaze of morning sunlight in the direction of St. Paul's, the river glistening towards it, and not a craft stirring.

Near Covent Garden he put her into a cab and they parted, looking into each other's faces like the very old friends they were. She reached home without adventure, limped to the door, and let herself in with her latchkey unseen.

The air and Sam's presence had revived her: her cheeks were quite pink—almost beautiful. She had something to live for in addition to her son. A woman of pure instincts, she knew there had been nothing really wrong in the journey, but supposed it conventionally to be very wrong indeed.

Soon however, she gave way to the temptation of going with him again, and on this occasion their conversation was distinctly tender, and Sam said he never should forget her, notwithstanding that she had served him rather badly at one time. After much hesitation he told her of a plan it was in his power to carry out and one he should like to take in hand, since he did not care for London work: it was to set up as a master-greengrocer down at Aldbrickham, the county-town of their native place. He knew of an opening—a shop kept by aged people who wished to retire.

"And why don't you do it then, Sam?" she asked with a slight heartsinking.

"Because I'm not sure if—you'd join me. I know you wouldn't—couldn't! Such a lady as ye've been so long, you couldn't be wife to a man like me."

"I hardly suppose I could!" she assented, also frightened at the idea.

"If you could," he said eagerly, "you'd on'y have to sit in the back parlour and look through the glass partition when I was away sometimes—just to keep an eye on things. The lameness wouldn't hinder that. . . . I'd keep you as genteel as ever I could, dear Sophy—if I might think of it!" he pleaded.

"Sam; I'll be frank," she said, putting her hand on his. "If it were only myself I would do it, and gladly; though everything I possess would be lost to me by marrying again."

"I don't mind that! It's more independent."

"That's good of you, dear dear Sam. But there's something else. I have a son. . . . I almost fancy when I am miserable sometimes that he is not really mine, but one I hold in trust for my late husband. He seems to belong so little to me personally, so entirely to his dead father. He is so much educated, and I so little, that I do not feel dignified enough to be his mother. . . . Well, he would have to be told."

"Yes. Unquestionably." Sam saw her thought, and her fear. "Still, you can do as you like, Sophy—Mrs Twycott," he added. "It is not you who are the child, but he."

"Ah—you don't know! Sam, if I could, I would marry you, some day. But you must wait a while, and let me think."

It was enough for him, and he was blithe at their parting. Not so she. To tell Randolph seemed impossible. She could wait till he had gone up to Oxford, when what she did would affect his life but little. But would he ever tolerate the idea? And if not, could she defy him?

She had not told him a word when the yearly cricket-match came on at Lord's between the public schools; though Sam had already gone back to Aldbrickham. Mrs Twycott felt stronger than usual: she went to the match with Randolph, and was able to leave her chair and walk about occasionally. The bright idea occurred to her that she could casually broach the subject while moving round among the spectators; when the boy's spirits were high with interest in the game, and he would weigh domestic matters as feathers in the scale beside the day's victory. They promenaded under the lurid July sun, this pair, so wide apart yet so near; and Sophy saw the large proportion of boys like her own, in their broad white collars and dwarf hats, and all around the rows of great coaches under which was jumbled the *débris* of luxurious luncheons; bones, pie-crusts, champagne-bottles, glasses, plates, napkins, and the family silver; while on the coaches sat the proud fathers and mothers; but never a poor mother like her. If Randolph had not appertained to these, had not centred all his interests in them, had not cared exclusively for the class they belonged to, how happy would things have been! A great huzza at some small performance with the bat burst from the multitude of relatives, and Randolph jumped

wildly into the air to see what had happened; Sophy fetched
up the sentence that had been already shaped; but she could
not get it out. The occasion was perhaps an inopportune one.
The contrast between her story, and the display of fashion
which Randolph had grown to regard himself as akin to,
would be fatal. She awaited a better time.

It was on an evening when they were alone in their plain
suburban residence, where life was not blue but brown, that
she ultimately broke silence, qualifying her announcement of
a probable second marriage by assuring him that it would not
take place for a long time to come, when he would be living
quite independently of her.

The boy thought the idea a very reasonable one, and asked
if she had chosen anybody? She hesitated; and he seemed to
have a misgiving. He hoped his step-father would be a gentleman? he said.

"Not what you call a gentleman," she answered timidly.
"He'll be much as I was before I knew your father." And by
degrees she acquainted him with the whole. The youth's face
remained fixed for a moment; then he flushed, leant on the
table, and burst into passionate tears.

His mother went up to him, kissed all of his face that she
could get at and patted his back as if he were still the baby he
once had been, crying herself the while. When he had somewhat recovered from his paroxysm he went hastily to his own
room and fastened the door.

Parleyings were attempted through the keyhole, outside
which she waited and listened. It was long before he would
reply, and when he did it was to say sternly at her from within:
"I am ashamed of you! It will ruin me! A miserable boor! a
churl! a clown! It will degrade me in the eyes of all the
gentlemen of England!"

"Say no more—perhaps I am wrong! I will struggle against
it!" she cried miserably.

Before Randolph left her that summer a letter arrived from
Sam to inform her that he had been unexpectedly fortunate
in obtaining the shop. He was in possession; it was the largest
in the town, combining fruit with vegetables, and he thought

it would form a home worthy even of her some day. Might he not run up to town to see her?

She met him by stealth, and said he must still wait for her final answer. The autumn dragged on, and when Randolph was home at Christmas for the holidays she broached the matter again. But the young gentleman was inexorable.

It was dropped for months; renewed again; abandoned under his repugnance; again attempted; and thus the gentle creature reasoned and pleaded till four or five long years had passed. Then the faithful Sam revived his suit with some peremptoriness. Sophy's son, now an undergraduate, was down from Oxford one Easter, when she again opened the subject. As soon as he was ordained, she argued, he would have a home of his own, wherein she, with her bad grammar and her ignorance, would be an encumbrance to him. Better obliterate her as much as possible.

He showed a more manly anger now, but would not agree. She on her side was more persistent, and he had doubts whether she could be trusted in his absence. But by indignation and contempt for her taste he completely maintained his ascendency; and finally taking her before a little cross and altar that he had erected in his bedroom for his private devotions, there bade her kneel, and swear that she would not wed Samuel Hobson without his consent. "I owe this to my father," he said.

The poor woman swore, thinking he would soften as soon as he was ordained and in full swing of clerical work. But he did not. His education had by this time sufficiently ousted his humanity to keep him quite firm; though his mother might have led an idyllic life with her faithful fruiterer and greengrocer, and nobody have been anything the worse in the world.

Her lameness became more confirmed as time went on, and she seldom or never left the house in the long southern thoroughfare, where she seemed to be pining her heart away. "Why mayn't I say to Sam that I'll marry him! Why mayn't I?" she would murmur plaintively to herself when nobody was near.

Some four years after this date a middle-aged man was standing at the door of the largest fruiterer's shop in Aldbrickham. He was the proprietor, but to-day instead of his usual business attire he wore a neat suit of black, and his window was partly shuttered. From the railway-station a funeral procession was seen approaching: it passed his door and went out of the town towards the village of Gaymead. The man, whose eyes were wet, held his hat in his hand as the vehicles moved by; while from the mourning-coach a young smooth-shaven priest in a high waistcoat looked black as a cloud at the shopkeeper standing there.

December 1891.

FOR CONSCIENCE' SAKE

I

WHETHER the utilitarian or the intuitive theory of the moral sense be upheld, it is beyond question that there are a few subtle-souled persons with whom the absolute gratuitousness of an act of reparation is an inducement to perform it; while exhortation as to its necessity would breed excuses for leaving it undone. The case of Mr Millborne and Mrs Frankland particularly illustrated this, and perhaps something more.

There were few figures better known to the local crossing-sweeper than Mr Millborne's in his daily comings and goings along a familiar and quiet London street, where he lived inside the door marked eleven, though not as householder. In age he was fifty at least, and his habits were as regular as those of a person can be who has no occupation but the study of how to keep himself employed. He turned almost always to the right on getting to the end of the street, then he went onward down Bond Street to his Club, whence he returned by precisely the same course about six o'clock, on foot; or if he went to dine, later on in a cab. He was known to be a man of some means, though apparently not wealthy. Being a bachelor he seemed to prefer his present mode of living as a lodger in Mrs Towney's best rooms, with the use of furniture which he had bought ten times over in rent during his tenancy, to having a house of his own.

None among his acquaintance tried to know him well, for his manner and moods did not excite curiosity or deep friendship. He was not a man who seemed to have anything on his mind, anything to conceal, anything to impart. From his casual remarks it was generally understood that he was country-born, a native of some place in Wessex, that he had come to London as a young man in a banking house and had risen to a post of responsibility; when, by the death of his father, who had been fortunate in his investments, the son succeeded to an income which led him to retire from a business-life somewhat early.

One evening, when he had been unwell for several days, Doctor Bindon came in after dinner from the adjoining medical quarter, and smoked with him over the fire. The patient's ailment was not such as to require much thought, and they talked together on indifferent subjects.

"I am a lonely man, Bindon; a lonely man," Millborne took occasion to say, shaking his head gloomily. "You don't know such loneliness as mine. . . . And the older I get the more I am dissatisfied with myself. And to-day I have been, through an accident, more than usually haunted by what above all other events of my life, causes that dissatisfaction—the recollection of an unfulfilled promise—made twenty years ago. In ordinary affairs I have always been considered a man of my word; and perhaps it is on that account that a particular vow I once made and did not keep comes back to me with a magnitude out of all proportion (I dare say) to its real gravity, especially at this time of day. You know the discomfort caused at night by the half-sleeping sense that a door or window has been left unfastened, or in the day by the remembrance of unanswered letters. So does that promise haunt me from time to time; and has done to-day particularly."

There was a pause, and they smoked on. Millborne's eyes, though fixed on the fire, were really regarding attentively a town in the West of England.

"Yes," he continued; "I have never quite forgotten it, though during the busy years of my life it was shelved and buried under the pressure of my pursuits. And, as I say, to-day in particular an incident in the law-report, of a somewhat similar kind, has brought it back again vividly. However, what it was I can tell you in a few words—though no doubt you, as a man of the world, will smile at the thinness of my skin when you hear it. . . . I came up to town at one-and-twenty, from Toneborough, in Outer Wessex, where I was born, and where, before I left, I had won the heart of a young woman my own age. I promised her marriage, took advantage of my promise, and—am a bachelor."

"The old story."

The other nodded. "I left the place and thought at the time I had done a very clever thing in getting so easily out of an entanglement. But I have lived long enough for that promise to return and bother me;—to be honest, not altogether as a pricking of the conscience, but as a dissatisfaction with myself as a specimen of the heap of flesh called humanity. If I were to ask you to lend me fifty pounds, which I would repay you next Midsummer, and I did not repay you, I should consider myself a shabby sort of fellow, especially if you wanted the money badly: yet I promised that girl just as distinctly; and then coolly broke my word, as if doing so were rather smart conduct than a mean action, for which the poor victim herself, encumbered with a child, and not I, had really to pay the penalty, in spite of certain pecuniary aid that was given. . . . There, that's the retrospective trouble that I am always unearthing; and you may hardly believe that though so many years have elapsed, and it is all gone by and done with, and she must be getting on for an old woman now, as I am for an old man, it really often destroys my sense of self-respect still."

"O I can understand it. All depends upon the temperament. Thousands of men would have forgotten all about it; so would you, perhaps, if you had married and had a family. . . . Did she ever marry?"

"I don't think so. O no—she never did. She left Toneborough, and later on appeared under another name at Exonbury in the next county, where she was not known. It is very seldom that I go down into that part of the country, but in passing through Exonbury on one occasion I learnt that she was quite a settled resident there, as a teacher of music or something of the kind. That much I casually heard when I was there, two or three years ago. But I have never set eyes on her since our original acquaintance, and should not know her if I met her."

"Did the child live?" asked the doctor.

"For several years certainly," replied his friend. "I cannot say if she is living now. It was a little girl. She might be married by this time as far as years go."

"And the mother—was she a decent, worthy young woman?"

"O yes. A sensible quiet girl, neither attractive nor unattractive to the ordinary observer; simply commonplace. Her position, at the time of our acquaintance was not so good as mine. My father was a solicitor, as I think I have told you. She was a young girl in a music-shop; and it was represented to me that it would be beneath my position to marry her; hence the result."

"Well, all I can say is that after twenty years it is probably too late to think of mending such a matter. It has doubtless by this time mended itself. You had better dismiss it from your mind as an evil past your control. Of course, if mother and daughter are alive, or either, you might settle something upon them, if you were inclined, and had it to spare."

"Well, I haven't much to spare; and I have relations in narrow circumstances—perhaps narrower than theirs. But that is not the point. Were I ever so rich I feel I could not rectify the past by money. I did not promise to enrich her. On the contrary, I told her it would probably be dire poverty for both of us. But I did promise to make her my wife."

"Then find her and do it," said the doctor jocularly, as he rose to leave.

"Ah, Bindon. That of course is the obvious jest. But I haven't the slightest desire for marriage; I am quite content to live as I have lived. I am a bachelor by nature, and instinct, and habit, and everything. Besides, though I respect her still (for she was not an atom to blame) I haven't any shadow of love for her; in my mind she exists as one of those women you think well of, but find uninteresting. It would be purely with the idea of putting wrong right that I should hunt her up, and propose to do it off-hand."

"You don't think of it seriously?" said his surprized friend.

"I sometimes think that I would, if it were practicable, simply, as I say, to recover my sense of being a man of honour."

"I wish you luck in the enterprise," said Doctor Bindon. "You'll soon be out of that chair, and then you can put your impulse to the test. But—after twenty years of silence—I should say, don't!"

II

THE Doctor's advice remained counterpoised, in Millborne's mind, by the aforesaid mood of seriousness and sense of principle, approximating often to religious sentiment, which had been evolving itself in his breast for months, and even years.

The feeling, however, had no immediate effect upon Mr Millborne's actions. He soon got over his trifling illness, and was vexed with himself for having, in a moment of impulse, confided such a case of conscience to anybody.

But the force which had prompted it, though latent, remained with him, and ultimately grew stronger. The upshot was that about four months after the date of his illness and disclosure, Millborne found himself on a mild spring morning at Paddington Station, in a train that was starting for the west. His many intermittent thoughts on his broken promise from time to time, in those hours when loneliness brought him face to face with his own personality, had at last resulted in this course.

The decisive stimulus had been given when, a day or two earlier, on looking into a Post-office Directory, he learnt that the woman he had not met for twenty years was still living on at Exonbury, under the name she had assumed when, a year or two after her disappearance from her native town and his, she had returned from abroad as a young widow with a child, and taken up her residence at the former city. Her condition was apparently but little changed, and her daughter seemed to be with her, their names standing in the Directory as "Mrs Leonora Frankland, and Miss Frankland: Teachers of Music and Dancing."

Mr Millborne reached Exonbury in the afternoon, and his first business, before even taking his luggage into the town, was to find the house occupied by the teachers. Standing in a central and open place it was not difficult to discover, a wellburnished brass door-plate bearing their names prominently. He hesitated to enter without further knowledge, and ultimately took lodgings over a toy-shop opposite, securing a sitting room which faced a similar drawing or sitting room at the Franklands', where the dancing-lessons were given. Installed here he was enabled to make indirectly, and without suspicion, inquiries and observations on the character of the ladies over the way, which he did with much deliberateness.

He learnt that the widow Mrs Frankland, with her one daughter Frances, was of cheerful and excellent repute, energetic and painstaking with her pupils, of whom she had a good many, and in whose tuition her daughter assisted her. She was quite a recognized townswoman, and though the dancing branch of her profession was perhaps a trifle worldly, she was really a serious-minded lady who, being obliged to live by what she knew how to teach, balanced matters by lending a hand at charitable bazaars, assisting at sacred concerts, and giving musical recitations in aid of funds for bewildering happy savages and other such enthusiasms of this enlightened country. Her daughter was one of the foremost of the bevy of young women who decorated the churches at Easter and Christmas, was organist in one of those edifices, and had subscribed to the testimonial of a silver broth-basin that was presented to the Reverend Mr Walker as a token of gratitude for his faithful and arduous intonations of six months as subprecentor in the Cathedral. Altogether mother and daughter appeared to be a typical and innocent pair among the genteel citizens of Exonbury.

As a natural and simple way of advertising their profession they allowed the windows of the music-room to be a little open, so that you had the pleasure of hearing all along the street at any hour between sunrise and sunset fragmentary gems of classical music as interpreted by the young people of twelve or fourteen who took lessons there. But it was said that Mrs Frankland made most of her income by letting out pianos on hire, and by selling them as agent for the makers.

The report pleased Millborne; it was highly creditable, and

far better than he had hoped. He was curious to get a view of the two women who led such blameless lives.

He had not long to wait to gain a glimpse of Leonora. It was when she was standing on her own doorstep, opening her parasol, on the morning after his arrival. She was thin, though not gaunt, with greying hair; and a good, well-wearing, thoughtful face had taken the place of the one which had temporarily attracted him in the days of his nonage. She wore black, and it became her in her character of widow. The daughter next appeared; she was a smoothed and rounded copy of her mother, with the same decision in her mien that Leonora had, and a bounding gait in which he traced a faint resemblance to his own at her age.

For the first time he absolutely made up his mind to call on them. But his antecedent step was to send Leonora a note the next morning, stating his proposal to visit her, and suggesting the evening as the time, because she seemed to be so greatly occupied in her professional capacity during the day. He purposely worded his note in such a form as not to require an answer from her which would be possibly awkward to write.

No answer came. Naturally he should not have been surprised at this; and yet he felt a little checked, even though she had only refrained from volunteering a reply that was not demanded.

At eight, the hour fixed by himself, he crossed over and was passively admitted by the servant. Mrs Frankland, as she called herself, received him in the large music-and-dancing room on the first-floor front, and not in any private little parlour as he had expected. This cast a distressingly business-like colour over their first meeting after so many years of severance. The woman he had wronged stood before him, well-dressed, even to his metropolitan eyes, and her manner as she came up to him was dignified even to hardness. She certainly was not glad to see him. But what could he expect after a neglect of twenty years?

"How do you do, Mr Millborne?" she said cheerfully, as to any chance caller. "I am obliged to receive you here because my daughter has a friend downstairs."

"Your daughter—and mine."

"Ah—yes, yes," she replied hastily, as if the addition had escaped her memory. "But perhaps the less said about that the better, in fairness to me. You will consider me a widow, please."

"Certainly, Leonora. . . ." He could not get on, her manner was so cold and indifferent. The expected scene of sad reproach, subdued to delicacy by the run of years, was absent altogether. He was obliged to come to the point without preamble.

"You are quite free, Leonora—I mean as to marriage? There is nobody who has your promise or—"

"O yes; quite free, Mr Millborne," she said somewhat surprized.

"Then I will tell you why I have come. Twenty years ago I promised to make you my wife; and I am here to fulfil that promise. Heaven forgive my tardiness!"

Her surprise was increased, but she was not agitated. She seemed to become gloomy, disapproving. "I—fear I could not entertain such an idea at this time of life," she said after a moment or two. "It would complicate matters too greatly. I have a very fair income, and require no help of any sort. I have no wish to marry. . . . What could have induced you to come on such an errand now? It seems quite extraordinary, if I may say so."

"It must—I dare say it does," Millborne replied vaguely. "And I must tell you that impulse—I mean in the sense of passion—has little to do with it. I wish to marry you, Leonora; I much desire to marry you. But it is as an affair of conscience, a case of fulfilment. I promised you; and it was dishonourable of me to go away. I want to remove that sense of dishonour before I die. No doubt we might get to love each other as warmly as we did in old times?"

She dubiously shook her head. "I appreciate your motives, Mr Millborne; but you must consider my position; and you will see that, short of the personal wish to marry, which I don't feel, there is no reason why I should change my state, even though by so doing I should ease your conscience. My position in this town is a respected one; I have built it up by my own hard labours, and, in short, I don't wish to alter it. My daughter, too, is just on the verge of an engagement to be married, to a young man who will make her an excellent husband. It will be in every way a desirable match for her. He is downstairs now."

"Does she know—anything about me?"

"O no no! God forbid. Her father is dead and buried to her. So that, you see, things are going on smoothly, and I don't want to disturb their progress."

He nodded. "Very well," he said; and rose to go. At the door however he came back again.

"Still, Leonora," he urged, "I have come on purpose. And I don't see what disturbance would be caused. You would simply marry an old friend. Won't you reconsider? It is no more than right that we should be united, remembering the girl."

She shook her head, and patted with her foot nervously.

"Well, I won't detain you," he added. "I shall not be leaving Exonbury yet. You will allow me to see you again?"

"Yes—I don't mind," she said reluctantly.

The obstacles he had encountered, though they did not reanimate his dead passion for Leonora, did certainly make it appear indispensable to his peace of mind to overcome her coldness. He called frequently. The first meeting with the daughter was a trying ordeal, though he did not feel drawn towards her as he had expected to be; she did not excite his sympathies. Her mother confided to Frances the errand of "her old friend", which was viewed by the daughter with strong disfavour. His desire being thus uncongenial to both, for a long time Millborne made not the least impression upon Mrs Frankland. His attentions pestered her rather than pleased her; he was surprised at her firmness, and it was only when he hinted at moral reasons for their union that she was ever shaken. "Strictly speaking," he would say, "we ought as honest persons to marry; and that's the truth of it, Leonora."

"I have looked at it in that light," she said quickly. "It struck me at the very first. But I don't see the force of the argument. I totally deny that after this interval of time I am bound to marry you for honour's sake. I would have married you, as you know well enough, at the proper time. But what is the use of remedies now?"

They were standing at the window. A scantly whiskered young man, in clerical attire, called at the door below. Leonora flushed with interest.

"Who is he?" said Mr Millborne.

"My Frances's lover. I am so sorry—she is not at home! Ah—they have told him where she is, and he has gone to find her. . . . I hope that suit will prosper, at any rate."

"Why shouldn't it?"

"Well—he cannot marry yet, and Frances sees but little of him now he has left Exonbury. He was formerly doing duty here, but now he is curate of St. John's, Ivell, fifty miles up the line. There is a tacit agreement between them; but—there have been friends of his who object, because of our vocation. However, he sees the absurdity of such an objection as that, and is not influenced by it."

"Your marriage with me would help the match, instead of hindering it, as you have said."

"Do you think it would?"

"It certainly would, by taking you out of this business altogether."

By chance he had found the way to move her somewhat, and he followed it up. This view was imparted to Mrs Frankland's daughter, and it led her to soften her opposition. Millborne, who had given up his lodging in Exonbury, journeyed to and fro regularly, till at last he overcame her negations, and she expressed a reluctant assent.

They were married at the nearest church; and the goodwill—whatever that was—of the music-and-dancing connection was sold to a successor only too ready to jump into the place, the Millbornes having decided to live in London.

III

MILLBORNE was a householder in his old district, though not in his old street, and Mrs Millborne and their daughter had turned themselves into Londoners. Frances was well reconciled to the removal by her lover's satisfaction at the change. It suited him better to travel from Ivell a hundred miles to see her in London, where he frequently had other engagements, than fifty in the opposite direction where nothing but herself required his presence. So here they were, furnished up to the attics, in one of the small but popular streets of the West district, in a house whose front, till lately of the complexion of a chimney-sweep, had been scraped to show to the surprized wayfarer the bright yellow and red brick that had lain lurking beneath the soot of fifty years.

The social lift that the two women had derived from the alliance was considerable; but when the exhilaration which accompanies a first residence in London, the sensation of standing on a pivot of the world, had passed, their lives promised to be somewhat duller than when, at despised Exonbury, they had enjoyed a nodding acquaintance with three-fourths of the town. Mr Millborne did not criticize his wife; he could not. Whatever defects of hardness and acidity his original treatment and the lapse of years might have developed in her, his sense of a realized idea, of a re-established self-satisfaction, was always thrown into the scale on her side, and outweighed all objections.

It was about a month after their settlement in town that the household decided to spend a week at a watering-place in the Isle of Wight and while there, the Reverend Percival Cope (the young curate aforesaid) came to see them, Frances in particular. No formal engagement of the young pair had been announced as yet, but it was clear that their mutual understanding could not end in anything but marriage without grievous disappointment to one of the parties at least. Not that Frances was sentimental; she was rather of the imperious sort, indeed; and, to say all, the young girl had not fulfilled her father's expectations of her. But he hoped and worked for her welfare as sincerely as any father could do.

Mr Cope was introduced to the new head of the family, and stayed with them in the Island two or three days. On the last day of his visit they decided to venture on a two-hour's sail in one of the small yachts which lay there for hire. The trip had

not progressed far before all, except the curate, found that
sailing in a breeze did not quite agree with them; but as he
seemed to enjoy the experience the other three bore their
condition as well as they could without grimace or complaint
till the young man, observing their discomfort, gave immediate directions to tack about. On the way back to port they sat
silent, facing each other.

Nausea in such circumstances, like midnight watchings,
fatigue, trouble, fright, has this marked effect upon the countenance, that it often brings out strongly the divergences of
the individual from the norm of his race, accentuating super-
ficial peculiarities to radical distinctions. Unexpected physi-
ognomies will uncover themselves at these times in
well-known faces; the aspect becomes invested with the spectral presence of entombed and forgotten ancestors; and
family lineaments of special or exclusive cast, which in ordinary moments are masked by a stereotyped expression and
mien, start up with crude insistence to the view.

Frances, sitting beside her mother's husband, with Mr
Cope opposite, was naturally enough much regarded by the
curate during the tedious sail home; at first with sympathetic
smiles; then, as the middle-aged father and his child grew
each grey-faced, as the pretty blush of Frances disintegrated
into spotty stains, and the soft rotundities of her features
diverged from their familiar and reposeful beauty into
elemental lines, Cope was gradually struck with the resemblance between a pair in their discomfort who in their ease
presented nothing to the eye in common. Mr Millborne
and Frances in their indisposition were strangely, startlingly,
alike.

The inexplicable fact absorbed Cope's attention quite: he
forgot to smile at Frances, to hold her hand; and when they
touched the shore he remained sitting for some moments like
a man in a trance.

As they went homeward, and recovered their complexions
and contours, the similarities one by one disappeared, and
Frances and Mr Millborne were again masked by the commonplace differences of sex and age. It was as if, during the
voyage, a mysterious veil had been lifted, temporarily reveal-
ing a strange pantomime of the past.

During the evening he said to her casually: "Is your step-father a cousin of your mother, dear Frances?"

"O no," said she. "There is no relationship. He was only an old friend of hers. Why did you suppose such a thing?"

He did not explain, and the next morning started to resume his duties at Ivell.

Cope was an honest young fellow, and shrewd withal. At home in his quiet rooms in St Peter's Street, Ivell, he pondered long and unpleasantly on the revelations of the cruise. The tale it told was distinct enough, and for the first time his position was an uncomfortable one. He had met the Franklands at Exonbury as parishioners, had been attracted by Frances, and had floated thus far into an engagement which was indefinite only because of his inability to marry just yet. The Franklands' past had apparently contained mysteries, and it did not coincide with his judgment to marry into a family whose mystery was of the sort suggested. So he sat and sighed, between his reluctance to lose Frances and his natural dislike of forming a connection with people whose antecedents would not bear the strictest investigation.

A passionate lover of the old-fashioned sort might possibly never have halted to weigh these doubts; but though he was in the church Cope's affections were fastidious—distinctly tempered with the alloys of the century's decadence. He delayed writing to Frances for some while, simply because he could not tune himself up to enthusiasm when worried by suspicions of such a kind.

Meanwhile the Millbornes had returned to London, and Frances was growing anxious. In talking to her mother of Cope she had innocently alluded to his curious inquiry if her mother and her step-father were connected by any tie of cousinship. Mrs Millborne made her repeat the words. Frances did so, and watched with inquisitive eye their effect upon her elder, which was a distinct one.

"What is there so startling in his inquiry then?" Frances asked. "Can it have anything to do with his not writing to me?"

Her mother flinched, but did not inform her, and Frances also was now drawn within the atmosphere of suspicion. That night when standing by chance outside the chamber of her parents she heard for the first time their voices engaged in a sharp altercation.

The apple of discord had, indeed, been dropped into the house of the Millbornes. The scene within the chamber-door was Mrs Millborne standing before her dressing-table, looking across to her husband in the dressing-room adjoining, where he was sitting down, his eyes fixed on the floor.

"Why did you come and disturb my life a second time?" she harshly asked. "Why did you pester me with your conscience, till I was driven to accept you to get rid of your importunity? Frances and I were doing well: the one desire of my life was that she should marry that good young man. And now the match is broken off by your cruel interference! Why did you show yourself in my world again, and raise this scandal upon my hard-won respectability—won by such weary years of labour as none will ever know!" She bent her face upon the table and wept passionately.

There was no reply from Mr Millborne. Frances lay awake nearly all that night, and when at breakfast-time the next morning still no letter appeared from Mr Cope, she entreated her mother to go to Ivell and see if the young man were ill.

Mrs Millborne went, returning the same day. Frances, anxious and haggard, met her at the station.

Was all well? Her mother could not say it was; though he was not ill.

One thing she had found out, that it was a mistake to hunt up a man when his inclinations were to hold aloof. Returning with her mother in the cab Frances insisted upon knowing what the mystery was which plainly had alienated her lover. The precise words which had been spoken at the interview with him that day at Ivell Mrs Millborne could not be induced to repeat; but thus far she admitted, that the estrangement was fundamentally owing to Mr Millborne having sought her out and married her.

"And why did he seek you out—and why were you obliged to marry him?" asked the distressed girl. Then the evidences pieced themselves together in her acute mind, and, her colour gradually rising, she asked her mother if what they pointed to was indeed the fact. Her mother admitted that it was.

A flush of mortification succeeded to the flush of shame upon the young woman's face. How could a scrupulously correct clergyman and lover like Mr Cope ask her to be his wife after this discovery of her irregular birth? She covered her eyes with her hands in a silent despair.

In the presence of Mr Millborne they at first suppressed their anguish. But by and by their feelings got the better of them, and when he was asleep in his chair after dinner Mrs Millborne's irritation broke out. The embittered Frances joined her in reproaching the man who had come as the spectre to their intended feast of Hymen, and turned its promise to ghastly failure.

"Why were you so weak, mother, as to admit such an enemy to your house—one so obviously your evil genius—much less accept him as a husband, after so long? If you had only told me all, I could have advised you better! But I suppose I have no right to reproach him, bitter as I feel, and even though he has blighted my life for ever!"

"Frances, I did hold out; I saw it was a mistake to have any more to say to a man who had been such an unmitigated curse to me! But he would not listen; he kept on about his conscience and mine, till I was bewildered, and said Yes! . . . Bringing us away from a quiet town where we were known and respected—what an ill-considered thing it was! O the content of those days! We had society there, people in our own position, who did not expect more of us than we expected of them. Here, where there is so much, there is nothing! He said London society was so bright and brilliant that it would be like a new world. It may be to those who are in it, but what is that to us two lonely women; we only see it flashing past! . . . O the fool, the fool that I was!"

Now Millborne was not so soundly asleep as to prevent his hearing these animadversions that were almost execrations, and many more of the same sort. As there was no peace for him at home he went again to his club, where, since his reunion with Leonora, he had seldom if ever been seen. But the shadow of the troubles in his household interfered with his comfort here also; he could not, as formerly, settle down into his favourite chair with the evening paper, reposeful in the celibate's sense that where he was his world's centre had its fixture. His world was now an ellipsoid, with a dual central-ity, of which his own was not the major.

The young curate of Ivell still held aloof, tantalizing Frances by his elusiveness. Plainly he was waiting upon events. Millborne bore the reproaches of his wife and daughter al-most in silence; but by degrees he grew meditative, as if revolving a new idea. The bitter cry about blighting their existence at length became so impassioned that one day Millborne calmly proposed to return again to the country; not necessarily to Exonbury, but, if they were willing, to a little old manor-house which he had found was to be let, standing a mile from Mr Cope's town of Ivell.

They were surprised, and, despite their view of him as the bringer of ill, were disposed to accede. "Though I suppose," said Mrs Millborne to him, "it will end in Mr Cope's asking you flatly about the past, and your being compelled to tell him; which may dash all my hopes for Frances. She gets more and more like you every day, particularly when she is in a bad temper. People will see you together, and notice it; and I don't know what may come of it."

"I don't think they will see us together," he said; but he entered into no argument when she insisted otherwise. The removal was eventually resolved on; the town-house was dis-posed of; and again came the invasion by furniture-men and vans, till all the moveables and servants were whisked away. He sent his wife and daughter to an hotel while this was going on, taking two or three journeys himself to Ivell to superin-tend the refixing, and the improvement of the grounds. When all was done he returned to them in town.

The house was ready for their reception, he told them, and there only remained the journey. He accompanied them and their personal luggage to the station only, having, he said, to remain in town a short time on business with his lawyer. They went, dubious and discontented; for the much-loved Cope had made no sign.

"If we were going down to live here alone," said Mrs Millborne to her daughter in the train; "and there was no intrusive tell-tale presence! . . . But let it be!"

The house was a lovely little place in a grove of elms, and they liked it much. The first person to call upon them as new residents was Mr Cope. He was delighted to find that they had come so near, and (though he did not say this) meant to live in such excellent style. He had not, however, resumed the manner of a lover.

"Your father spoils all!" murmured Mrs Millborne.

But three days later she received a letter from her husband, which caused her no small degree of astonishment. It was written from Boulogne.

It began with a long explanation of settlements of his property, in which he had been engaged since their departure. The chief feature in the business was that Mrs Millborne found herself the absolute mistress of a comfortable sum in personal estate, and Frances of a life-interest in a larger sum, the principal to be afterwards divided amongst her children if she had any. The remainder of his letter ran as hereunder:

"I have learnt that there are some derelictions of duty which cannot be blotted out by tardy accomplishment. Our evil actions do not remain isolated in the past, waiting only to be reversed: like locomotive plants they spread and re-root till to destroy the original stem has no material effect in killing them. I made a mistake in searching you out; I admit it; whatever the remedy may be in such cases, it is not marriage, and the best thing for you and me is that you do not see me more. You had better not seek me, for you will not be likely to find me: you are well provided for, and we may do ourselves more harm than good by meeting again.

"F. M."

Millborne, in short, disappeared from that day forward. But a searching inquiry would have revealed that soon after the Millbornes went to Ivell, an Englishman, who did not give the name of Millborne, took up his residence in Brussels; a man who might have been recognized by Mrs Millborne if she had met him. One afternoon in the ensuing summer, when this gentleman was looking over the English papers, he saw the announcement of Miss Frances Frankland's marriage. She had become the Reverend Mrs Cope.

"Thank God!" said the gentleman.

But his momentary satisfaction was far from being happiness. As he formerly had been weighted with a bad conscience, so now was he burdened with the heavy thought which oppressed Antigone, that by honourable observance of a rite he had obtained for himself the reward of dishonourable laxity. Occasionally he had to be helped to his lodgings by his servant from the *Cercle* he frequented, through having imbibed a little too much liquor to be able to take care of himself. But he was harmless, and even when he had been drinking said little.

March 1891.

A TRAGEDY OF TWO AMBITIONS

I

THE shouts of the village-boys came in at the window, accompanied by broken laughter from loungers at the inn-door; but the brothers Halborough worked on.

They were sitting in a bedroom of the master-millwright's house, engaged in the untutored reading of Greek and Latin. It was no tale of Homeric blows and knocks, Argonautic voyaging, or Theban family woe that inflamed their imaginations and spurred them onward. They were plodding away at the Greek Testament, immersed in a chapter of the idiomatic and difficult Epistle to the Hebrews.

The Dog-day sun in its decline reached the low ceiling with slanting sides, and the shadows of the great goat's-willow swayed and interchanged upon the wall like a spectral army manœuvring. The open casement which admitted the remoter sounds now brought the voice of some one close at hand. It was their sister, a pretty girl of fourteen, who stood in the court below.

"I can see the tops of your heads! What's the use of staying up there? I like you not to go out with the street-boys; but do come and play with me!"

They treated her as an inadequate interlocutor, and put her off with some slight word. She went away disappointed. Presently there was a dull noise of heavy footsteps at the side of the house, and one of the brothers sat up. "I fancy I hear him coming," he murmured, his eyes on the window.

A man in the light drab clothes of an old-fashioned country tradesman approached from round the corner, reeling as he came. The elder son flushed with anger, rose from his books, and descended the stairs. The younger sat on, till, after the lapse of a few minutes, his brother re-entered the room.

"Did Rosa see him?"

"No."

"Nor anybody?"

"No."

"What have you done with him?"

"He's in the straw-shed. I got him in with some trouble, and he has fallen asleep. I thought this would be the explanation of his absence! No stones dressed for Miller Kench, the great wheel of the saw-mills waiting for new float-boards, even the poor folk not able to get their waggons wheeled."

"What *is* the use of poring over this!" said the younger, shutting up Donnegan's *Lexicon* with a slap . . . . "O, if we had only been able to keep mother's nine-hundred pound, what we could have done!"

"How well she had estimated the sum necessary. Four-hundred-and-fifty each, she thought. And I have no doubt that we could have done it on that, with care."

This loss of the nine hundred pounds was the sharp thorn of their crown. It was a sum which their mother had amassed with great exertion and self-denial, by adding to a chance legacy such other small amounts as she could lay hands on from time to time; and she had intended with the hoard to indulge the dear wish of her heart, that of sending her sons Joshua and Cornelius to one of the Universities, having been informed that from four-hundred to four-hundred-and-fifty each might carry them through their terms with such great economy as she knew she could trust them to practise. But she had died a year or two before this time, worn out by too keen a strain towards these ends; and the money, coming unreservedly into the hands of their father, had been nearly dissipated. With its exhaustion went all opportunity and hope of a University degree for the sons.

"It drives me mad when I think of it," said Joshua, the elder. "And here we work and work in our own bungling way, and the utmost we can hope for is a term of years as national schoolmasters, and possible admission to a Theological college, and ordination as despised licentiates."

The anger of the elder was reflected as simple sadness in the face of the other. "We çan preach the Gospel as well without a hood on our surplices as with one," he said with feeble consolation.

"Preach the Gospel—true," said Joshua with a slight pursing of mouth. "But we can't rise."

"Let us make the best of it, and grind on."

The other was silent, and they drearily bent over their books again.

The cause of all this gloom, the Millwright Halborough, now snoring in the shed, had been a thriving master-mechanist, notwithstanding his free and careless disposition, till a taste for a more than adequate quantity of strong liquor took hold of him; since when his habits had interfered with his business sadly. Already millers went elsewhere for their gear, and only one set of hands was now kept going, though there were formerly two. Already he found a difficulty in meeting his men at the week's end, and though they had been reduced in number there was barely enough work to do for those who remained.

The sun dropped lower and vanished, the shouts of the village children ceased to resound, darkness cloaked the students' bedroom, and all the scene outwardly breathed peace. None knew of the fevered youthful ambitions that throbbed in two breasts within the quiet creeper-covered walls of the millwright's house.

In a few months the brothers left the village of their birth to enter themselves as students in a Training College for school-masters; first having placed their young sister Rosa under as efficient a tuition at a fashionable watering-place as the means at their disposal could command.

II

A MAN in semi-clerical dress was walking along the road which led from the railway-station into a provincial town. As he walked he read persistently, only looking up once now and then to see that he was keeping on the foot-track, or to avoid other passengers. At those moments, whoever had known the former students at the millwright's would have perceived that one of them, Joshua Halborough, was the peripatetic reader here.

What had been simple force in the youth's face was energized judgment in the man's. His character was gradually writing itself out in his countenance. That he was watching his own career with deeper and deeper interest, that he continually "heard his days before him," and cared to hear little else, might have been hazarded from what was seen there. His ambitions were, in truth, passionate, yet controlled; so that the germs of many more plans than ever blossomed to maturity had place in him; and forward visions were kept purposely in twilight, to avoid distraction.

Events so far had been encouraging. Shortly after assuming the mastership of his first school he had obtained an introduction to the Bishop of a diocese far from his native county, who had looked upon him as a promising young man and taken him in hand. He was now in the second year of his residence at the Theological College of the cathedral-town, and would soon be presented for ordination.

He entered the town, turned into a back street, and then into a yard, keeping his book before him till he set foot under the arch of the latter place. Round the arch was written "National School", and the stonework of the jambs was worn away as nothing but boys and the waves of ocean will wear it. He was soon amid the sing-song accents of the scholars.

His brother Cornelius, who was the schoolmaster here, laid down the pointer with which he was directing attention to the capes of Europe, and came forward.

"That's his brother Jos!" whispered one of the sixth-standard boys. "He's going to be a pa'son. He's now at College."

"Corney is going to be one too, when he's saved enough money," said another.

After greeting his brother, whom he had not seen for several months, the junior began to explain his system of teaching geography.

But Halborough the elder took no interest in the subject. "How about your own studies?" he asked. "Did you get the books I sent?"

Cornelius had received them, and he related what he was doing.

"Mind you work in the morning. What time do you get up?"

The younger replied: "Half-past five."

"Half-past four is not a minute too soon this time of the year. There is no time like the morning for construing. I don't know why, but when I feel even too dreary to read a novel I can translate—there is something mechanical about it I suppose. Now Cornelius, you are rather behindhand, and have some heavy reading before you if you mean to get out of this next Christmas."

"I am afraid I have."

"We must soon sound the Bishop. I am sure you will get a title without difficulty when he has heard all. The sub-dean, the principal of my College, says that the best plan will be for you to come there when his lordship is present at an examination, and he'll get you a personal interview with him. Mind you make a good impression upon him. I found in my case that that was everything, and doctrine almost nothing. You'll do for a deacon, Corney, if not for a priest."

The younger remained thoughtful. "Have you heard from Rosa lately?" he asked. "I had a letter this morning."

"Yes. The little minx writes rather too often. She is homesick—though Brussels must be an attractive place enough. But she must make the most of her time over there. I thought a year would be enough for her, after that high-class school at Sandbourne, but I have decided to give her two, and make a good job of it, expensive as the establishment is."

Their two rather harsh faces had softened directly they began to speak of their sister, whom they loved more ambitiously than they loved themselves.

"But where is the money to come from Joshua?"

"I have already got it." He looked round, and finding that some boys were near withdrew a few steps. "I have borrowed it at five-per-cent from the farmer who used to occupy the farm next our field. You remember him."

"But about paying him?"

"I shall pay him by degrees out of my stipend. No, Cornelius, it was no use to do the thing by halves. She promises to be a most attractive, not to say beautiful, girl. I have seen that for years; and if her face is not her fortune, her face and her brains together will be, if I observe and contrive aright. That she should be, every inch of her, an accomplished and refined woman, was indispensable for the fulfilment of her destiny, and for moving onwards and upwards with us; and she'll do it, you will see. I'd half starve myself rather than take her away from that school now."

They looked round the school they were in. To Cornelius it was natural and familiar enough, but to Joshua, with his limited human sympathies, who had just dropped in from a superior sort of place, the sight jarred unpleasantly, as being that of something he had left behind. "I shall be glad when you are out of this," he said; "and in your pulpit, and well through your first sermon."

"You may as well say inducted into my fat living, while you are about it."

"Ah, well—don't think lightly of the Church. There's a fine work for any man of energy in the Church, as you'll find," he said fervidly. "Torrents of infidelity to be stemmed, new views of old subjects to be expounded, truths in spirit to be substituted for truths in the letter. . . ." He lapsed into reverie with the vision of his career, persuading himself that it was ardour for Christianity which spurred him on, and not pride of place. He had shouldered a body of doctrine, and was prepared to defend it tooth and nail, solely for the honour and glory that warriors win.

"If the Church is elastic, and stretches to the shape of the time, she'll last I suppose," said Cornelius. "If not—. Only think, I bought a copy of Paley's *Evidences*, best edition, broad margins, excellent preservation, at a bookstall the other day for—ninepence; and I thought that at this rate Christianity must be in rather a bad way."

"No, no!" said the other, almost angrily. "It only shows that such defences are no longer necessary. Men's eyes can see the truth without extraneous assistance. Besides, we are in for Christianity, and must stick to her, whether or no. I am just now going right through Pusey's *Library of the Fathers*."

"You'll be a bishop, Joshua, before you have done!"

"Ah!" said the other bitterly, shaking his head. "Perhaps I might have been—I might have been! But where is my D.D. or LL.D., and how be a bishop without that kind of appendage? Archbishop Tillotson was the son of a Sowerby clothier, but he was sent to Clare College. To hail Oxford or Cambridge as *alma mater* is not for me—for us. My God, when I think of what we should have been—what fair promise has been blighted by that cursed, worthless—"

"Hush, hush! . . . But I feel it, too, as much as you. I have seen it more forcibly lately. You would have obtained your degree long before this time—possibly fellowship—and I should have been on my way to mine."

"Don't talk of it," said the other. "We must do the best we can."

They looked out of the window sadly, through the dusty panes, so high up that only the sky was visible. By degrees the haunting trouble loomed again, and Cornelius broke the silence with a whisper: "He has called on me!"

The living pulses died in Joshua's face, which grew arid as a clinker. "When was that?" he asked quickly.

"Last week."

"How did he get here—so many miles?"

"Came by railway. He came to ask for money."

"Ah!"

"He says he will call on you."

Joshua replied resignedly. The theme of their conversation spoilt his buoyancy for that afternoon. He returned in the evening, Cornelius accompanying him to the station; but he did not read in the train which took him back to the Fountall Theological College as he had done on the way out. That ineradicable trouble still remained as a squalid spot in the expanse of his life. He sat with the other students in the Cathedral Choir next day; and the recollection of the trouble obscured the purple splendour thrown by the panes upon the floor.

It was afternoon. All was as still in the Close as a Cathedral-green can be between the Sunday services, and the incessant cawing of the rooks was the only sound. Joshua Halborough had finished his ascetic lunch, and had gone into the library, where he stood for a few moments looking out of the large window facing the green. He saw walking slowly across it a man in a fustian coat, and battered white hat with a much ruffled nap, having upon his arm a tall gipsy-woman wearing long brass earrings. The man was staring quizzically at the west front of the Cathedral, and Halborough recognized in him the form and features of his father. Who the woman was he knew not. Almost as soon as Joshua became conscious of these things, the sub-dean, who was also the principal of the College, and of whom the young man stood in more awe than of the Bishop himself, emerged from the gate, and entered a path across the Close. The pair met the dignitary, and to Joshua's horror his father turned and addressed the sub-dean.

What passed between them he could not tell. But as he stood in a cold sweat he saw his father place his hand familiarly on the sub-dean's shoulder; the shrinking response of the latter, and his quick withdrawal, told his feeling. The woman seemed to say nothing, but when the sub-dean had passed by they came on towards the college gate.

Halborough flew along the corridor and out at a side door, so as to intercept them before they could reach the front entrance for which they were making. He caught them behind a clump of laurel.

"By Jerry, here's the very chap! Well, you're a fine fellow Jos, never to send your father as much as a twist o' baccy on such an occasion, and to leave him to travel all these miles to find 'ee out!"

"First, who is this?" said Joshua Halborough with pale dignity, waving his hand towards the buxom woman with the great earrings.

"Dammy, the mis'ess! Your step-mother. Didn't you know I'd married? She helped me home from market one night, and we came to terms, and struck the bargain. Didn't we Selinar?"

"Oi, by the great Lord an' we did!" simpered the lady.

"Well, what sort of a place is this you are living in?" asked the millwright. "A kind of house-of-correction, apparently?"

Joshua listened abstractedly, his features set to resignation. Sick at heart he was going to ask them if they were in want of any necessary, any meal, when his father cut him short by saying, "Why we've called to ask ye to come round and take pot-luck with us at the Cock-and-Bottle, where we've put up for the day, on our way to see Mis'ess's friends at Binegar Fair, where they'll be lying under canvas for a night or two. As for the victuals at the Cock I can't testify to 'em at all; but for the drink, they've the rarest drop of Old Tom that I've tasted for many a year."

"Thanks; but I am a teetotaller; and I have lunched," said Joshua, who could fully believe his father's testimony to the gin, from the odour of his breath. "You see, we have to observe regular habits here; and—I couldn't be seen at the Cock-and-Bottle just now."

"O dammy, then don't come, your reverence. Perhaps you won't mind standing treat for those who can be seen there?"

"Not a penny!" said the younger firmly. "You've had enough already."

"Thank you for nothing! By the by, who was that spindle-legged, shoe-buckled parson-feller we met by now? He seemed to think we should poison him!"

Joshua remarked coldly that it was the principal of his College, guardedly enquiring, "Did you tell him whom you were come to see?"

His father did not reply. He and his strapping gipsy wife—if she were his wife—stayed no longer, and disappeared in the direction of the high-street. Joshua Halborough went back to the library. Determined as was his nature he wept hot tears upon the books, and was immeasurably more wretched that afternoon than the unwelcome mill-wright. In the evening he sat down and wrote a letter to his brother, in which, after stating what had happened, and expatiating upon this new disgrace in the gipsy wife, he propounded a plan for raising money sufficient to induce the couple to emigrate to Canada. "It is our only chance," he said. "The case as it stands is maddening. For a successful painter, sculptor, musician, author, who takes society by storm, it is no drawback, it is sometimes even a romantic recommendation, to hail from outcasts and profligates. But for a clergyman of the Church of England! Cornelius—it is fatal! To succeed in the Church people must believe in you, first of all, as a gentleman, sec-ondly as a man of means, thirdly as a scholar, fourthly as a preacher, fifthly, perhaps, as a Christian,—but always first as a gentleman, with all their heart and soul and strength. I would have faced the fact of being a small machinist's son, and have taken my chance, if he'd been in any sense respectable and decent. The essence of Christianity is humility, and by the help of God I would have brazened it out. But this terrible vagabondage and disreputable connexion: if he does not accept my terms and leave the country it will extinguish us and kill me! For how can we live, and relinquish our high aim, and bring down our dear sister Rosa to the level of a gipsy's step-daughter?"

III

THERE was excitement in the parish of Narrobourne one day. The congregation had just come out from morning service, and the whole conversation was of the new curate Mr Halborough, who had officiated for the first time, in the absence of the rector.

Never before had the feelings of the villagers approached a level which could be called excitement on such a matter as this. The droning which had been the rule in that quiet old place for a century seemed ended at last. They repeated the text to each other as a refrain: "O Lord be thou my helper!" Not within living memory till to-day had the subject of the sermon formed the topic of conversation from the church-door to churchyard-gate, to the exclusion of personal remarks on those who had been present, and on the week's news in general.

The thrilling periods of the preacher hung about their minds all that day. The parish being steeped in indifferentism it happened that when the youths and maidens, middle-aged and old people, who had attended church that morning, recurred as by a fascination to what Halborough had said, they did so more or less indirectly, and even with the subterfuge of a light laugh that was not real, so great was their shyness under the novelty of their sensations.

What was more curious than that these unconventional villagers should have been excited by a preacher of a new school after forty years of familiarity with the old hand who had had charge of their souls, was the effect of Halborough's address upon the occupants of the manor-house pew, including the owner of the estate. These thought they knew how to discount the mere sensational sermon, how to minimize flash oratory to its bare proportions; but they had yielded like the rest of the assembly to the charm of the newcomer.

Mr Fellmer, the landowner, was a young widower, whose mother, still in the prime of life, had returned to her old position in the family mansion since the death of her son's wife in the year after her marriage, at the birth of a fragile little girl. From the date of his loss to the present time Fellmer had led an inactive existence in the seclusion of the parish; a lack of motive seemed to leave him listless; he had gladly reinstated his mother in the gloomy house, and his main occupation now lay in stewarding his estate, which was not large. Mrs Fellmer, who had sat beside him under Halborough this morning, was a cheerful, straightforward woman, who did her marketing and her almsgiving in person, was fond of old-fashioned flowers, and walked about the village on very wet days visiting the parishioners. These, the only two great ones of Narrobourne, were impressed by Joshua's eloquence as much as the cottagers.

Halborough had been briefly introduced to them on his arrival some days before, and their interest being kindled they waited a few moments till he came out of the vestry, to walk down the churchyard-path with him. Mrs Fellmer spoke warmly of the sermon, of the good fortune of the parish in his advent, and hoped he had found comfortable quarters.

Halborough, faintly flushing, said that he had obtained very fair lodgings in the roomy house of a farmer whom he named.

She feared he would find it very lonely, especially in the evenings, and hoped they would see a good deal of him. When would he dine with them? Could he not come that very day—it must be so dull for him, the first Sunday evening in country lodgings?

Halborough replied that it would give him much pleasure, but that he feared he must decline. "I am not altogether alone," he said. "My sister, who has just returned from

Brussels, and who felt as you do, that I should be rather dismal by myself, has accompanied me hither, to stay a few days till she has put my rooms in order and set me going. She was too fatigued to come to church, and is waiting for me now at the farm."

"Oh, but bring your sister—that will be still better! I shall be delighted to know her. How I wish I had been aware—Do tell her, please, that we had no idea of her presence."

Halborough assured Mrs Fellmer that he would certainly bear the message; but as to her coming he was not so sure. The real truth was, however, that the matter would be decided by him, Rosa having an almost filial respect for his wishes. But he was uncertain as to the state of her wardrobe, and had determined that she should not enter the manor-house at a disadvantage that evening, when there would probably be plenty of opportunities in the future of her doing so becomingly.

He walked to the farm in long strides. This, then, was the outcome of his first morning's work as curate here. Things had gone fairly well with him. He had been ordained; he was in a comfortable parish, where he would exercise almost sole supervision, the rector being infirm; he had made a deep impression at starting; and the absence of a hood seemed to have done him no harm. Moreover, by considerable persuasion and payment his father and the dark woman had been shipped off to Canada, where they were not likely to interfere greatly with his interests.

Rosa came out to meet him. "Ah, you should have gone to church, like a good girl," he said.

"Yes—I wished I had afterwards. But I do so hate church as a rule that even your preaching was underestimated in my mind. It was too bad of me!"

The girl who spoke thus playfully was fair, tall, and sylph-like—in a muslin dress, and with just the coquettish *désinvolture* which an English girl brings home from abroad and loses again after a few months of native life. Joshua was the reverse of playful: the world was too important a concern for him to indulge in light moods. He told her in decided practical phraseology of the invitation.

"Now, Rosa, we must go—that's settled—if you've a dress that can be made fit to wear all on the hop like this. You didn't, of course, think of bringing an evening dress to such an out-of-the-way place?"

But Rosa had come from the wrong city to be caught napping in those matters. "Yes I did," said she. "One never knows what may turn up."

"Well done! Then off we go at seven."

The evening drew on, and at dusk they started on foot, Rosa pulling up the edge of her skirt under her cloak, out of the way of the dews, so that it formed a great wind-bag all round her, and carrying her satin shoes under her arm. Joshua would not let her wait till she got indoors before changing them, as she proposed, but insisted on her performing that operation under a tree, so that they might enter as if they had not walked. He was nervously formal about such trifles, while Rosa took the whole proceeding—walk, dressing, dinner, and all—as a pastime. To Joshua it was a serious step in life.

A more unexpected kind of person for a curate's sister was never presented at a dinner. The surprise of Mrs Fellmer was unconcealed. She had looked forward to a Dorcas, or Martha, or Rhoda at the outside, and a shade of misgiving crossed her face. It was possible that, had the young lady accompanied her brother to church there would have been no dining at Narrobourne House that day.

Not so with the young widower her son. He resembled a sleeper who had awaked in a summer noon expecting to find it only dawn. He could scarcely help stretching his arms and yawning in their faces, so strong was his sense of being suddenly aroused to an unforeseen thing. When they had sat down to table he at first talked to Rosa somewhat with the air of a ruler in the land; but the woman lurking in the acquaintance soon brought him to his level; and the girl from Brussels saw him looking at her mouth, her hands, her contour, as if he could not quite comprehend how they got created: then he dropped into the more satisfactory stage which discerns no particulars.

He talked but little; she said much. The homeliness of the

Fellmers, to her view, though they were regarded with such awe down here, quite disembarrassed her. The squire had become so unpractised, had dropped so far into the shade during the last year or so of his life, that he had almost forgotten what the world contained till this evening reminded him. His mother, after her first moments of doubt, appeared to think that he must be left to his own guidance, and gave her attention to Joshua.

With all his foresight and doggedness of aim the result of that dinner exceeded Halborough's expectations. In weaving his ambitions he had viewed his sister Rosa as a slight bright thing to be helped into notice by his abilities; but it now began to dawn upon him that the physical gifts of Nature to her might do more for them both than Nature's intellectual gifts to himself. While he was patiently boring the tunnel Rosa seemed about to fly over the mountain.

He wrote the next day to his brother—now occupying his own old rooms in the Theological College, telling him exultingly of the unanticipated *début* of Rosa at the manor-house. The next post brought him a reply of congratulation— dashed with the counteracting intelligence that his father did not like Canada—that his gipsy wife had deserted him, which made him feel so dreary that he thought of returning home.

In his recent satisfaction at his own successes Joshua Halborough had well-nigh forgotten his chronic trouble— latterly screened by distance. But it now returned upon him; he saw more in this brief announcement than his brother seemed to see. It was the cloud no bigger than a man's hand.

IV

THE following December, a day or two before Christmas, Mrs Fellmer and her son were walking up and down the broad gravel path which bordered the east front of the house. Till within the last half-hour the morning had been a drizzling one, and they had just emerged for a short turn before luncheon.

"You see, dear mother," the son was saying, "it is the peculiarity of my position which makes her appear to me in such a desirable light. When you consider how I have been crippled at starting, how my life has been maimed, that I feel anything like publicity distasteful, that I have no political ambition, and that my chief aim and hope lie in the education of the little thing Annie has left me, you must see how desirable a wife like Miss Halborough would be, to prevent my becoming a mere vegetable."

"If you adore her I suppose you must have her!" replied his mother with dry indirectness. "But you'll find that she will not be content to live on here as you do, giving her whole mind to a young child."

"That's just where we differ. Her very disqualification, that of being a nobody, as you call it, is her recommendation in my eyes. Her lack of influential connections limits her ambition. From what I know of her a life in this place is all that she would wish for. She would never care to go outside the park-gates if it were necessary to stay within."

"Being in love with her, Albert, and meaning to marry her, you invent your practical reasons to make the case respectable. Well, do as you will—I have no authority over you, so why should you consult me? You mean to propose on this very occasion, no doubt. Don't you, now?"

"By no means. I am merely revolving the idea in my mind. If on further acquaintance she turns out to be as good as she has hitherto seemed—well, I shall see. Admit, now, that you like her."

"I readily admit it. She is very captivating at first sight. But as a stepmother to your child—. You seem mighty anxious, Albert, to get rid of me!"

"Not at all. And I am not so reckless as you think. I don't make up my mind in a hurry. But the thought having occurred to me I mention it to you at once, mother. If you dislike it, say so."

"I don't say anything. I will try to make the best of it, if you are determined. When does she come?"

"To-morrow."

All this time there were great preparations in train at the

curate's—who was now a householder. Rosa, whose two or three weeks' stay on two occasions earlier in the year had so affected the squire, was coming again, and at the same time her younger brother Cornelius, to make up a family-party. Rosa, who journeyed from the Midlands, could not arrive till late in the evening, but Cornelius was to get there in the afternoon, Joshua going out to meet him in his walk across the fields from the railway.

Everything being ready in Joshua's modest abode he started on his way, his heart buoyant and thankful if ever it was in his life. He was of such good report himself that his brother's path into holy orders promised to be unexpectedly easy, and he longed to compare experiences with him, even though there was on hand a more exciting matter still. From his youth he had held that, in old-fashioned country places, the Church conferred social prestige up to a certain point at a cheaper price than any other profession or pursuit; and events seemed to be proving him right.

He had walked about half-an-hour when he saw Cornelius coming along the path; and in a few minutes the two brothers met. The experiences of Cornelius had been less immediately interesting than those of Joshua, but his personal position was satisfactory, and there was nothing to account for the singularly subdued manner that he exhibited, which at first Joshua set down to the fatigue of over-study, and he proceeded to the subject of Rosa's arrival in the evening, and the probable consequences of this her third visit. "Before next Easter she'll be his wife, my boy," said Joshua with grave exultation.

Cornelius shook his head. "She comes too late!" he returned.

"What do you mean?"

"Look here." He produced the Fountall paper, and placed his finger on a paragraph, which Joshua read. It appeared under the report of Petty Sessions, and was a commonplace case of disorderly conduct, in which a man was sent to prison for seven days for breaking windows in that town.

"Well?" said Joshua.

"It happened during an evening that I was in the street; and the offender is our father."

"Not—how—I sent him more money on his promising to stay in Canada?"

"He is home, safe enough." Cornelius in the same gloomy tone gave the remainder of his information. He had witnessed the scene, unobserved of his father, and had heard him say that he was on his way to see his daughter, who was going to marry a rich gentleman. The only good fortune attending the untoward incident was that the millwright's name had been printed as Joshua Alborough.

"Beaten! We are to be beaten on the eve of our expected victory!" said the elder brother. "How did he guess that Rosa was likely to marry? Good Heaven! Cornelius, you seem doomed to bring bad news always, do you not!"

"I do," said Cornelius. "Poor Rosa!"

It was almost in tears, so great was their heart-sickness and shame, that the brothers walked the remainder of the way to Joshua's dwelling. In the evening they set out to meet Rosa, bringing her to the village in a fly; and when she had come into the house, and was sitting down with them, they almost forgot their secret anxiety in contemplating her, who knew nothing about it.

Next day the Fellmers came, and the two or three days after that were a lively time. That the squire was yielding to his impulses—making up his mind—there could be no doubt. On Sunday Cornelius read the service and Joshua preached. Mrs Fellmer was quite maternal towards Rosa, and it appeared that she had decided to welcome the inevitable with a good grace. The pretty girl was to spend yet another afternoon with the elder lady, superintending some parish treat at the house in observance of Christmas, and afterwards to stay on to dinner, her brothers to fetch her in the evening. They were also invited to dine, but they could not accept owing to an engagement.

The engagement was of a sombre sort. They were going to meet their father, who would that day be released from Fountall Gaol, and try to persuade him to keep away from Narrobourne. Every exertion was to be made to get him back to Canada, to his old home in the Midlands—anywhere; so that he would not impinge disastrously upon their courses, and blast their sister's prospects of the auspicious marriage which was just then hanging in the balance.

As soon as Rosa had been fetched away by her friends at the manor-house her brothers started on their expedition without waiting for dinner or tea. Cornelius, to whom the millwright always addressed his letters when he wrote any, drew from his pocket and re-read as he walked the curt note which had led to this journey being undertaken; it was despatched by their father the night before, immediately upon his liberation; and stated that he was setting out for Narrobourne at the moment of writing; that having no money he would be obliged to walk all the way; that he calculated on passing through the intervening town of Ivell about six on the following day, where he should sup at the Castle Inn, and where he hoped they would meet him with a carriage-and-pair, or some other such conveyance, that he might not disgrace them by arriving like a tramp.

"That sounds as if he gave a thought to our position," said Cornelius.

Joshua knew the satire that lurked in the paternal words, and said nothing. Silence prevailed during the greater part of their journey. The lamps were lighted in Ivell when they entered the streets, and Cornelius, who was quite unknown in this neighbourhood, and who, moreover, was not in clerical attire, decided that he should be the one to call at the Castle Inn. Here, in answer to his inquiry under the darkness of the archway, they told him that such a man as he had described left the house about a quarter of an hour earlier, after making a meal in the kitchen-settle. He was rather the worse for liquor.

"Then," said Joshua, when Cornelius joined him outside with this intelligence, "we must have met and passed him. And now that I think of it we did meet some one who was unsteady in his gait, under the trees on the other side of Hendford Hill, where it was too dark to see him."

They rapidly retraced their steps; but for a long stretch of the way home could discern nobody. When however they had gone about three-quarters of the distance they became conscious of an irregular footfall in front of them, and could see a whitish figure in the gloom. They followed dubiously. The figure met another wayfarer—the single one that had been encountered upon this lonely road—and they distinctly heard him ask the way to Narrobourne. The stranger replied—what was quite true—that the nearest way was by turning in at the stile by the next bridge, and following the foot-path which branched thence across the meadows.

When the brothers reached the stile they also entered the path, but did not overtake the subject of their worry till they had crossed two or three meads, and the lights from Narrobourne Manor-House were visible before them through the trees. Their father was no longer walking; he was seated against the wet bank of an adjoining hedge. Observing their forms he shouted, "I'm going to Narrobourne. Who may you be?"

They went up to him, and revealed themselves, reminding him of the plan which he had himself proposed in his note, that they should meet him at Ivell.

"By Jerry, I'd forgot it!" he said. "Well, what do you want me to do?" His tone was distinctly quarrelsome.

A long conversation followed, which became embittered at the first hint from them that he should not come to the village. The millwright drew a quart bottle from his pocket, and challenged them to drink if they meant friendly and called themselves men. Neither of the two had touched alcohol for years, but for once they thought it best to accept, so as not to needlessly provoke him.

"What's in it?" said Joshua.

"A drop of weak gin-and-water. It won't hurt 'ee. Drink from the bottle." Joshua did so, and his father pushed up the bottom of the vessel, so as to make him swallow a good deal in spite of himself. It went down into his stomach like molten lead.

"Ha-ha—that's right!" said old Halborough. "But 'twas raw spirit—ha-ha!"

"Why should you take me in so!" said Joshua, losing his self-command, try as he would to keep calm.

"Because you took me in, my lad, in banishing me to that cursed country under pretence that it was for my good. You

were a pair of hypocrites to say so. It was done to get rid of
me—no more nor less. But by Jerry I'm a match for ye now!
I'll spoil your souls for preaching. My daughter is going to be
married to the squire here—I've heard the news—I saw it in
a paper!"

"It is premature—"

"I know it is true, and I'm her father, and I shall give her
away, or there'll be a hell of a row I can assure 'ee. Is that
where the gennleman lives?"

Joshua Halborough writhed in impotent despair. Fellmer
had not yet positively declared himself, his mother was hardly
won round; a scene with their father in the parish would
demolish as fair a palace of hopes as was ever builded. The
millwright rose. "If that's where the squire lives I'm going to
call. Just arrived from Canady with her fortune—ha-ha! I wish
no harm to the gennleman, and the gennleman will wish no
harm to me. But I like to take my place in the family, and
stand upon my rights, and lower people's pride!"

"You've succeeded already! Where's that woman you took
with you—"

"Woman! She was my wife as lawful as the Constitution—a
sight more lawful than your mother was till some time after
you were born!"

Joshua had many years before heard whispers that his
father had cajoled his mother in their early acquaintance, and
had made somewhat tardy amends; but never from his
father's lips till now. It was the last stroke, and he could not
bear it. He sank back against the hedge. "It is over!" he said.
"He ruins us all!"

The millwright moved on, waving his stick triumphantly,
and the two brothers stood still. They could see his drab
figure stalking along the path, and over his head the lights
from the conservatory of Narrobourne House; inside which
Albert Fellmer might possibly be sitting with Rosa at that
moment, holding her hand, and asking her to share his home
with him.

The staggering whitey-brown form, advancing to put a blot
upon all this, had been diminishing in the shade, and now
suddenly disappeared beside a weir. There was the noise of a
flounce in the water.

"He has fallen in!" said Cornelius, starting forward to run for the place at which his father had vanished.

Joshua, awakening from the stupefied reverie into which he had sunk, rushed to the other's side before he had taken ten steps. "Stop, stop, what are you thinking of!" he whispered hoarsely, grasping Cornelius's arm.

"Pulling him out!"

"Yes, yes—so am I. But—wait a moment—"

"But Joshua!"

"Her life and happiness you know—Cornelius—and your reputation and mine—and our chance of rising together, all three—"

He clutched his brother's arm to the bone; and as they stood breathless the splashing and floundering in the weir continued; and over it they saw the hopeful lights from the manor-house conservatory winking through the trees as their bare branches waved to and fro. In their pause there had been time to save him twice over.

The floundering and splashing grew weaker, and they could hear gurgling words: "Help—I'm drownded! Rosie—Rosie!"

"We'll go—we *must* save him. O Joshua!"

"Yes, yes; we must!"

Still they did not move, but waited, holding each other, each thinking the same thought. Weights of lead seemed to be affixed to their feet, which would no longer obey their wills. The mead became silent. Over it they fancied they could see figures moving in the conservatory. The air up there seemed to emit gentle kisses.

Cornelius started forward at last, and Joshua almost simultaneously. Two or three minutes brought them to the brink of the stream. At first they could see nothing in the water, though it was not so deep nor the night so dark but that their father's light kerseymere coat would have been visible if he had lain at the bottom. Joshua looked this way and that.

"He has drifted into the culvert," he said.

Below the foot-bridge of the weir the stream suddenly narrowed to half its width, to pass under a barrel-arch or culvert constructed for waggons to cross into the middle of the mead in haymaking time. It being at present the season of high water the arch was full to the crown, against which the ripples clucked every now and then. At this point he had just caught sight of a pale object slipping under. In a moment it was gone.

They went to the lower end, but nothing emerged. For a long time they tried at both ends to effect some communication with the interior, but to no purpose.

"We ought to have come sooner!" said the conscience-stricken Cornelius, when they were quite exhausted, and dripping wet.

"I suppose we ought," replied Joshua heavily. He perceived his father's walking-stick on the bank; hastily picking it up he stuck it into the mud among the sedge. Then they went on.

"Shall we—say anything about this accident?" whispered Cornelius as they approached the door of Joshua's house.

"What's the use? It can do no good. We must wait until he is found."

They went indoors, and changed their clothes: after which they started for the manor-house, reaching it about ten o'clock. Besides their sister there were only three guests; an adjoining landowner and his wife, and the infirm old rector.

Rosa, although she had parted from them so recently, grasped their hands in an ecstatic, brimming, joyful manner, as if she had not seen them for years. "You look pale," she said.

The brothers answered that they had had a long walk, and were somewhat tired. Everybody in the room seemed charged full with some sort of interesting knowledge: the squire's neighbour and neighbour's wife looked wisely around; and Fellmer himself played the part of host with a preoccupied bearing which approached fervour. They left at eleven, not accepting the carriage offered, the distance being so short, and the roads dry. The squire came rather further into the dark with them than he need have done, and wished Rosa good-night in a mysterious manner, slightly apart from the rest.

When they were walking along Joshua said with a desperate attempt at joviality, "Rosa, what's going on?"

"O, I—" she began between a gasp and a titter. "He—"

"Never mind—if it disturbs you."

She was so excited that she could not speak connectedly at first, the practised air which she had brought home with her having disappeared. Calming herself she added, "I am not disturbed, and nothing has happened. Only he said he wanted to ask me *something*, some day; and I said, never mind that now. He hasn't asked yet, and is coming to speak to you about it. He would have done so to-night, only I asked him not to be in a hurry. But he will come to-morrow I am sure!"

V

IT was summer-time, six months later, and mowers and hay-makers were at work in the meads. The manor-house, being opposite them, frequently formed a peg for conversation during these operations; and the doings of the squire, and the squire's young wife, the curate's sister—who was at present the admired of most of them, and the interest of all—met with their due amount of criticism.

Rosa was happy, if ever woman could be said to be so. She had not learnt the fate of her father, and sometimes wondered—perhaps with a sense of relief—why he did not write to her from his supposed home in Canada. Her brother Joshua had been presented to a living in a small town, shortly after her marriage, and Cornelius had thereupon succeeded to the vacant curacy of Narrobourne.

These two had awaited in deep suspense the discovery of their father's body; and yet the discovery had not been made. Every day they expected a man or a boy to run up from the meads with the intelligence; but he had never come. Days had accumulated to weeks and months; the wedding had come and gone; Joshua had tolled and read himself in at his new parish; and never a shout of amazement over the millwright's remains.

But now, in June, when they were mowing the meads, the hatches had to be drawn, and the water let out of its channels for the convenience of the mowers. It was thus that the discovery was made. A man, stooping low with his scythe, caught a view of the culvert lengthwise, and saw something entangled in the recently bared weeds of its bed. A day or two after there was an inquest; but the body was unrecognizable. Fish and flood had been busy with the millwright; he had no watch or marked article which could be identified; and a verdict of the accidental drowning of a person unknown settled the matter.

As the body was found in Narrobourne parish there it had to be buried. Cornelius wrote to Joshua, begging him to come and read the service, or to send some one; he himself could not do it. Rather than let in a stranger Joshua came; and silently scanned the coroner's order handed him by the undertaker:

"I, Henry Giles, Coroner for the Mid-Division of Outer Wessex, do hereby order the Burial of the Body now shown to the Inquest Jury as the Body of an Adult Male Person Unknown . . . ," etc.

Joshua Halborough got through the service in some way, and rejoined his brother Cornelius at his house. Neither accepted an invitation to lunch at their sister's; they wished to discuss parish matters together. In the afternoon she came down, though they had already called on her, and had not expected to see her again. Her bright eyes, brown hair, flowery bonnet, lemon-coloured gloves, and flush beauty, were like an irradiation into the apartment which they in their gloom could hardly bear.

"I forgot to tell you," she said, "of a curious thing which happened to me a month or two before my marriage—something which I have thought may have had a connection with the accident to the poor man you have buried to-day. It was on that evening I was at the manor-house waiting for you to fetch me; I was in the winter-garden with Albert, and we were sitting silent together, when we fancied we heard a cry in the distant meadow. We opened the door, and while Albert ran to fetch his hat, leaving me standing there, the cry was repeated, and my excited senses made me think I heard my own name. When Albert came back all was silent, and we decided that it was only a drunken shout, and not a cry for help. We both forgot the incident; and it never has occurred to me till since the funeral to-day that it might have been this stranger's cry. The name of course was only fancy—or he might have had a wife or child with a name something like mine, poor man!"

When she was gone the brothers were silent till Cornelius said, "Now mark this, Joshua. Sooner or later she'll know."

"How?"

"From one of us. Do you think human hearts are iron-cased safes, that you suppose we can keep this secret for ever?"

"Yes—I think they are, sometimes," said Joshua.

"No. It will out. We shall tell."

"What, and ruin her—kill her? Disgrace her children, and pull down the whole auspicious house of Fellmer about our ears? No! May I—drown where he was drowned before I do it. Never, never. Surely you can say the same, Cornelius!"

Cornelius seemed fortified, and no more was said. For a long time after that day he did not see Joshua, and before the next year was out a son and heir was born to the Fellmers. The villagers rang the three bells every evening for a week and more, and were made merry by Mr Fellmer's ale; and when the christening came on Joshua paid Narrobourne another visit.

Among all the people who assembled on that day the brother clergymen were the least interested. Their minds were haunted by a spirit in kerseymere. In the evening they walked together in the fields.

"She's all right," said Joshua. "But here are you doing journey-work, Cornelius, and likely to continue at it till the end of the day, as far as I can see. I, too, with my petty living— what am I after all? . . . To tell the truth, the Church is a poor forlorn hope for people without influence, particularly when their enthusiasm begins to flag. A social regenerator has a better chance outside, where he is unhampered by dogma and tradition. As for me, I would rather have gone on mending mills, with my crust of bread and liberty."

Almost automatically they had bent their steps along the margin of the river; they now paused. They were standing on the brink of the well-known weir. There were the hatches, there was the culvert; they could see the pebbly bed of the stream through the pellucid water. The notes of the church-bells were audible, still jangled by the enthusiastic villagers.

"Why see—it was there I hid his walking-stick!" said Joshua, looking towards the sedge. The next moment, during a passing breeze, something flashed white on the spot to which the attention of Cornelius was drawn.

From the sedge rose a straight little silver-poplar, and it was the leaves of this sapling which caused the flicker of whiteness.

"His walking-stick has grown!" Joshua added. "It was a rough one—cut from the hedge, I remember."

At every puff of wind the tree turned white, till they could not bear to look at it; and they walked away.

"I see him every night," Cornelius murmured.... "Ah, we read our *Hebrews* to little account, Jos! "Ὑπέμεινε σταυρὸν, αἰσχύνης καταφρονήσας. To have *endured* the cross, *despising* the shame—there lay greatness! But now I often feel that I should like to put an end to trouble here in this self-same spot."

"I have thought of it myself," said Joshua.

"Perhaps we shall, some day," murmured his brother.

"Perhaps," said Joshua moodily.

With that contingency to consider in the silence of their nights and days they bent their steps homewards.

December 1888.

ON THE WESTERN CIRCUIT

I

THE man who played the disturbing part in the two quiet feminine lives hereunder depicted—no great man, in any sense, by the way—first had knowledge of them on an October evening, in the city of Melchester. He had been standing in the Close, vainly endeavouring to gain amid the darkness a glimpse of the most homogeneous pile of mediaeval architecture in England, which towered and tapered from the damp and level sward in front of him. While he stood the presence of the Cathedral walls was revealed rather by the ear than by the eyes; he could not see them, but they reflected sharply a roar of sound which entered the Close by a street leading from the city square, and, falling upon the building, was flung back upon him.

He postponed till the morrow his attempt to examine the deserted edifice, and turned his attention to the noise. It was compounded of steam barrel-organs, the clanging of gongs, the ringing of hand-bells, the clack of rattles, and the undistinguishable shouts of men. A lurid light hung in the air in the direction of the tumult. Thitherward he went, passing under the arched gateway, along a straight street, and into the square.

He might have searched Europe over for a greater contrast between juxtaposed scenes. The spectacle was that of the eighth chasm of the Inferno as to colour and flame, and, as to mirth, a development of the Homeric heaven. A smoky glare, of the complexion of brass-filings, ascended from the fiery tongues of innumerable naphtha lamps affixed to booths, stalls, and other temporary erections which crowded the spacious market-square. In front of this irradiation scores of human figures, more or less in profile, were darting athwart and across, up, down, and around, like gnats against a sunset.

Their motions were so rhythmical that they seemed to be

moved by machinery. And it presently appeared that they were moved by machinery indeed; the figures being those of the patrons of swings, see-saws, flying-leaps, above all of the three steam roundabouts which occupied the centre of the position. It was from the latter that the din of steam-organs came.

Throbbing humanity in full light was, on second thoughts, better than architecture in the dark. The young man, lighting a short pipe and putting his hat on one side and one hand in his pocket, to throw himself into harmony with his new environment, drew near to the largest and most patronized of the steam-circuses (as the roundabouts were called by their owners). This was one of brilliant finish, and it was now in full revolution. The musical instrument in the midst, to whose tones the riders revolved, directed its trumpet-mouths of brass upon the young man, and the long plate-glass mirrors set at angles, which revolved with the machine, flashed the gyrating personages and hobby-horses kaleidoscopically into his eyes.

It could now be seen that he was unlike the majority of the crowd. He was a gentlemanly young fellow, one of the species found in large towns only, and London particularly, built on delicate lines, well though not fashionably dressed, and appeared to belong to the professional class. Yet he had nothing square or practical about his look, much that was curvilinear and sensuous. Indeed, some would have called him a man not altogether typical of the middle-class male of a century wherein sordid ambition is the master-passion that seems to be taking the time-honoured place of love.

The revolving figures passed before his eyes with an unexpected and quiet grace in a throng whose natural movements did not suggest gracefulness or quietude as a rule. By some contrivance there was imparted to each of the hobby-horses a motion which was really the triumph and perfection of roundabout inventiveness—a galloping rise and fall, so timed that, of each pair of steeds, one was on the spring while the other was on the pitch. The riders were quite fascinated by these equine undulations in this most delightful fair-day-game of our times. There were riders as young as six, and as old as sixty years, with every age between. At first it was difficult to catch a personality, but by-and-by the observer's eyes centred on the prettiest girl out of the several pretty ones revolving.

It was not that one with the light frock and light hat whom he had been at first attracted by: no, it was the one with the brown cape, crimson skirt, light gloves and—no, not even she; but the one behind her; she with the black skirt, grey jacket, black and white hat and white cotton gloves. Unmistakably that was the prettiest girl.

Having finally selected her this idle spectator studied her as well as he was able during each of her brief transits across his visual field. She was absolutely unconscious of everything save the act of riding: her features were rapt in an ecstatic dreaminess; for the moment she did not know her age or her history or her lineaments, much less her troubles. He himself was full of vague latter-day glooms and popular melancholies, and it was a refreshing sensation to behold this young thing then and there, absolutely as happy as if she were in a Paradise.

Dreading the moment when the inexorable stoker, grimily lurking behind the glittering rococo-work, should decide that this set of riders had had their pennyworth, and bring the whole concern of steam-engine, horses, mirrors, trumpets, drums, cymbals, and such-like to pause and silence, he waited for her every reappearance, glancing indifferently over the intervening series, including the two plainer girls, the old woman and child, the two youngsters, the newly-married couple, the old man with a clay pipe, the sparkish youth with a ring, the young ladies in the chariot, the pair of journeyman-carpenters, and others, till his select country beauty followed on again in her place. He had never seen a fairer product of nature, and at each round she made a deeper mark in his sentiments. The stoppage then came, and the sighs of the riders were audible.

He moved round to the place at which he reckoned she would alight, but she retained her seat. The empty saddles began to refill, and she plainly was deciding to have another turn. The young man drew up to the side of her steed, and pleasantly asked her if she had enjoyed her ride.

"O yes!" she said, with dancing eyes. "It has been quite unlike anything I have ever felt in my life before!"

It was not difficult to fall into conversation with her. Unreserved—too unreserved—by nature, she was not experienced enough to be reserved by art, and after a little coaxing she answered his remarks readily. She had come to live in Melchester from a village on the Great Plain, and this was the first time that she had ever seen a steam-circus: she could not understand how such wonderful machines were made. She had come to the city on the invitation of Mrs Harnham, who had taken her into her household to train her as a servant if she showed any aptitude. Mrs Harnham was a young lady who before she married had been Miss Edith White, living in the country near the speaker's cottage; and was now very kind to her through knowing her in childhood so well. She was even taking the trouble to educate her. Mrs Harnham was the only friend she had in the world, and being without children had wished to have her near her in preference to anybody else, though she had only lately come; allowed her to do almost as she liked, and to have a holiday whenever she asked for it. The husband of this kind young lady was a rich wine-merchant of the town, but Mrs Harnham did not care much about him. In the daytime you could see the house from where they were talking. She, the speaker, liked Melchester better than the lonely country, and she was going to have a new hat for next Sunday that was to cost fifteen and ninepence.

Then she inquired of her acquaintance where he lived, and he told her in London, that ancient and smoky city, where everybody lived who lived at all, and died because they could not live there. He came into Wessex two or three times a year for professional reasons; he had arrived from Wintoncester yesterday, and was going on into the next county in a day or two. For one thing he did like the country better than the town, and it was because it contained such girls as herself.

Then the pleasure-machine started again, and, to the light-hearted girl, the figure of the handsome young man, the market-square with its lights and crowd, the houses beyond, and the world at large, began moving round as before, countermoving in the revolving mirrors on her right hand, she being as it were the fixed point in an undulating, dazzling, lurid universe, in which loomed forward most prominently of all the form of her late interlocutor. Each time that she approached the half of her orbit that lay nearest him they gazed at each other with smiles, and with that unmistakable expression which means so little at the moment, yet so often leads up to passion, heart-ache, union, disunion, devotion, overpopulation, drudgery, discontent, resignation, despair.

When the horses slowed anew he stepped to her side and proposed another heat. "Hang the expense for once," he said. "I'll pay."

She laughed till the tears came.

"Why do you laugh, dear?" said he.

"Because—you are so genteel that you must have plenty o' money, and only say that for fun!" she returned.

"Ha-ha!" laughed the young man in unison, and gallantly producing his money she was enabled to whirl on again.

As he stood smiling there in the motley crowd, with his pipe in his hand, and clad in the rough pea-jacket and wideawake that he had put on for his stroll, who would have supposed him to be Charles Bradford Raye, Esquire, stuff-gownsman, educated at Wintoncester, called to the Bar at Lincoln's-Inn, now going the Western Circuit, merely detained in Melchester by a small arbitration after his brethren had moved on to the next county-town?

II

THE square was overlooked from its remoter corner by the house of which the young girl had spoken—a dignified residence of considerable size, having several windows on each floor. Inside one of these, on the first floor, the apartment being a large drawing-room, sat a lady, in appearance from twenty-eight to thirty years of age. The blinds were still undrawn, and the lady was absently surveying the weird scene without, her cheek resting on her hand. The room was unlit from within, but enough of the glare from the market-place entered it to reveal the lady's face. She was what is called an interesting creature rather than a handsome woman; dark-eyed, thoughtful, and with sensitive lips.

A man sauntered into the room from behind and came forward.

"O Edith—I didn't see you," he said. "Why are you sitting here in the dark?"

"I am looking at the fair," replied the lady in a languid voice.

"Oh? Horrid nuisance every year! I wish it could be put a stop to."

"I like it."

"H'm. There's no accounting for taste." For a moment he gazed from the window with her, for politeness sake, and then went out again.

In a few minutes she rang. "Hasn't Anna come in?" asked Mrs Harnham.

"No m'm."

"She ought to be in by this time. I meant her to go for ten minutes only."

"Shall I go and look for her m'm?" said the housemaid alertly.

"No. It is not necessary. She is a good girl and will come soon."

However, when the servant had gone Mrs Harnham arose, went up to her room, cloaked and bonneted herself, and proceeded downstairs, where she found her husband.

"I want to see the fair," she said, "and I am going to look for Anna. I have made myself responsible for her, and must see she comes to no harm. She ought to be indoors. Will you come with me?"

"Oh—she's all right. I saw her on one of those whirligig things, talking to her young man as I came in. But I'll go if you wish, though I'd rather go a hundred miles the other way."

"Then please do so. I shall come to no harm alone."

She left the house and entered the crowd which thronged the market-place, where she soon discerned Anna, seated on the revolving horse. As soon as it stopped Mrs Harnham advanced and said severely, "Anna, how can you be such a wild girl? You were only to be out for ten minutes."

Anna looked blank, and the young man, who had dropped into the background, came to help her alight. "Please don't blame her," he said politely. "It is my fault that she has stayed. She looked so graceful on the horse that I induced her to go round again. I assure you that she has been quite safe."

"In that case I'll leave her in your hands," said Mrs Harnham, turning to retrace her steps. But this, for the moment, it was not so easy to do. Something had attracted the crowd to a spot in their rear, and the wine-merchant's wife, caught by its sway, found herself pressed against Anna's acquaintance without power to move away. Their faces were within a few inches of each other, his breath fanned her cheek as well as Anna's. They could do no other than smile at the accident; but neither spoke and each waited passively. Mrs Harnham then felt a man's hand clasping her fingers, and from the look of consciousness on the young fellow's face she knew the hand to be his: she also knew that from the position of the girl he had no other thought than that the imprisoned hand was Anna's. What prompted her to refrain from undeceiving him she could hardly tell. Not content with holding the hand, he playfully slipped two of his fingers inside her glove, against her palm. Thus matters continued till the pressure lessened; but several minutes passed before the crowd thinned sufficiently to allow Mrs Harnham to withdraw.

"How did they get to know each other, I wonder?" she mused as she retreated. "Anna is really very forward—and he very wicked and nice."

She was so gently stirred with the stranger's manner and voice, with the tenderness of his idle touch, that instead of re-entering the house she turned back again and observed the pair from a screened nook. Really she argued (being little less impulsive than Anna herself) it was very excusable in Anna to encourage him, however she might have contrived to make his acquaintance; he was so gentlemanly, so fascinating, had such beautiful eyes. The thought that he was several years her junior produced a reasonless sigh.

At length the couple turned from the roundabout towards the door of Mrs Harnham's house and the young man could be heard saying that he would accompany her home. Anna, then, had found a lover, apparently a very devoted one. Mrs Harnham was quite interested in him. When they drew near the door of the wine-merchant's house, a comparatively deserted spot by this time, they stood invisible for a little while in the shadow of a wall, where they separated, Anna going on to the entrance, and her acquaintance returning across the square.

"Anna," said Mrs Harnham, coming up. "I've been looking at you. That young man kissed you at parting, I am almost sure."

"Well," stammered Anna; "he said, if I didn't mind—it would do me no harm, and, and, him a great deal of good."

"Ah, I thought so. And he was a stranger till to-night?"

"Yes ma'am."

"Yet I warrant you told him your name and everything about yourself?"

"He asked me."

"But he didn't tell you his?"

"Yes ma'am, he did!" cried Anna victoriously. "It is Charles Bradford of London."

"Well, if he's respectable, of course I've nothing to say against your knowing him," remarked her mistress, prepossessed, in spite of general principles, in the young man's favour. "But I must re-consider all that, if he attempts to renew your acquaintance. A country-bred girl like you, who has never lived in Melchester till this month, who had hardly ever seen a black-coated man till you came here, to be so sharp as to capture a young Londoner like him!"

"I didn't capture him. I didn't do anything," said Anna, in confusion.

When she was indoors and alone Mrs Harnham thought what a well-bred and chivalrous young man Anna's companion had seemed. There had been a magic in his wooing touch of her hand; and she wondered how he had come to be attracted by the girl.

The next morning the emotional Edith Harnham went to the usual week-day service in Melchester Cathedral. In crossing the Close through the fog she again perceived him who had interested her the previous evening, gazing up thoughtfully at the high-piled architecture of the nave: and as soon as she had taken her seat he entered and sat down in a stall opposite hers.

He did not particularly heed her; but Mrs Harnham was continually occupying her eyes with him, and wondered more than ever what had attracted him in her unfledged maidservant. The mistress was almost as unaccustomed as the maiden herself to the end-of-the-age young man, or she might have wondered less. Raye, having looked about him awhile, left abruptly, without regard to the service that was proceeding; and Mrs Harnham, lonely, impressionable creature that she was, took no further interest in praising the Lord. She wished she had married a London man who knew the subtleties of love-making as they were evidently known to him who had mistakenly caressed her hand.

III

THE calendar at Melchester had been light, occupying the court only a few hours; and the assizes at Casterbridge, the next county-town on the Western Circuit, having no business for Raye, he had not gone thither. At the next town after that they did not open till the following Monday, trials to begin on Tuesday morning. In the natural order of things Raye would have arrived at the latter place on Monday afternoon; but it was not till the middle of Wednesday that his gown and grey wig, curled in tiers, in the best fashion of Assyrian bas-reliefs, were seen blowing and bobbing behind him as he hastily walked up the High-street from his lodgings. But though he entered the assize building there was nothing for him to do, and sitting at the blue baize table in the well of the court he mended pens with a mind far away from the case in progress.

Thoughts of unpremeditated conduct, of which a week earlier he would not have believed himself capable, threw him into a mood of dissatisfied depression.

He had contrived to see again the pretty rural maiden Anna the day after the fair, had walked out of the city with her to the earthworks of Old Melchester, and feeling a violent fancy for her had remained in Melchester all Sunday, Monday, and Tuesday; by persuasion obtaining walks and meetings with the girl six or seven times during the interval; had in brief won her, body and soul.

He supposed it must have been owing to the seclusion in which he had lived of late in town that he had given way so unrestrainedly to a passion for an artless creature whose inexperience had, from the first, led her to place herself unreservedly in his hands. Much he deplored trifling with her feelings for the sake of a passing desire; and he could only hope that she might not live to suffer on his account.

She had begged him to come to her again; entreated him; wept. He had promised that he would do so, and he meant to carry out that promise. He could not desert her now. Awkward as such unintentional connections were, the interspace of a hundred miles—which to a girl of her limited capabilities was like a thousand—would effectually hinder this summer fancy from greatly encumbering his life; while thought of her simple love might do him the negative good of keeping him from idle pleasures in town when he wished to work hard. His circuit journeys would take him to Melchester three or four times a year; and then he could always see her.

The pseudonym, or rather partial name, that he had given her as his, before knowing how far the acquaintance was going to carry him, had been spoken on the spur of the moment, without any ulterior intention whatever. He had not afterwards disturbed Anna's error, but on leaving her he had felt bound to give her an address at a stationer's not far from his chambers, at which she might write to him under the initials "C.B."

In due time Raye returned to his London abode, having called at Melchester on his way and spent a few additional hours with his fascinating child of nature. In town he lived monotonously every day. Often he and his rooms were enclosed by a tawny fog from all the world besides, and when he lighted the gas to read or write by, his situation seemed so unnatural that he would look into the fire and think of that trusting girl at Melchester again and again. Often, oppressed by absurd fondness for her, he would enter the dim religious nave of the Law Courts because it was something like her cathedral, elbow other juniors habited like himself, and like him unretained; edge himself into this or that crowded court where a sensational case was going on, just as if he were in it, though the police officers at the door knew as well as he knew himself that he had no more concern with the business in hand than the patient idlers at the gallery door outside, who had waited to enter since eight in the morning because, like him, they belonged to the classes that live on expectation. But he would do these things to no purpose, and think how greatly the characters in such scenes contrasted with the pink and breezy Anna.

An unexpected feature in that peasant maiden's conduct was that she had not as yet written to him, though he had told her she might do so if she wished. Surely a young creature had never before been so reticent in such circumstances. At length he sent her a brief line, positively requesting her to write. There was no answer by the return post, but the day after a letter in a neat feminine hand, and bearing the Melchester post-mark, was handed to him by the stationer.

The fact alone of its arrival was sufficient to satisfy his imaginative sentiment. He was not anxious to open the epistle and in truth did not begin to read it for nearly half-an-hour, anticipating readily its terms of passionate retrospect and tender adjuration. When at last he turned his feet to the fireplace and unfolded the sheet he was surprized and pleased to find that neither extravagance nor vulgarity was there. It was the most charming little missive he had ever received from woman. To be sure the language was simple and the ideas were slight; but it was so self-possessed; so purely that of a young girl who felt her womanhood to be enough for her dignity that he read it through twice. Four sides were filled; and a few lines written across, after the fashion of former days; the paper, too, was common, and not of the latest shade and surface. But what of those things? He had received letters from women who were fairly called ladies, but never so sensible, so human a letter as this. He could not single out any one sentence and say it was at all remarkable or clever; the *ensemble* of the letter it was which won him; and beyond the one request that he would write or come to her again soon there was nothing to show her sense of a claim upon him.

To write again and develop a correspondence was the last thing Raye would have preconceived as his conduct in such a situation; yet he did send a short, encouraging line or two, signed with his pseudonym, in which he asked for another letter, and cheeringly promised that he would try to see her again on some near day, and would never forget how much they had been to each other during their short acquaintance.

IV

To return now to the moment at which Anna, at Melchester, had received Raye's letter.

It had been put into her own hand by the postman on his morning rounds. She flushed down to her neck on receipt of it, and turned it over and over. "Is it mine?" she said.

"Why yes—can't you see it is?" said the postman, smiling as he guessed the nature of the document and the cause of her confusion.

"O yes—of course!" replied Anna, looking at the letter, forcedly tittering, and blushing still more.

Her look of embarrassment did not leave her with the postman's departure. She opened the envelope, kissed its contents, put away the letter in her pocket, and remained musing, till her eyes filled with tears.

A few minutes later she carried up a cup of tea to Mrs Harnham in her bed-chamber. Anna's mistress looked at her, and said, "How dismal you seem this morning, Anna. What's the matter?"

"I'm not dismal—I'm glad; only I—" She stopped to stifle a sob.

"Well?"

"I've got a letter—and what good is it to me, if I can't read a word in it!"

"Why, I'll read it child, if necessary."

"But this is from somebody—I don't want anybody to read it but myself," Anna murmured.

"I shall not tell anybody. Is it from that young man?"

"I think so."

Anna slowly produced the letter, saying, "Then will you read it to me, ma'am?"

This was the secret of Anna's embarrassment and flutterings. She could neither read nor write. She had grown up under the care of an aunt by marriage, at one of the lonely hamlets on the Great Mid-Wessex Plain where, even in days of National education, there had been no school within a distance of two miles. Her aunt was an ignorant woman; there had been nobody to investigate Anna's circumstances, nobody to care about her learning the rudiments; though, as often in such cases, she had been well fed and clothed and not unkindly treated. Since she had come to live at Melchester with Mrs Harnham, the latter, who took a kindly interest in the girl, had taught her to speak correctly, in which accomplishment Anna showed considerable readiness, as is not unusual with the illiterate; and soon became quite fluent in the use of her mistress's phraseology. Mrs Harnham also insisted upon her getting a spelling and copybook, and beginning to practise in these. Anna was slower in this branch of her education, and meanwhile here was the letter.

Edith Harnham's large dark eyes expressed some interest in the contents, though, in her character of mere interpreter she threw into her tone as much as she could of mechanical passiveness. She read the short epistle on to its concluding sentence, which idly requested Anna to send him a tender answer.

"Now—you'll do it for me, won't you, dear mis'ess?" said Anna eagerly. "And you'll do it as well as ever you can, please? Because I couldn't bear him to think I am not able to do it myself. I should sink into the earth with shame if he knew that."

From some words in the letter Mrs Harnham was led to ask questions, and the answers she received confirmed her suspicions. Deep concern filled Edith's heart at perceiving how the girl had committed her happiness to the issue of this new-sprung attachment. She blamed herself for not interfering in a flirtation which had resulted so seriously for the poor little creature in her charge; though at the time of seeing the pair together she had a feeling that it was hardly within her province to nip young affection in the bud. However, what was done could not be undone; and it behoved her now, as Anna's only protector, to help her as much as she could. To Anna's eager request that she, Mrs Harnham, should compose and write the answer to this young London man's letter, she felt bound to accede, to keep alive his passion for the girl if possible; though in other circumstances she might have suggested the cook as an amanuensis.

A tender reply was thereupon concocted, and set down in Edith Harnham's hand. This letter it had been which Raye had received and delighted in. Written in the presence of Anna it certainly was, and on Anna's humble note-paper, and in a measure indited by the young girl; but the life, the spirit, the individuality, were Edith Harnham's.

"Won't you at least put your name yourself?" she said. "You can manage to write that by this time?"

"No, no," said Anna, shrinking back. "I should do it so bad. He'd be ashamed of me, and never see me again."

The note, so prettily requesting another from him, had, as we have seen, power enough in its pages to bring one. He declared it to be such a pleasure to hear from her that she must write every week. The same process of manufacture was accordingly repeated by Anna and her mistress, and continued for several weeks in succession; each letter being penned and suggested by Edith, the girl standing by; the answer read and commented on by Edith, Anna standing by and listening again.

Late on a winter evening, after the dispatch of the sixth letter, Mrs Harnham was sitting alone by the remains of her fire. Her husband had retired to bed, and she had fallen into that fixity of musing which takes no count of hour or temperature. This state of mind had been brought about in Edith by a strange thing which she had done that day. For the first time since Raye's visit Anna had gone to stay over a night or two with her cottager friends on the Plain, and in her absence had arrived, out of its time, a letter from Raye. To this Edith had replied on her own responsibility, from the depths of her own heart, without waiting for her maid's collaboration. The luxury of writing to him what would be known to no consciousness but his, was great, and she had indulged herself therein.

Why was it a luxury?

Edith Harnham led a lonely life. Influenced by the belief of the British parent that a bad marriage with its aversions is better than free womanhood with its interests, dignity, and leisure, she had consented to marry the elderly wine-merchant as a *pis aller*, at the age of seven-and-twenty—some three years before this date—to find afterwards that she had made a mistake. That contract had left her still a woman whose deeper nature had never been stirred.

She was now clearly realizing that she had become possessed to the bottom of her soul with the image of a man to whom she was hardly so much as a name. From the first he had attracted her by his looks and voice; above all by his wooing touch; and, with these as generators, the writing of letter after letter and the reading of their soft answers had insensibly developed on her side an emotion which fanned his; till there had resulted a magnetic reciprocity between the correspondents, notwithstanding that one of them wrote in a character not her own. That he had been able to seduce another woman in two days was his crowning though unrecognized fascination for her as the she-animal.

They were her own impassioned and pent up ideas—lowered to monosyllabic phraseology in order to keep up the disguise—that Edith put into letters signed with another name, much to the shallow Anna's delight, who, unassisted, could not for the world have conceived such pretty fancies for winning him, even had she been able to write them. Edith found that it was these, her own foisted in sentiments, to which the young barrister mainly responded. The few sentences occasionally added from Anna's own lips made apparently no impression upon him.

The letter-writing in her absence Anna never discovered; but on her return the next morning she declared she wished to see her lover about something at once, and begged Mrs Harnham to ask him to come.

There was a strange anxiety in her manner which did not escape Mrs Harnham, and ultimately resolved itself into a flood of tears. Sinking down at Edith's knees, she made confession that the result of her relations with her lover it would soon become necessary to disclose.

Edith Harnham was generous enough to be very far from inclined to cast Anna adrift at this conjuncture. No true woman ever is so inclined from her own personal point of view, however prompt she may be in taking such steps to safeguard those dear to her. Although she had written to Raye so short a time previously, she instantly penned another Anna-note hinting clearly though delicately the state of affairs.

Raye replied by a hasty line to say how much he was concerned at her news: he felt that he must run down to see her almost immediately.

But a week later the girl came to her mistress's room with another note, which on being read informed her that after all he could not find time for the journey. Anna was broken with grief; but by Mrs Harnham's counsel strictly refrained from hurling at him the reproaches and bitterness customary from young women so situated. One thing was imperative: to keep the young man's romantic interest in her alive. Rather therefore did Edith, in the name of her *protégée*, request him on no account to be distressed about the looming event, and not to inconvenience himself to hasten down. She desired above everything to be no weight upon him in his career, no clog upon his high activities. She had wished him to know what had befallen: he was to dismiss it again from his mind. Only he must write tenderly as ever, and when he should come again on the Spring circuit it would be soon enough to discuss what had better be done.

Male contra female naturalness

It may well be supposed that Anna's own feelings had not been quite in accord with these generous expressions; but the mistress's judgment had ruled, and Anna had acquiesced. "All I want is that *niceness* you can so well put into your letters, my dear, dear mistress, and that I can't for the life o' me make up out of my own head; though I mean the same thing and feel it exactly when you've written it down!"

When the letter had been sent off, and Edith Harnham was left alone, she bowed herself on the back of her chair and wept.

"I wish his child was mine—I wish it was!" she murmured. "Yet how can I say such a wicked thing!"

V

THE letter moved Raye considerably when it reached him. The intelligence itself had affected him less than her un-expected manner of treating him in relation to it. The absence of any word of reproach, the devotion to his interests, the self-sacrifice apparent in every line, all made up a no-bility of character that he had never dreamt of finding in womankind.

"God forgive me!" he said tremulously. "I have been a wicked wretch. I did not know she was such a treasure as this!"

He reassured her instantly, declaring that he would not of course desert her, that he would provide a home for her somewhere. Meanwhile she was to stay where she was as long as her mistress would allow her.

But a misfortune supervened in this direction. Whether an inkling of Anna's circumstances reached the knowledge of Mrs Harnham's husband or not cannot be said, but the girl was compelled, in spite Edith's entreaties, to leave the house. By her own choice she decided to go back for a while to the cottage on the Plain. This arrangement led to a consultation as to how the correspondence should be carried on; and in the girl's inability to continue personally what had been begun in her name, and in the difficulty of their acting in concert as heretofore, she requested Mrs Harnham—the only well-to-do friend she had in the world—to receive the letters and reply to them off hand, sending them on afterwards to herself on the Plain, where she might at least get some neighbour to read them to her, if a trustworthy one could be met with. Anna and her box then departed for the Plain.

Thus it befel that Edith Harnham found herself in the strange position of having to correspond, under no supervision by the real woman, with a man not her husband, in terms which were virtually those of a wife, concerning a corporeal condition that was not Edith's at all; the man being one for whom, mainly through the sympathies involved in playing this part, she secretly cherished a predilection, subtle and imaginative truly, but strong and absorbing. She opened each letter, read it, as if intended for herself, and replied from the promptings of her own heart and no other.

Throughout this correspondence, carried on in the girl's absence, the high-strung Edith Harnham lived in the ecstasy of fancy: the vicarious intimacy engendered such a flow of passionateness as was never exceeded. For conscience' sake Edith at first sent on each of his letters to Anna, and even rough copies of her replies; but later on these so-called copies were much abridged, and many letters on both sides were not sent on at all.

Though sensuous, and, superficially at least, infested with the self-indulgent vices of artificial society, there was a substratum of honesty and fairness in Raye's character. He had really a tender regard for the country girl, and it grew more tender than ever when he found her apparently capable of expressing the deepest sensibilities in the simplest words. He meditated, he wavered; and finally resolved to consult his sister, a maiden lady much older than himself, of lively sympathies and good intent. In making this confidence he showed her some of the letters.

"She seems fairly educated," Miss Raye observed. "And bright in ideas. She expresses herself with a taste that must be innate."

"Yes. She writes very prettily, doesn't she, thanks to these elementary schools?"

"One is drawn out towards her, in spite of one's self, poor thing."

The upshot of the discussion was that though he had not been directly advised to do it, Raye wrote, in his real name, what he would never have decided to write on his own responsibility; namely that she should not suffer for his sake; he would come down in the Spring and shelve her looming difficulty by marrying her.

This bold acceptance of the situation was made known to Anna by Mrs Harnham driving out immediately to the cottage on the Plain. Anna jumped for joy like a little child. And poor, crude directions for answering appropriately were given to Edith Harnham, who on her return to the city carried them out, with warm intensifications.

"O!" she groaned, as she threw down the pen. "Anna—poor good little fool—hasn't intelligence enough to appreciate him! How should she? While I—don't bear his child!"

It was now February. The correspondence had continued altogether for four months; and the next letter from Raye contained incidentally a statement of his position and prospects. He said that, in offering to wed her he had, at first, contemplated the step of retiring from a profession which hitherto had brought him very slight emolument, and which, to speak plainly, he had thought might be difficult of practice after his union with her. But the unexpected mines of brightness and warmth that her letters had disclosed to be lurking in her sweet nature had led him to abandon that somewhat sad prospect. He felt sure that, with her powers of development, after a little private training in the social forms of London under his supervision, and a little help from a governess if necessary, she would make as good a professional man's wife as could be desired, even if he should rise to the woolsack. Many a Lord Chancellor's wife had been less intuitively a lady than she had shown herself to be in her lines to him.

"O—poor fellow, poor fellow!" mourned Edith Harnham.

Her distress now raged as high as her infatuation. It was she who had wrought him to this pitch—to a marriage which meant his ruin; yet she could not, in mercy to her maid, do anything to hinder his plan. Anna was coming to Melchester that week, but she could hardly show the girl this last reply from the young man: it told too much of the second individuality that had usurped the place of the first.

Anna came, and her mistress took her into her own room for privacy. Anna began by saying with some anxiety that she was glad the wedding was so near.

"O Anna!" replied Mrs Harnham. "I think we must tell him all—that I have been doing your writing for you?—lest he should not know it till after you become his wife, and it might lead to dissension and recriminations—"

"O mis'ess, dear mis'ess—please don't tell him now!" cried Anna in distress. "If you were to do it, perhaps he would not marry me; and what should I do then? It would be terrible what would come to me! And I am getting on with my writing, too. I have brought with me the copybook you were so good as to give me, and I practise every day. And though it is so, so hard, I shall do it well at last, I believe, if I keep on trying."

Edith looked at the copybook. The copies had been set by herself, and such progress as the girl had made was in the way of grotesque fac-simile of her mistress's hand. But even if Edith's flowing caligraphy were reproduced, the inspiration would be another thing.

"You do it so beautifully," continued Anna, "and say all that I want to say so much better than I could say it, that I do hope you won't leave me in the lurch just now!"

"Very well," replied the other. "But I—but I thought I ought not to go on!"

"Why?"

Her strong desire to confide her sentiments led Edith to answer truly:

"Because of its effect upon me."

"But it *can't* have any!"

"Why, child?"

"Because you are married already!" said Anna with lucid simplicity.

"Of course it can't," said her mistress hastily; yet glad, despite her conscience, that two or three outpourings still remained to her. "But you must concentrate your attention on writing your name as I write it here."

VI

Soon Raye wrote about the wedding. Having decided to make the best of what he feared was a piece of romantic folly he had acquired more zest for the grand experiment. He wished the ceremony to be in London, for greater privacy. Edith Harnham would have preferred it at Melchester; Anna was passive. His reasoning prevailed, and Mrs Harnham threw herself with mournful zeal into the preparations for Anna's departure. In a last desperate feeling that she must, at every hazard, be in at the death of her dream, and see once again the man who by a species of telepathy had exercised such an influence on her, she offered to go up with Anna and be with her through the ceremony—"to see the end of her," as her mistress put it with forced gaiety; an offer which the girl gratefully accepted; for she had no other friend capable of playing the part of companion and witness, in the presence of a gentlemanly bridegroom, in such a way as not to hasten an opinion that he had made an irremediable social blunder.

It was a muddy morning in March when Raye alighted from a four-wheel cab at the door of a registry-office in the S.W. district of London, and carefully handed down Anna, and her companion Mrs Harnham. Anna looked attractive in the somewhat fashionable clothes which Mrs Harnham had helped her to buy, though not quite so attractive as, an innocent child, she had appeared in her country gown on the back of the wooden horse at Melchester Fair.

Mrs Harnham had come up this morning by an early train, and a young man—a friend of Raye's—having met them at the door, all four entered the registry-office together. Till an hour before this time Raye had never known the wine-merchant's wife except at that first casual encounter, and in the flutter of the performance before them he had little opportunity for more than a brief acquaintance. The contract of marriage at a registry is soon got through; but somehow, during its progress, Raye discovered a strange and secret gravitation between himself and Anna's friend.

The formalities of the wedding—or rather ratification of a previous union—being concluded, the four went in one cab to Raye's lodgings, newly taken in a near suburb, in preference to a house, the rent of which he could ill afford just then. Here Anna cut the little cake which Raye had bought at a pastrycook's on his way home from Lincoln's-Inn the night before. But she did not do much besides. Raye's friend was obliged to depart almost immediately, and when he had left the only ones virtually present were Edith and Raye, who exchanged ideas with much animation. The conversation was indeed theirs only, Anna being as a domestic animal, who humbly heard but understood not. Raye seemed startled in awakening to this fact and began to feel dissatisfied with her inadequacy.

At last, more disappointed than he cared to own, he said, "Mrs Harnham, my darling is so flurried that she doesn't know what she is doing or saying. I see that, after this event, a little quietude will be necessary before she gives tongue to that tender philosophy which she used to treat me to in her letters."

They had planned to start early that afternoon for Knollsea, to spend the few opening days of their married life there, and as the hour for departure was drawing near Raye asked his wife if she would go to the writing-desk in the next room and scribble a little note to his sister, who had been unable to attend through indisposition, informing her that the ceremony was over, thanking her for her kind presents and hoping to know her well, now that she was the writer's sister as well as Charles's.

"Say it in the pretty poetical way you know so well how to adopt," he added: "for I want you particularly to win her, and both of you to be dear friends."

Anna looked uneasy, but departed to her task, Raye remaining to talk to their guest. Anna was a long while absent, and her husband suddenly rose and went to her.

He found her still bending over the writing-table, with tears brimming up in her eyes; and he looked down upon the sheet of note-paper with some interest, to discover with what tact

she had expressed her good-will in the delicate circumstances. To his surprise she had progressed but a few lines, in
the characters and spelling of a child of eight, and with the
ideas of a goose.

"Anna?" he said, staring. "What's this?"

"It only means—that I can't do it any better!" she answered
through her tears.

"Eh? Nonsense!"

"I can't!" she insisted, with miserable, sobbing hardihood.
"I—I—didn't write those letters, Charles! I only told *her* what
to write! And not always that! But I am learning—O so fast—
my dear dear husband! And you'll forgive me, won't you, for
not telling you before?" She slid to her knees, abjectly clasped
his waist and laid her face against him.

He stood a few moments, raised her, abruptly turned, and
shut the door upon her, rejoining Edith in the drawing-room.
She saw that something untoward had been discovered, and
their eyes remained fixed on each other.

"Do I guess rightly?" he asked with wan quietude. "*You* were
her scribe through all this?"

"It was necessary," said Edith.

"Did she dictate every word you ever wrote to me?"

"Not every word."

"In fact, very little?"

"Very little."

"You wrote a great part of those pages every week from your
own conceptions, though in her name?"

"Yes."

"Perhaps you wrote many of the letters when you were
alone, without communication with her?"

"I did."

He turned to the bookcase, and leant with his hand over
his face; and Edith, seeing his distress, became white as a
sheet.

"You have deceived me—ruined me!" he murmured.

"O don't say it!" she cried in her anguish, jumping up and
putting her hand on his shoulder. "I can't bear that!"

"Delighting me deceptively! Why did you do it—why did
you?"

"I began doing it in kindness to her. How could I do

otherwise than try to save such a simple girl from misery? But I admit that I continued it for—pleasure to myself."

Raye looked up. "Why did it give you pleasure?" he asked.

"I must not tell," said she.

He continued to regard her, and saw that her lips suddenly began to quiver under his scrutiny, and her eyes to fill and droop. She started aside and said that she must go to the station to catch the return train: could a cab be called immediately?

But Raye went up to her, and took her unresisting hand. "Well—to think of such a thing as this," he said. "Why—you and I are friends—lovers—devoted lovers—by correspondence."

"Yes—I suppose."

"More."

"More?"

"Plainly more. It is no use blinking that. Legally I have married her—God help us both!—in soul and spirit I have married you, and no other woman in the world."

"Hush."

"But I will not hush! Why should you try to disguise the full truth, when you have already owned half of it? Yes, it is between you and me that the bond is—not between me and her. Now I'll say no more. . . . But, O my cruel one, I think I have one claim upon you."

She did not say what, and he drew her towards him, and bent over her. "If it was all pure invention in those letters," he said emphatically, "give me your cheek only. If you meant what you said, let it be lips. It is for the first and last time, remember."

She put up her mouth, and he kissed her long. "You forgive me?" she said, crying.

"Yes."

"But you are ruined!"

"What matter!" he said shrugging his shoulders. "It serves me right."

She withdrew, wiped her eyes, entered and bade good-bye to Anna, who had not expected her to go so soon, and was still wrestling with the letter. Raye followed Edith downstairs, and in three minutes she was in a hansom driving to the Waterloo station.

He went back to his wife. "Never mind the letter, Anna, to-day," he said gently. "Put on your things. We, too, must be off shortly."

The simple girl, upheld by the sense that she was indeed married, showed her delight at finding that he was as kind as ever after the disclosure. She did not know that before his eyes he beheld as it were a galley, in which he, the fastidious urban, was chained to work for the remainder of his life, with her, the unlettered peasant, chained to his side.

Edith travelled back to Melchester that day with a face that showed the very stupor of grief, her lips still tingling from the desperate pressure of his kiss. The end of her impassioned dream had come. When at dusk she reached the Melchester station her husband was there to meet her, but in his perfunctoriness and her preoccupation they did not see each other, and she went out of the station alone.

She walked mechanically homewards without calling a fly. Entering, she could not bear the silence of the house, and went up in the dark to where Anna had slept, where she remained thinking awhile. She then returned to the drawing-room and not knowing what she did crouched down upon the floor.

"I have ruined him!" she kept repeating. "I have ruined him; because I would not deal treacherously towards her!"

In the course of half an hour a figure opened the door of the apartment.

"Ah—who's that?" she said, starting up, for it was dark.

"Your husband—who should it be?" said the worthy merchant.

"Ah—my husband!—I forgot I had a husband!" she whispered to herself.

"I missed you at the station," he continued. "Did you see Anna safely tied up? I hope so, for 'twas time."

"Yes—Anna is married."

Simultaneously with Edith's journey home Anna and her husband were sitting at the opposite windows of a second class carriage which sped along to Knollsea. In his hand was a pocket-book full of creased sheets closely written over. Unfolding them one after another he read them in silence, and sighed.

"What are you doing, dear Charles?" she said timidly from the other window, and drew nearer to him as if he were a god.

"Reading over all those sweet letters to me signed 'Anna'," he replied with dreary resignation.

Autumn: 1891.

TO PLEASE HIS WIFE

I

THE interior of St. James's Church, in Havenpool Town, was slowly darkening under the close clouds of a winter afternoon. It was Sunday: service had just ended, the face of the parson in the pulpit was buried in his hands, and the congregation, with a cheerful sigh of release, were rising from their knees to depart.

For the moment the stillness was so complete that the surging of the sea could be heard outside the harbour-bar. Then it was broken by the footsteps of the clerk going towards the west door to open it in the usual manner for the exit of the assembly. Before, however, he had reached the doorway, the latch was lifted from without, and the dark figure of a man in a sailor's garb appeared against the light.

The clerk stepped aside, the sailor closed the door gently behind him, and advanced up the nave till he stood at the chancel-step. The parson looked up from the private little prayer which, after so many for the parish, he quite fairly took for himself, rose to his feet, and stared at the intruder.

"I beg your pardon, sir," said the sailor, addressing the minister in a voice distinctly audible to all the congregation. "I have come here to offer thanks for my narrow escape from shipwreck. I am given to understand that it is a proper thing to do, if you have no objection?"

The parson, after a moment's pause, said hesitatingly, "I have no objection; certainly. It is usual to mention any such wish before service, so that the proper words may be used in the General Thanksgiving. But, if you wish, we can read from the form for use after a storm at sea."

"Ay, sure; I ain't particular," said the sailor.

The clerk thereupon directed the sailor to the page in the prayer-book where the collect of thanksgiving would be found, and the rector began reading it, the sailor kneeling where he stood, and repeating it after him word by word in a distinct voice. The people, who had remained agape and motionless at the proceeding, mechanically knelt down likewise; but they continued to regard the isolated form of the sailor who, in the precise middle of the chancel-step, remained fixed on his knees, facing the east, his hat beside him, his hands joined, and he quite unconscious of his appearance in their regard.

When his thanksgiving had come to an end he rose; the people rose also, and all went out of church together. As soon as the sailor emerged, so that the remaining daylight fell upon his face, old inhabitants began to recognize him as no other than Shadrach Jolliffe, a young man who had not been seen at Havenpool for several years. A son of the town, his parents had died when he was quite young, on which account he had early gone to sea, in the Newfoundland trade.

He talked with this and that townsman as he walked, informing them that, since leaving his native place years before, he had become captain and owner of a small coasting-ketch, which had providentially been saved from the gale as well as himself. Presently he drew near to two girls who were going out of the churchyard in front of him; they had been sitting in the nave at his entry, and had watched his doings with deep interest, afterwards discussing him as they moved out of church together. One was a slight and gentle creature, the other a tall, large-framed, deliberative girl. Captain Jolliffe regarded the loose curls of their hair, their backs and shoulders, down to their heels, for some time.

"Who may them two maids be?" he whispered to his neighbour.

"The little one is Emily Hanning; the tall one Joanna Phippard."

"Ah! I recollect 'em now, to be sure."

He advanced to their elbow, and genially stole a gaze at them.

"Emily, you don't know me?" said the sailor, turning his beaming brown eyes on her.

"I think I do, Mr Jolliffe," said Emily shyly.

The other girl looked straight at him with her dark eyes.

"The face of Miss Joanna I don't call to mind so well," he continued. "But I know her beginnings and kindred."

They walked and talked together, Jolliffe narrating particulars of his late narrow escape, till they reached the corner of Sloop-lane, in which Emily Hanning dwelt, when, with a nod and smile, she left them. Soon the sailor parted also from Joanna, and, having no especial errand or appointment, turned back towards Emily's house. She lived with her father, who called himself an accountant, the daughter, however, keeping a little stationery-shop as a supplemental provision for the gaps of his somewhat uncertain business. On entering Jolliffe found father and daughter about to begin tea.

"O, I didn't know it was tea-time," he said. "Ay, I'll have a cup with much pleasure."

He remained to tea and long afterwards, telling more tales of his seafaring life. Several neighbours called to listen, and were asked to come in. Somehow Emily Hanning lost her heart to the sailor that Sunday night, and in the course of a week or two there was a tender understanding between them.

One moonlight evening in the next month Shadrach was ascending out of the town by the long straight road eastward, to an elevated suburb where the more fashionable houses stood—if anything near this ancient port could be called fashionable—when he saw a figure before him whom, from her manner of glancing back, he took to be Emily. But, on coming up, he found she was Joanna Phippard. He gave a gallant greeting, and walked beside her.

"Go along," she said, "or Emily will be jealous!"

He seemed not to like the suggestion, and remained.

What was said and what was done on that walk never could be clearly recollected by Shadrach; but in some way or other Joanna contrived to wean him away from her gentler and younger rival. From that week onwards, Jolliffe was seen more and more in the wake of Joanna Phippard and less in the company of Emily; and it was soon rumoured about the quay that old Jolliffe's son, who had come home from sea, was going to be married to the former young woman, to the great disappointment of the latter.

Just after this report had gone about, Joanna dressed herself for a walk one morning, and started for Emily's house in the little cross-street. Intelligence of the deep sorrow of her friend on account of the loss of Shadrach had reached her ears also, and her conscience reproached her for winning him away.

Joanna was not altogether satisfied with the sailor. She liked his attentions, and she coveted the dignity of matrimony; but she had never been deeply in love with Jolliffe. For one thing, she was ambitious, and socially his position was hardly so good as her own, and there was always the chance of an attractive woman mating considerably above her. It had long been in her mind that she would not strongly object to give him back again to Emily if her friend felt so very badly about him. To this end she had written a letter of renunciation to Shadrach, which letter she carried in her hand, intending to send it if personal observation of Emily convinced her that her friend was suffering.

Joanna entered Sloop-lane and stepped down into the stationery-shop, which was below the pavement level. Emily's father was never at home at this hour of the day, and it seemed as though Emily were not at home either, for the visitor could make nobody hear. Customers came so seldom hither that a five minutes' absence of the proprietor counted for little. Joanna waited in the little shop, where Emily had tastefully set out—as women can—articles in themselves of slight value, so as to obscure the meagreness of the stock-in-trade; till she saw a figure pausing without the window apparently absorbed in the contemplation of the sixpenny books, packets of paper, and prints hung on a string. It was Captain Shadrach Jolliffe, peering in to ascertain if Emily were there alone. Moved by an impulse of reluctance to meet him in a spot which breathed of Emily, Joanna slipped through the door that communicated with the parlour at the back. She had frequently done so before, for in her friendship with Emily she had the freedom of the house without ceremony.

Jolliffe entered the shop. Through the thin blind which screened the glass partition she could see that he was disappointed at not finding Emily there. He was about to go out again, when Emily's form darkened the doorway, hastening home from some errand. At sight of Jolliffe she started back as if she would have gone out again.

"Don't run away, Emily; don't!" said he. "What can make 'ee afraid?"

"I'm not afraid, Captain Jolliffe. Only—only I saw you all of a sudden, and—it made me jump!" Her voice showed that her heart had jumped even more than the rest of her.

"I just called as I was passing," he said.

"For some paper?" She hastened behind the counter.

"No, no, Emily; why do you get behind there? Why not stay by me? You seem to hate me."

"I don't hate you. How can I?"

"Then come out, so that we can talk like Christians."

Emily obeyed with a fitful laugh, till she stood again beside him in the open part of the shop.

"There's a dear," he said.

"You mustn't say that, Captain Jolliffe; because the words belong to somebody else."

"Ah! I know what you mean. But, Emily, upon my life I didn't know till this morning that you cared one bit about me, or I should not have done as I have done. I have the best of feelings for Joanna, but I know that from the beginning she hasn't cared for me more than in a friendly way; and I see now the one I ought to have asked to be my wife. You know, Emily, when a man comes home from sea after a long voyage he's as blind as a bat—he can't see who's who in women. They are all alike to him, beautiful creatures, and he takes the first that comes easy, without thinking if she loves him, or if he might not soon love another better than her. From the first I inclined to you most, but you were so backward and shy that I thought you didn't want me to bother 'ee, and so I went to Joanna."

"Don't say any more, Mr Jolliffe, don't!" said she, choking. "You are going to marry Joanna next month, and it is wrong to—to—"

"O, Emily, my darling!" he cried, and clasped her little figure in his arms before she was aware.

Joanna, behind the curtain, turned pale, tried to withdraw
her eyes, but could not.

"It is only you I love as a man ought to love the woman he
is going to marry; and I know this from what Joanna has said,
that she will willingly let me off! She wants to marry higher I
know, and only said 'Yes' to me out of kindness. A fine, tall
girl like her isn't the sort for a plain sailor's wife: you be the
best suited for that."

He kissed her and kissed her again, her flexible form quivering in the agitation of his embrace.

"I wonder—are you sure—Joanna is going to break off with
you? O, are you sure? Because—"

"I know she would not wish to make us miserable. She will
release me."

"O, I hope—I hope she will! Don't stay any longer, Captain
Jolliffe!"

He lingered, however, till a customer came for a penny
stick of sealing-wax, and then he withdrew.

Green envy had overspread Joanna at the scene. She
looked about for a way of escape. To get out without Emily's
knowledge of her visit was indispensable. She crept from the
parlour into the passage, and thence to the back door of the
house, where she let herself noiselessly into the street.

The sight of that caress had reversed all her resolutions.
She could not let Shadrach go. Reaching home she burnt the
letter, and told her mother that if Captain Jolliffe called she
was too unwell to see him.

Shadrach, however, did not call. He sent her a note expressing in simple language the state of his feelings; and
asked to be allowed to take advantage of the hints she had
given him that her affection, too, was little more than
friendly, by cancelling the engagement.

Looking out upon the harbour and the island beyond he
waited and waited in his lodgings for an answer that did not
come. The suspense grew to be so intolerable that after dark
he went up the High-street. He could not resist calling at
Joanna's to learn his fate.

Her mother said her daughter was too unwell to see him,
and to his questioning admitted that it was in consequence of

a letter received from himself, which had distressed her deeply.

"You know what it was about, perhaps, Mrs Phippard?" he said.

Mrs Phippard owned that she did, adding that it put them in a very painful position. Thereupon Shadrach, fearing that he had been guilty of an enormity, explained that if his letter had pained Joanna it must be owing to a misunderstanding, since he had thought it would be a relief to her. If otherwise, he would hold himself bound by his word, and she was to think of the letter as never having been written.

Next morning he received an oral message from the young woman, asking him to fetch her home from a meeting that evening. This he did, and while walking from the Town Hall to her door, with her hand in his arm, she said:

"It is all the same as before between us, isn't it, Shadrach? Your letter was sent in mistake?"

"It is all the same as before," he answered, "if you say it must be."

"I wish it to be," she murmured, with hard lineaments, as she thought of Emily.

Shadrach was a religious and scrupulous man, who respected his word as his life. Shortly afterwards the wedding took place, Jolliffe having conveyed to Emily as gently as possible the error he had fallen into when estimating Joanna's mood as one of indifference.

II

A MONTH after the marriage Joanna's mother died, and the couple were obliged to turn their attention to very practical matters. Now that she was left without a parent, Joanna could not bear the notion of her husband going to sea again, but the question was, What could he do at home? They finally decided to take on a small grocer's shop in High-street, the goodwill and stock of which were waiting to be disposed of at that time. Shadrach knew nothing of shopkeeping, and Joanna very little, but they hoped to learn.

To the management of this grocery business they now

devoted all their energies, and continued to conduct it for many succeeding years, without great success. Two sons were born to them, whom their mother loved to idolatry, although she had never passionately loved her husband; and she lavished upon them all her forethought and care. But the shop did not thrive, and the large dreams she had entertained of her sons' education and career became attenuated in the face of realities. Their schooling was of the plainest, but, being by the sea, they grew alert in all such nautical arts and enterprises as were attractive to their age.

The great interest of the Jolliffes' married life, outside their own immediate household, had lain in the marriage of Emily. By one of those odd chances which lead those that lurk in unexpected corners to be discovered, while the obvious are passed by, the gentle girl had been seen and loved by a thriving merchant of the town, a widower, some years older than herself, though still in the prime of life. At first Emily had declared that she never, never could marry any one; but Mr Lester had quietly persevered, and had at last won her reluctant assent. Two children also were the fruits of this union, and, as they grew and prospered, Emily declared that she had never supposed that she could live to be so happy.

The worthy merchant's home, one of those large, substantial brick mansions frequently jammed up in old-fashioned towns, faced directly on the High-street, nearly opposite to the grocery shop of the Jolliffes, and it now became the pain of Joanna to behold the woman whose place she had usurped out of pure covetousness, looking down from her position of comparative wealth upon the humble shop-window with its dusty sugar-loaves, heaps of raisins, and canisters of tea, over which it was her own lot to preside. The business having so dwindled, Joanna was obliged to serve in the shop herself, and it galled and mortified her that Emily Lester, sitting in her large drawing-room over the way, could witness her own dancings up and down behind the counter at the beck and call of wretched twopenny customers, whose patronage she was driven to welcome gladly: persons to whom she was compelled to be civil in the street, while Emily was bounding along with her children and her governess, and conversing with the genteelest people of the town and neighbourhood. This was what she had gained by not letting Shadrach Jolliffe, whom she had so faintly loved, carry his affection elsewhere.

Shadrach was a good and honest man, and he had been faithful to her in heart and in deed. Time had clipped the wings of his love for Emily in his devotion to the mother of his boys: he had quite lived down that impulsive earlier fancy, and Emily had become in his regard nothing more than a friend. It was the same with Emily's feelings for him. Possibly, had she found the least cause for jealousy, Joanna would almost have been better satisfied. It was in the absolute acquiescence of Emily and Shadrach in the results she herself had contrived that her discontent found nourishment.

Shadrach was not endowed with the narrow shrewdness necessary for developing a retail business in the face of many competitors. Did a customer inquire if the grocer could really recommend the wondrous substitute for eggs which a persevering bagman had forced into his stock, he would answer that "when you did not put eggs into a pudding it was difficult to taste them there"; and when he was asked if his "real Mocha coffee" was real Mocha, he would say grimly, "as understood in small shops." The way to wealth was not by this route.

One summer day, when the big brick house opposite was reflecting the oppressive sun's heat into the shop, and nobody was present but husband and wife, Joanna looked across at Emily's door, where a wealthy visitor's carriage had drawn up. Traces of patronage had been visible in Emily's manner of late.

"Shadrach, the truth is, you are not a business-man," his wife sadly murmured. "You were not brought up to shopkeeping, and it is impossible for a man to make a fortune at an occupation he has jumped into, as you did into this."

Jolliffe agreed with her, in this as in everything else. "Not that I care a rope's end about making a fortune," he said cheerfully. "I am happy enough, and we can rub on somehow."

She looked again at the great house through the screen of bottled pickles.

"Rub on—yes," she said bitterly. "But see how well off Emmy Lester is, who used to be so poor! Her boys will go to College, no doubt; and think of yours—obliged to go to the Parish School!"

Shadrach's thoughts had flown to Emily.

"Nobody," he said good-humouredly, "ever did Emily a better turn than you did, Joanna, when you warned her off me and put an end to that little simpering nonsense between us, so as to leave it in her power to say 'Aye' to Lester when he came along."

This almost maddened her.

"Don't speak of bygones!" she implored, in stern sadness. "But think, for the boys' and my sake, if not for your own, what are we to do to get richer?"

"Well," he said, becoming serious, "to tell the truth, I have always felt myself unfit for this business, though I've never liked to say so. I seem to want more room for sprawling; a more open space to strike out in than here among friends and neighbours. I could get rich as well as any man, if I tried my own way."

"I wish you would! What is your way?"

"To go to sea again."

She had been the very one to keep him at home, hating the semi-widowed existence of sailors' wives. But her ambition checked her instincts now, and she said:

"Do you think success really lies that way?"

"I am sure it lies in no other."

"Do you want to go, Shadrach?"

"Not for the pleasure of it, I can tell 'ee. There's no such pleasure at sea, Joanna, as I can find in my back parlour here. To speak honest, I have no love for the brine. I never had much. But if it comes to a question of a fortune for you and the lads, it is another thing. That's the only way to it for one born and bred a seafarer as I."

"Would it take long to earn?"

"Well, that depends; perhaps not."

The next morning Shadrach pulled from a chest of drawers

the nautical jacket he had worn during the first months of his return, brushed out the moths, donned it, and walked down to the quay. The port still did a fair business in the Newfoundland trade, though not so much as formerly.

It was not long after this that he invested all he possessed in purchasing a part-ownership in a brig, of which he was appointed captain. A few months were passed in coast-trading, during which interval Shadrach wore off the land-rust that had accumulated upon him in his grocery phase; and in the spring the brig sailed for Newfoundland.

Joanna lived on at home with her sons, who were now growing up into strong lads, and occupying themselves in various ways about the harbour and quay.

"Never mind, let them work a little," their fond mother said to herself. "Our necessities compel it now, but when Shadrach comes home they will be only seventeen and eighteen, and they shall be removed from the port, and their education thoroughly taken in hand by a tutor; and with the money they'll have they will perhaps be as near to gentlemen as Emmy Lester's precious two, with their algebra and their Latin!"

The date for Shadrach's return drew near and arrived, and he did not appear. Joanna was assured that there was no cause for anxiety, sailing-ships being so uncertain in their coming; which assurance proved to be well-grounded, for late one wet evening, about a month after the calculated time, the ship was announced as at hand, and presently the slip-slop step of Shadrach as the sailor sounded in the passage, and he entered. The boys had gone out and had missed him, and Joanna was sitting alone.

As soon as the first emotion of reunion between the couple had passed, Jolliffe explained the delay as owing to a small speculative contract, which had produced good results.

"I was determined not to disappoint 'ee," he said; "and I think you'll own that I haven't!"

With this he pulled out an enormous canvas bag, full and rotund as the money-bag of the giant whom Jack slew, untied it, and shook the contents out into her lap as she sat in her low chair by the fire. A mass of sovereigns and guineas (there

were guineas on the earth in those days) fell into her lap with
a sudden thud, weighing down her gown to the floor.

"There!" said Shadrach complacently. "I told 'ee, dear, I'd
do it; and have I done it or no?"

Somehow her face, after the first excitement of possession,
did not retain its glory.

"It is a lot of gold, indeed," she said. "And—is this *all*?"

"All? Why, dear Joanna, do you know you can count to
three hundred in that heap? It is a fortune!"

"Yes—yes. A fortune—judged by sea; but judged by
land—"

However, she banished considerations of the money for the
nonce. Soon the boys came in, and next Sunday Shadrach
returned thanks to God—this time by the more ordinary
channel of the italics in the General Thanksgiving. But a few
days after, when the question of investing the money arose, he
remarked that she did not seem so satisfied as he had hoped.

"Well you see, Shadrach," she answered, "*we* count by hundreds; *they* count by thousands" (nodding towards the other
side of the street). "They have set up a carriage and pair since
you left."

"O, have they?"

"My dear Shadrach, you don't know how the world moves.
However, we'll do the best we can with it. But they are rich,
and we are poor still!"

The greater part of a year was desultorily spent. She moved
sadly about the house and shop, and the boys were still occupying themselves in and around the harbour.

"Joanna," he said, one day, "I see by your movements that it
is not enough."

"It is not enough," said she. "My boys will have to live by
steering the ships that the Lesters own; and I was once above
her!"

Jolliffe was not an argumentative man, and he only murmured that he thought he would make another voyage. He
meditated for several days, and coming home from the quay
one afternoon said suddenly:

"I could do it for 'ee dear, in one more trip, for certain, if—
if—"

"Do what, Shadrach?"

"Enable 'ee to count by thousands instead of hundreds."

"If what?"

"If I might take the boys."

She turned pale.

"Don't say that, Shadrach," she answered hastily.

"Why?"

"I don't like to hear it! There's danger at sea. I want them to be something genteel, and no danger to them. I couldn't let them risk their lives at sea. O, I couldn't ever, ever!"

"Very well, dear, it shan't be done."

Next day, after a silence, she asked a question:

"If they were to go with you it would make a great deal of difference, I suppose, to the profit?"

"'Twould treble what I should get from the venture single-handed. Under my eye they would be as good as two more of myself."

Later on she said: "Tell me more about this."

"Well, the boys are almost as clever as master-mariners in handling a craft, upon my life! There isn't a more cranky place in the Northern Seas than about the sand-banks of this harbour, and they've practised here from their infancy. And they are so steady. I couldn't get their steadiness and their trustworthiness in half-a-dozen men twice their age."

"And is it *very* dangerous at sea; now, too, there are rumours of war?" she asked uneasily.

"O, well, there be risks. Still . . ."

The idea grew and magnified, and the mother's heart was crushed and stifled by it. Emmy was growing *too* patronizing; it could not be borne. Shadrach's wife could not help nagging him about their comparative poverty. The young men, amiable as their father, when spoken to on the subject of a voyage of enterprise, were quite willing to embark; and though they, like their father, had no great love for the sea, they became quite enthusiastic when the proposal was detailed.

Everything now hung upon their mother's assent. She withheld it long, but at last gave the word: the young men might accompany their father. Shadrach was unusually cheerful about it: Heaven had preserved him hitherto, and he had uttered his thanks. God would not forsake those who were faithful to him.

All that the Jolliffes possessed in the world was put into the enterprise. The grocery stock was pared down to the least that possibly could afford a bare sustenance to Joanna during the absence, which was to last through the usual "New-f'nland spell." How she would endure the weary time she hardly knew, for the boys had been with her formerly; but she nerved herself for the trial.

The ship was laden with boots and shoes, ready-made clothing, fishing-tackle, butter, cheese, cordage, sailcloth, and many other commodities; and was to bring back oil, furs, skins, fish, cranberries, and what else came to hand. But much speculative trading to other ports was to be undertaken between the voyages out and homeward, and thereby much money made.

III

THE brig sailed on a Monday morning in spring; but Joanna did not witness its departure. She could not bear the sight that she had been the means of bringing about. Knowing this, her husband told her overnight that they were to sail some time before noon next day; hence when, awakening at five the next morning, she heard them bustling about downstairs, she did not hasten to descend, but lay trying to nerve herself for the parting, imagining they would leave about nine, as her husband had done on his previous voyage. When she did descend she beheld words chalked upon the sloping face of the bureau; but no husband or sons. In the hastily-scrawled lines Shadrach said they had gone off thus not to pain her by a leave-taking; and the sons had chalked under his words: "Good-bye, mother!"

She rushed to the quay, and looked down the harbour towards the blue rim of the sea, but she could only see the masts and bulging sails of the *Joanna*; no human figures. "'Tis I have sent them!" she said wildly, and burst into tears. In the house the chalked "Good-bye" nearly broke her heart. But when she had re-entered the front room, and looked across at

Emily's, a gleam of triumph lit her thin face at her anticipated release from the thraldom of subservience.

To do Emily Lester justice, her assumption of superiority was mainly a figment of Joanna's brain. That the circumstances of the merchant's wife were more luxurious than Joanna's, the former could not conceal; though whenever the two met, which was not very often now, Emily endeavoured to subdue the difference by every means in her power.

The first summer lapsed away; and Joanna meagrely maintained herself by the shop, which now consisted of little more than a window and a counter. Emily was, in truth, her only large customer; and Mrs Lester's kindly readiness to buy anything and everything without questioning the quality had a sting of bitterness in it, for it was the uncritical attitude of a patron, and almost of a donor. The long dreary winter moved on; the face of the bureau had been turned to the wall to protect the chalked words of farewell, for Joanna could never bring herself to rub them out; and she often glanced at them with wet eyes. Emily's handsome boys came home for the Christmas holidays; the University was talked of for them; and still Joanna subsisted as it were with held breath, like a person submerged. Only one summer more, and the "spell" would end. Towards the close of the time Emily called on her quondam friend. She had heard that Joanna began to feel anxious; she had received no letter from husband or sons for some months. Emily's silks rustled arrogantly when, in response to Joanna's almost dumb invitation, she squeezed through the opening of the counter and into the parlour behind the shop.

"*You* are all success, and *I* am all the other way!" said Joanna.

"But why do you think so?" said Emily. "They are to bring back a fortune I hear."

"Ah! will they come? The doubt is more than a woman can bear. All three in one ship—think of that! And I have not heard of them for months!"

"But the time is not up. You should not meet misfortune half-way."

"Nothing will repay me for the grief of their absence!"

"Then why did you let them go? You were doing fairly well."

"I *made* them go!" she said, turning vehemently upon Emily. "And I'll tell you why! I could not bear that we should be only muddling on, and you so rich and thriving! Now I have told you, and you may hate me if you will!"

"I shall never hate you, Joanna."

And she proved the truth of her words afterwards. The end of autumn came, and the brig should have been in port; but nothing like the *Joanna* appeared in the channel between the sands. It was now really time to be uneasy. Joanna Jolliffe sat by the fire, and every gust of wind caused her a cold thrill. She had always feared and detested the sea; to her it was a treacherous, restless, slimy creature, glorying in the griefs of women. "Still," she said, "they *must* come!"

She recalled to her mind that Shadrach had said before starting that if they returned safe and sound, with success crowning their enterprise, he would go as he had gone after his shipwreck, and kneel with his sons in the church, and offer sincere thanks for their deliverance. She went to church regularly morning and afternoon, and sat in the most forward pew, nearest the chancel-step. Her eyes were mostly fixed on that step, where Shadrach had knelt in the bloom of his young manhood: she knew to an inch the spot which his knees had pressed twenty winters before; his outline as he had knelt, his hat on the step beside him. God was good. Surely her husband must kneel there again: a son on each side as he had said; George just here, Jim just there. By long watching the spot as she worshipped, it became as if she saw the three returned ones there kneeling; the two slim outlines of her boys, the more bulky form between them; their hands clasped, their heads shaped against the eastern wall. The fancy grew almost to an hallucination: she could never turn her worn eyes to the step without seeing them there.

Nevertheless they did not come. Heaven was merciful, but it was not yet pleased to relieve her soul. This was her purgation for the sin of making them the slaves of her ambition. But it became more than purgation soon, and her mood approached despair. Months had passed since the brig had been due, but it had not returned.

Joanna was always hearing or seeing evidences of their arrival. When on the hill behind the port, whence a view of the open Channel could be obtained, she felt sure that a little speck on the horizon, breaking the eternally level waste of waters southward, was the truck of the *Joanna's* mainmast. Or when indoors, a shout or excitement of any kind at the corner of the Town Cellar, where the High-street joined the Quay, caused her to spring to her feet and cry: "'Tis they!"

But it was not. The visionary forms knelt every Sunday afternoon on the chancel-step, but not the real. Her shop had, as it were, eaten itself hollow. In the apathy which had resulted from her loneliness and grief she had ceased to take in the smallest supplies, and thus had sent away her last customer.

In this strait Emily Lester tried by every means in her power to aid the afflicted woman; but she met with constant repulses.

"I don't like you! I can't bear to see you!" Joanna would whisper hoarsely when Emily came to her and made advances.

"But I want to help and soothe you, Joanna," Emily would say.

"You are a lady, with a rich husband and fine sons. What can you want with a bereaved crone like me!"

"Joanna, I want this: I want you to come and live in my house, and not stay alone in this dismal place any longer."

"And suppose they come and don't find me at home? You wish to separate me and mine! No, I'll stay here. I don't like you, and I can't thank you, whatever kindness you do me!"

However, as time went on Joanna could not afford to pay the rent of the shop and house without an income. She was assured that all hope of the return of Shadrach and his sons was vain, and she reluctantly consented to accept the asylum of the Lesters' house. Here she was allotted a room of her own on the second floor, and went and came as she chose, without contact with the family. Her hair greyed and whitened, deep lines channeled her forehead, and her form grew gaunt and stooping. But she still expected the lost ones, and when she met Emily on the staircase she would say morosely: "I know why you've got me here! They'll come, and be disappointed at not finding me at home, and perhaps go away again; and then you'll be revenged for my taking Shadrach away from 'ee!"

Emily Lester bore these reproaches from the grief-stricken soul. She was sure—all the people of Havenpool were sure—that Shadrach and his sons had gone to the bottom. For years the vessel had been given up as lost. Nevertheless, when awakened at night by any noise, Joanna would rise from bed and glance at the shop opposite by the light from the flickering lamp, to make sure it was not they.

It was a damp and dark December night, six years after the departure of the brig *Joanna*. The wind was from the sea, and brought up a fishy mist which mopped the face like moist flannel. Joanna had prayed her usual prayer for the absent ones with more fervour and confidence than she had felt for months, and had fallen asleep about eleven. It must have been between one and two when she suddenly started up. She had certainly heard steps in the street, and the voices of Shadrach and her sons calling at the door of the grocery shop. She sprang out of bed, and, hardly knowing what clothing she dragged on herself, hastened down Emily's large and carpeted staircase, put the candle on the hall-table, unfastened the bolts and chain, and stepped into the street. The mist, blowing up the street from the Quay, hindered her seeing the shop, although it was so near; but she had crossed to it in a moment. How was it? Nobody stood there. The wretched woman walked wildly up and down with her bare feet—there was not a soul. She returned and knocked with all her might at the door which had once been her own—they might have been admitted for the night, unwilling to disturb her till the morning. It was not till several minutes had elapsed that the young man who now kept the shop looked out of an upper window, and saw the skeleton of something human standing below half-dressed.

"Has anybody come?" asked the form.

"O, Mrs Jolliffe, I didn't know it was you," said the young man kindly, for he was aware how her baseless expectations moved her. "No; nobody has come."

June 1891.

THE FIDDLER OF THE REELS

"TALKING of Exhibitions, World's Fairs, and what not," said the old gentleman, "I would not go round the corner to see a dozen of them nowadays. The only exhibition that ever made, or ever will make, any impression upon my imagination was the first of the series, the parent of them all, and now a thing of old times—the Great Exhibition of 1851, in Hyde Park, London. None of the younger generation can realize the sense of novelty it produced in us who were then in our prime. A noun substantive went so far as to become an adjective in honour of the occasion. It was 'exhibition' hat, 'exhibition' razor-strop, 'exhibition' watch; nay, even 'exhibition' weather, 'exhibition' spirits, sweethearts, babies, wives—for the time.

"For South Wessex, the year formed in many ways an extraordinary chronological frontier or transit-line, at which there occurred what one might call a precipice in Time. As in a geological 'fault,' we had presented to us a sudden bringing of ancient and modern into absolute contact, such as probably in no other single year since the Conquest was ever witnessed in this part of the country."

These observations led us onward to talk of the different personages, gentle and simple, who lived and moved within our narrow and peaceful horizon at that time; and of three people in particular, whose queer little history was oddly touched at points by the Exhibition, more concerned with it than that of anybody else who dwelt in those outlying shades of the world, Stickleford, Mellstock, and Egdon. First in prominence among these three came Wat Ollamoor—if that were his real name—whom the seniors in our party had known well.

He was a woman's man, they said,—supremely so—externally little else. To men he was not attractive; perhaps a little repulsive at times. Musician, dandy, and company-man in practice; veterinary surgeon in theory, he lodged awhile in Mellstock village, coming from nobody knew where; though some said his first appearance in this neighbourhood had been as fiddle-player in a show at Greenhill Fair.

Many a worthy villager envied him his power over unsophisticated maidenhood—a power which seemed sometimes to have a touch of the weird and wizardly in it. Personally he was not ill-favoured, though rather un-English, his complexion being a rich olive, his rank hair dark and rather clammy—made still clammier by secret ointments, which, when he came fresh to a party, caused him to smell like "boys'-love" (southernwood) steeped in lamp-oil. On occasion he wore curls—a double row—running almost horizontally around his head. But as these were sometimes noticeably absent, it was concluded that they were not altogether of Nature's making. By girls whose love for him had turned to hatred he had been nicknamed "Mop," from this abundance of hair, which was long enough to rest upon his shoulders; as time passed the name more and more prevailed.

His fiddling possibly had the most to do with the fascination he exercised, for, to speak fairly, it could claim for itself a most peculiar and personal quality, like that in a moving preacher. There were tones in it which bred the immediate conviction that indolence and averseness to systematic application were all that lay between "Mop" and the career of a second Paganini.

While playing he invariably closed his eyes; using no notes, and, as it were, allowing the violin to wander on at will into the most plaintive passages ever heard by rustic man. There was a certain lingual character in the supplicatory expressions he produced, which would well-nigh have drawn an ache from the heart of a gate-post. He could make any child in the parish, who was at all sensitive to music, burst into tears in a few minutes by simply fiddling one of the old dance-tunes he almost entirely affected—country jigs, reels, and "Favourite Quick Steps" of the last century—some mutilated remains of which even now reappear as nameless phantoms in new quadrilles and gallops, where they are recognized only by the curious, or by such old-fashioned and far-between people as have been thrown with men like Wat Ollamoor in their early life.

His date was a little later than that of the old Mellstock quire-band which comprised the Dewys, Mail, and the rest— in fact, he did not rise above the horizon thereabout till those well-known musicians were disbanded as ecclesiastical functionaries. In their honest love of thoroughness they despised the new man's style. Theophilus Dewy (Reuben the tranter's younger brother) used to say there was no "plumness" in it— no bowing, no solidity—it was all fantastical. And probably this was true. Anyhow, Mop had, very obviously, never bowed a note of church-music from his birth; he never once sat in the gallery of Mellstock church where the others had tuned their venerable psalmody so many hundreds of times; had never, in all likelihood, entered a church at all. All were devil's tunes in his repertory. "He could no more play the Wold Hundredth to his true time than he could play the brazen serpent," the tranter would say. (The brazen serpent was supposed in Mellstock to be a musical instrument particularly hard to blow.)

Occasionally Mop could produce the aforesaid moving effect upon the souls of grown-up persons, especially young women of fragile and responsive organization. Such an one was Car'line Aspent. Though she was already engaged to be married before she met him, Car'line, of them all, was the most influenced by Mop Ollamoor's heart-stealing melodies, to her discomfort, nay, positive pain and ultimate injury. She was a pretty, invocating, weak-mouthed girl, whose chief defect as a companion with her sex was a tendency to peevishness now and then. At this time she was not a resident in Mellstock parish where Mop lodged, but lived some miles off at Stickleford, further down the river.

How and where she first made acquaintance with him and his fiddling is not truly known, but the story was that it either began or was developed on one spring evening, when, in passing through Lower Mellstock, she chanced to pause on the bridge near his house to rest herself, and languidly leaned over the parapet. Mop was standing on his door-step, as was his custom, spinning the insidious thread of semi- and demi-semiquavers from the E string of his fiddle for the benefit of passers-by, and laughing as the tears rolled down the cheeks of the little children hanging around him. Car'line pretended to be engrossed with the rippling of the stream under the arches, but in reality she was listening, as he knew. Presently the aching of the heart seized her simultaneously with a wild desire to glide airily in the mazes of an infinite dance. To shake off the fascination she resolved to go on, although it would be necessary to pass him as he played. On stealthily glancing ahead at the performer, she found to her relief that his eyes were closed in abandonment to instrumentation, and she strode on boldly. But when closer her step grew timid, her tread convulsed itself more and more accordantly with the time of the melody, till she very nearly danced along. Gaining another glance at him when immediately opposite, she saw that *one* of his eyes was open, quizzing her as he smiled at her emotional state. Her gait could not divest itself of its compelled capers till she had gone a long way past the house; and Car'line was unable to shake off the strange infatuation for hours.

After that day, whenever there was to be in the neighbourhood a dance to which she could get an invitation, and where Mop Ollamoor was to be the musician, Car'line contrived to be present, though it sometimes involved a walk of several miles; for he did not play so often in Stickleford as elsewhere.

The next evidences of his influence over her were singular enough, and it would require a neurologist to fully explain them. She would be sitting quietly, any evening after dark, in the house of her father, the parish clerk, which stood in the middle of Stickleford village street, this being the highroad between Lower Mellstock and Moreford, five miles eastward. Here, without a moment's warning, and in the midst of a general conversation between her father, sister, and the young man before alluded to, who devotedly wooed her in ignorance of her infatuation, she would start from her seat in the chimney-corner as if she had received a galvanic shock, and spring convulsively towards the ceiling; then she would burst into tears, and it was not till some half-hour had passed that she grew calm as usual. Her father, knowing her hysterical tendencies, was always excessively anxious about this trait in his youngest girl, and feared the attack to be a species of epileptic fit. Not so her sister Julia. Julia had found out what was the cause. At the moment before the jumping, only an exceptionally sensitive ear situated in the chimney-nook could have caught from down the flue the beat of a man's footstep along the highway without. But it was in that footfall, for which she had been waiting, that the origin of Car'line's involuntary springing lay. The pedestrian was Mop Ollamoor, as the girl well knew; but his business that way was not to visit her; he sought another woman whom he spoke of as his Intended, and who lived at Moreford, two miles further on. On one, and only one, occasion did it happen that Car'line could not control her utterance; it was when her sister alone chanced to be present. "O—O—O—!" she cried. "He's going to *her*, and not coming to *me!*"

To do the fiddler justice he had not at first thought greatly of, or spoken much to, this girl of impressionable mould. But he had soon found out her secret, and could not resist a little by-play with her too easily hurt heart, as an interlude between his more serious lovemakings at Moreford. The two became well acquainted, though only by stealth, hardly a soul in Stickleford except her sister, and her lover Ned Hipcroft, being aware of the attachment. Her father disapproved of her coldness to Ned; her sister, too, hoped she might get over this nervous passion for a man of whom so little was known. The ultimate result was that Car'line's manly and simple wooer Edward found his suit becoming practically hopeless. He was a respectable mechanic, in a far sounder position than Mop the nominal horse-doctor; but when, before leaving her, Ned put his flat and final question, would she marry him, then and there, now or never, it was with little expectation of obtaining more than the negative she gave him. Though her father supported him and her sister supported him, he could not play the fiddle so as to draw your soul out of your body like a spider's thread, as Mop did, till you felt as limp as withywind and yearned for something to cling to. Indeed, Hipcroft had not the slightest ear for music; could not sing two notes in tune, much less play them.

The No he had expected and got from her, in spite of a preliminary encouragement, gave Ned a new start in life. It had been uttered in such a tone of sad entreaty that he resolved to persecute her no more; she should not even be distressed by a sight of his form in the distant perspective of the street and lane. He left the place, and his natural course was to London.

The railway to South Wessex was in process of construction, but it was not as yet opened for traffic; and Hipcroft reached the capital by a six days' trudge on foot, as many a better man had done before him. He was one of the last of the artisan class who used that now extinct method of travel to the great centres of labour, so customary then from time immemorial.

In London he lived and worked regularly at his trade. More fortunate than many, his disinterested willingness recommended him from the first. During the ensuing four years he was never out of employment. He neither advanced nor receded in the modern sense; he improved as a workman, but he did not shift one jot in social position. About his love for Car'line he maintained a rigid silence. No doubt he often thought of her; but being always occupied, and having no relations at Stickleford, he held no communication with that part of the country, and showed no desire to return. In his quiet lodging in Lambeth he moved about after working-hours with the facility of a woman, doing his own cooking, attending to his stocking-heels, and shaping himself by degrees to a life-long bachelorhood. For this conduct one is bound to advance the canonical reason that time could not efface from his heart the image of little Car'line Aspent—and it may be in part true; but there was also the inference that his was a nature not greatly dependent upon the ministrations of the other sex for its comforts.

The fourth year of his residence as a mechanic in London was the year of the Hyde-Park Exhibition already mentioned, and at the construction of this huge glass-house, then unexampled in the world's history, he worked daily. It was an era of great hope and activity among the nations and industries. Though Hipcroft was, in his small way, a central man in the movement, he plodded on with his usual outward placidity. Yet for him, too, the year was destined to have its surprises, for when the bustle of getting the building ready for the opening day was past, the ceremonies had been witnessed, and people were flocking thither from all parts of the globe, he received a letter from Car'line. Till that day the silence of four years between himself and Stickleford had never been broken.

She informed her old lover, in an uncertain penmanship which suggested a trembling hand, of the trouble she had been put to in ascertaining his address, and then broached the subject which had prompted her to write. Four years ago, she said, with the greatest delicacy of which she was capable, she had been so foolish as to refuse him. Her wilful wrong-headedness had since been a grief to her many times, and of late particularly. As for Mr Ollamoor, he had been absent almost as long as Ned—she did not know where. She would gladly marry Ned now if he were to ask her again, and be a tender little wife to him till her life's end.

A tide of warm feeling must have surged through Ned Hipcroft's frame on receipt of this news, if we may judge by the issue. Unquestionably he loved her still, even if not to the exclusion of every other happiness. This from his Car'line, she who had been dead to him these many years, alive to him again as of old, was in itself a pleasant, gratifying thing. Ned had grown so resigned to, or satisfied with, his lonely lot, that he probably would not have shown much jubilation at anything. Still, a certain ardour of preoccupation, after his first surprise, revealed how deeply her confession of faith in him had stirred him. Measured and methodical in his ways, he did not answer the letter that day, nor the next, nor the next. He was having "a good think." When he did answer it, there was a great deal of sound reasoning mixed in with the unmistakable tenderness of his reply; but the tenderness itself was sufficient to reveal that he was pleased with her straightforward frankness; that the anchorage she had once obtained in his heart was renewable, if it had not been continuously firm.

He told her—and as he wrote his lips twitched humorously over the few gentle words of raillery he indited among the rest of his sentences—that it was all very well for her to come round at this time of day. Why wouldn't she have him when he wanted her? She had no doubt learned that he was not married, but suppose his affections had since been fixed on another? She ought to beg his pardon. Still, he was not the man to forget her. But considering how he had been used, and what he had suffered, she could not quite expect him to go down to Stickleford and fetch her. But if she would come to him, and say she was sorry, as was only fair; why, yes, he would marry her, knowing what a good little woman she was at the core. He added that the request for her to come to him was a less one to make than it would have been when he first left Stickleford, or even a few months ago; for the new railway into South Wessex was now open, and there had just begun to be run wonderfully contrived special trains, called excursion-trains, on account of the Great Exhibition; so that she could come up easily alone.

She said in her reply how good it was of him to treat her so generously, after her hot and cold treatment of him; that though she felt frightened at the magnitude of the journey, and was never as yet in a railway-train, having only seen one pass at a distance, she embraced his offer with all her heart; and would, indeed, own to him how sorry she was, and beg his pardon, and try to be a good wife always, and make up for lost time.

The remaining details of when and where were soon settled, Car'line informing him, for her ready identification in the crowd, that she would be wearing "my new sprigged-laylock cotton gown," and Ned gaily responding that, having married her the morning after her arrival, he would make a day of it by taking her to the Exhibition. One early summer afternoon, accordingly, he came from his place of work, and hastened towards Waterloo Station to meet her. It was as wet and chilly as an English June day can occasionally be, but as he waited on the platform in the drizzle he glowed inwardly, and seemed to have something to live for again.

The "excursion-train"—an absolutely new departure in the history of travel—was still a novelty on the Wessex line, and probably everywhere. Crowds of people had flocked to all the stations on the way up to witness the unwonted sight of so long a train's passage, even where they did not take advantage of the opportunity it offered. The seats for the humbler class of travellers in these early experiments in steam-locomotion were open trucks, without any protection whatever from the wind and rain; and damp weather having set in with the afternoon, the unfortunate occupants of these vehicles were, on the train drawing up at the London terminus, found to be in a pitiable condition from their long journey; blue-faced, stiff-necked, sneezing, rain-beaten, chilled to the marrow, many of the men being hatless; in fact, they resembled people who had been out all night in an open boat on a rough sea, rather than inland excursionists for pleasure. The women had in some degree protected themselves by turning up the skirts of their gowns over their heads, but as by this arrangement they were additionally exposed about the hips, they were all more or less in a sorry plight.

In the bustle and crush of alighting forms of both sexes which followed the entry of the huge concatenation into the station, Ned Hipcroft soon discerned the slim little figure his eye was in search of, in the sprigged lilac, as described. She came up to him with a frightened smile—still pretty, though so damp, weather-beaten, and shivering from long exposure to the wind.

"O Ned!" she sputtered, "I—I—" He clasped her in his arms and kissed her, whereupon she burst into a flood of tears.

"You are wet, my poor dear! I hope you'll not get cold," he said. And surveying her and her multifarious surrounding packages, he noticed that by the hand she led a toddling child—a little girl of three or so—whose hood was as clammy and tender face as blue as those of the other travellers.

"Who is this—somebody you know?" asked Ned, curiously.

"Yes, Ned. She's mine."

"Yours?"

"Yes—my own."

"Your own child?"

"Yes!"

"But who's the father?"

"The young man I had after you courted me."

"Well—as God's in—"

"Ned, I didn't name it in my letter, because, you see, it would have been so hard to explain! I thought that when we met I could tell you how she happened to be born, so much better than in writing! I hope you'll excuse it this once, dear Ned, and not scold me, now I've come so many, many miles!"

"This means Mr Mop Ollamoor, I reckon!" said Hipcroft, gazing palely at them from the distance of the yard or two to which he had withdrawn with a start.

Car'line gasped. "But he's been gone away for years!" she supplicated. "And I never had a young man before! And I was so onlucky to be catched the first time he took advantage o' me, though some of the girls down there go on like anything!"

Ned remained in silence, pondering.

"You'll forgive me, dear Ned?" she added, beginning to sob outright. "I haven't taken 'ee in after all, because—because you can pack us back again, if you want to; though 'tis hundreds o' miles, and so wet, and night a-coming on, and I with no money!"

"What the devil can I do!" Hipcroft groaned.

A more pitiable picture than the pair of helpless creatures presented was never seen on a rainy day, as they stood on the great, gaunt, puddled platform, a whiff of drizzle blowing under the roof upon them now and then; the pretty attire in which they had started from Stickleford in the early morning bemuddled and sodden, weariness on their faces, and fear of him in their eyes; for the child began to look as if she thought she too had done some wrong, remaining in an appalled silence till the tears rolled down her chubby cheeks.

"What's the matter, my little maid?" said Ned, mechanically.

"I do want to go home!" she let out, in tones that told of a bursting heart. "And my totties be cold, an' I shan't have no bread an' butter no more!"

"I don't know what to say to it all!" declared Ned, his own eye moist as he turned and walked a few steps with his head down; then regarded them again point blank. From the child escaped troubled breaths and silently welling tears.

"Want some bread and butter, do 'ee?" he said, with fac-
titious hardness.

"Ye—e—s!"

"Well, I dare say I can get 'ee a bit. Naturally, you must want
some. And you, too, for that matter, Car'line."

"I do feel a little hungered. But I can keep it off," she
murmured.

"Folk shouldn't do that," he said gruffly. . . . "There, come
along!" He caught up the child, as he added, "You must bide
here to-night, anyhow, I s'pose! What can you do otherwise?
I'll get 'ee some tea and victuals; and as for this job, I'm sure
I don't know what to say! This is the way out."

They pursued their way, without speaking, to Ned's lodgings, which were not far off. There he dried them and made
them comfortable, and prepared tea; they thankfully sat
down. The ready-made household of which he suddenly
found himself the head imparted a cosy aspect to his room,
and a paternal one to himself. Presently he turned to the
child and kissed her now blooming cheeks; and, looking
wistfully at Car'line, kissed her also.

"I don't see how I can send you back all them miles," he
growled, "now you've come all the way o' purpose to join me.
But you must trust me, Car'line, and show you've real faith in
me. Well, do you feel better now, my little woman?"

The child nodded beamingly, her mouth being otherwise
occupied.

"I did trust you, Ned, in coming; and I shall always!"

Thus, without any definite agreement to forgive her, he
tacitly acquiesced in the fate that Heaven had sent him; and
on the day of their marriage (which was not quite so soon as
he had expected it could be, on account of the time necessary
for banns) he took her to the Exhibition when they came
back from church, as he had promised. While standing near
a large mirror in one of the courts devoted to furniture,
Car'line started, for in the glass appeared the reflection of a
form exactly resembling Mop Ollamoor's— so exactly, that it
seemed impossible to believe anybody but that artist in person to be the original. On passing round the objects which
hemmed in Ned, her, and the child from a direct view, no

Mop was to be seen. Whether he were really in London or not at that time was never known; and Car'line always stoutly denied that her readiness to go and meet Ned in town arose from any rumour that Mop had also gone thither; which denial there was no reasonable ground for doubting.

And then the year glided away, and the Exhibition folded itself up and became a thing of the past. The park trees that had been enclosed for six months were again exposed to the winds and storms, and the sod grew green anew. Ned found that Car'line resolved herself into a very good wife and companion, though she had made herself what is called cheap to him; but in that she was like another domestic article, a cheap tea-pot, which often brews better tea than a dear one. One autumn Hipcroft found himself with but little work to do, and a prospect of less for the winter. Both being country born and bred, they fancied they would like to live again in their natural atmosphere. It was accordingly decided between them that they should leave the pent-up London lodging, and that Ned should seek out employment near his native place, his wife and her daughter staying with Car'line's father during the search for occupation and an abode of their own.

Tinglings of pride pervaded Car'line's spasmodic little frame as she journeyed down with Ned to the place she had left two or three years before, in silence and under a cloud. To return to where she had once been despised, a smiling London wife with a distinct London accent, was a triumph which the world did not witness every day.

The train did not stop at the petty roadside station that lay nearest to Stickleford, and the trio went on to Casterbridge. Ned thought it a good opportunity to make a few preliminary inquiries for employment at workshops in the borough where he had been known; and feeling cold from her journey, and it being dry underfoot and only dusk as yet, with a moon on the point of rising, Car'line and her little girl walked on towards Stickleford, leaving Ned to follow at a quicker pace, and pick her up at a certain half-way house, widely known as an inn.

The woman and child pursued the well-remembered way comfortably enough, though they were both becoming wearied. In the course of three miles they had passed Heed-less-William's Pond, the familiar landmark by Bloom's End, and were drawing near the Quiet Woman, a lone roadside hostel on the lower verge of the Egdon Heath, since and for many years abolished. In stepping up towards it Car'line heard more voices within than had formerly been customary at such an hour, and she learned that an auction of fat stock had been held near the spot that afternoon. The child would be the better for a rest as well as herself, she thought, and she entered.

The guests and customers overflowed into the passage, and Car'line had no sooner crossed the threshold than a man whom she remembered by sight came forwards with a glass and mug in his hands towards a friend leaning against the wall; but, seeing her, very gallantly offered her a drink of the liquor, which was gin-and-beer hot, pouring her out a tumblerful and saying, in a moment or two: "Surely, 'tis little Car'line Aspent that was—down at Stickleford?"

She assented, and, though she did not exactly want this beverage, she drank it since it was offered, and her enter-tainer begged her to come in further and sit down. Once within the room she found that all the persons present were seated close against the walls, and there being a chair vacant she did the same. An explanation of their position occurred the next moment. In the opposite corner stood Mop, rosining his bow and looking just the same as ever. The company had cleared the middle of the room for dancing, and they were about to dance again. As she wore a veil to keep off the wind she did not think he had recognized her, or could possibly guess the identity of the child; and to her satisfied surprise she found that she could confront him quite calmly—mistress of herself in the dignity her London life had given her. Before she had quite emptied her glass the dance was called, the dancers formed in two lines, the music sounded, and the figure began.

Then matters changed for Car'line. A tremor quickened itself to life in her, and her hand so shook that she could hardly set down her glass. It was not the dance nor the dancers, but the notes of that old violin which thrilled the

London wife, these having still all the witchery that she had so well known of yore, and under which she had used to lose her power of independent will. How it all came back! There was the fiddling figure against the wall; the large, oily, mop-like head of him, and beneath the mop the face with closed eyes.

After the first moments of paralyzed reverie the familiar tune in the familiar rendering made her laugh and shed tears simultaneously. Then a man at the bottom of the dance, whose partner had dropped away, stretched out his hand and beckoned to her to take the place. She did not want to dance; she entreated by signs to be left where she was, but she was entreating of the tune and its player rather than of the dancing man. The saltatory tendency which the fiddler and his cunning instrument had ever been able to start in her was seizing Car'line just as it had done in earlier years, possibly assisted by the gin-and-beer hot. Tired as she was she grasped her little girl by the hand, and plunging in at the bottom of the figure, whirled about with the rest. She found that her companions were mostly people of the neighbouring hamlets and farms—Bloom's End, Mellstock, Lewgate, and elsewhere; and by degrees she was recognized as she convulsively danced on, wishing that Mop would cease and let her heart rest from the aching he caused, and her feet also.

After long and many minutes the dance ended, when she was urged to fortify herself with more gin-and-beer; which she did, feeling very weak and overpowered with hysteric emotion. She refrained from unveiling, to keep Mop in ignorance of her presence, if possible. Several of the guests having left, Car'line hastily wiped her lips and also turned to go; but, according to the account of some who remained, at that very moment a five-handed reel was proposed, in which two or three begged her to join.

She declined on the plea of being tired and having to walk to Stickleford, when Mop began aggressively tweedling "My Fancy-Lad," in D major, as the air to which the reel was to be footed. He must have recognized her, though she did not know it, for it was the strain of all seductive strains which she was least able to resist—the one he had played when she was leaning over the bridge at the date of their first acquaintance. Car'line stepped despairingly into the middle of the room with the other four.

Reels were resorted to hereabouts at this time by the more robust spirits, for the reduction of superfluous energy which the ordinary figure-dances were not powerful enough to exhaust. As everybody knows, or does not know, the five reelers stood in the form of a cross, the reel being performed by each line of three alternately, the persons who successively came to the middle place dancing in both directions. Car'line soon found herself in this place, the axis of the whole performance, and could not get out of it, the tune turning into the first part without giving her opportunity. And now she began to suspect that Mop did know her, and was doing this on purpose, though whenever she stole a glance at him his closed eyes betokened obliviousness to everything outside his own brain. She continued to wend her way through the figure of 8 that was formed by her course, the fiddler introducing into his notes the wild and agonizing sweetness of a living voice in one too highly wrought; its pathos running high and running low in endless variation, projecting through her nerves excruciating spasms, a sort of blissful torture. The room swam, the tune was endless; and in about a quarter of an hour the only other woman in the figure dropped out exhausted, and sank panting on a bench.

The reel instantly resolved itself into a four-handed one. Car'line would have given anything to leave off; but she had, or fancied she had, no power, while Mop played such tunes; and thus another ten minutes slipped by, a haze of dust now clouding the candles, the floor being of stone, sanded. Then another dancer fell out—one of the men—and went into the passage, in a frantic search for liquor. To turn the figure into a three-handed reel was the work of a second, Mop modulating at the same time into "The Fairy Dance," as better suited to the contracted movement, and no less one of those foods of love which, as manufactured by his bow, had always intoxicated her.

In a reel for three there was no rest whatever, and four or five minutes were enough to make her remaining two partners, now thoroughly blown, stamp their last bar, and, like their predecessors, limp off into the next room to get something to drink. Car'line, half-stifled inside her veil, was left dancing alone, the apartment now being empty of everybody save herself, Mop, and their little girl.

She flung up the veil, and cast her eyes upon him, as if imploring him to withdraw himself and his acoustic magnetism from the atmosphere. Mop opened one of his own orbs, as though for the first time, fixed it peeringly upon her, and smiling dreamily, threw into his strains the reserve of expression which he could not afford to waste on a big and noisy dance. Crowds of little chromatic subtleties, capable of drawing tears from a statue, proceeded straightway from the ancient fiddle, as if it were dying of the emotion which had been pent up within it ever since its banishment from some Italian or German city where it first took shape and sound. There was that in the look of Mop's one dark eye which said: "You cannot leave off, dear, whether you would or no!" and it bred in her a paroxysm of desperation that defied him to tire her down.

She thus continued to dance alone, defiantly as she thought, but in truth slavishly and abjectly, subject to every wave of the melody, and probed by the gimlet-like gaze of her fascinator's open eye; keeping up at the same time a feeble smile in his face, as a feint to signify it was still her own pleasure which led her on. A terrified embarrassment as to what she could say to him if she were to leave off, had its unrecognized share in keeping her going. The child, who was beginning to be distressed by the strange situation, came up and whimpered: "Stop, mother, stop, and let's go home!" as she seized Car'line's hand.

Suddenly Car'line sank staggering to the floor; and rolling over on her face, prone she remained. Mop's fiddle thereupon emitted an elfin shriek of finality; stepping quickly down from the nine-gallon beer-cask which had formed his rostrum, he went to the little girl, who disconsolately bent over her mother.

The guests who had gone into the back-room for liquor and change of air, hearing something unusual, trooped back hitherward, where they endeavoured to revive poor, weak Car'line by blowing her with the bellows and opening the window. Ned, her husband, who had been detained in Casterbridge, as aforesaid, came along the road at this juncture, and hearing excited voices through the open casement, and to his great surprise, the mention of his wife's name, he entered amid the rest upon the scene. Car'line was now in convulsions, weeping violently, and for a long time nothing could be done with her. While he was sending for a cart to take her onward to Stickleford Hipcroft anxiously inquired how it had all happened; and then the assembly explained that a fiddler formerly known in the locality had lately revisited his old haunts, and had taken upon himself without invitation to play that evening at the inn and raise a dance.

Ned demanded the fiddler's name, and they said Ollamoor.

"Ah!" exclaimed Ned, looking round him. "Where is he, and where—where's my little girl?"

Ollamoor had disappeared, and so had the child. Hipcroft was in ordinary a quiet and tractable fellow, but a determination which was to be feared settled in his face now. "Blast him!" he cried. "I'll beat his skull in for'n, if I swing for it to-morrow!"

He had rushed to the poker which lay on the hearth, and hastened down the passage, the people following. Outside the house, on the other side of the highway, a mass of dark heath-land rose sullenly upward to its not easily accessible interior, a ravined plateau, whereon jutted into the sky, at the distance of a couple of miles, the fir-woods of Mistover backed by the Yalbury coppices—a place of Dantesque gloom at this hour, which would have afforded secure hiding for a battery of artillery, much less a man and a child.

Some other men plunged thitherward with him, and more went along the road. They were gone about twenty minutes altogether, returning without result to the inn. Ned sat down in the settle, and clasped his forehead with his hands.

"Well—what a fool the man is, and hev been all these years,

if he thinks the child his, as a' do seem to!" they whispered. "And everybody else knowing otherwise!"

"No, I don't think 'tis mine!" cried Ned, hoarsely, as he looked up from his hands. "But she *is* mine, all the same!

"Ha'n't I nussed her? Ha'n't I fed her and teached her? Ha'n't I played wi' her? O, little Carry—gone with that rogue—gone!"

"You ha'n't lost your mis'ess, anyhow," they said to console him. "She's throwed up the sperrits, and she is feeling better, and she's more to 'ee than a child that isn't yours."

"She isn't! She's not so particular much to me, especially now she's lost the little maid! But Carry's the whole world to me!"

"Well, ver' like you'll find her to-morrow."

"Ah—but shall I? Yet he *can't* hurt her—surely he can't! Well—how's Car'line now? I am ready. Is the cart here?"

She was lifted into the vehicle, and they sadly lumbered on towards Stickleford. Next day she was calmer; but the fits were still upon her; and her will seemed shattered. For the child she appeared to show singularly little anxiety, though Ned was nearly distracted by his passionate paternal love for a child not his own. It was nevertheless quite expected that the impish Mop would restore the lost one after a freak of a day or two; but time went on, and neither he nor she could be heard of, and Hipcroft murmured that perhaps he was exercising upon her some unholy musical charm, as he had done upon Car'line herself. Weeks passed, and still they could obtain no clue either to the fiddler's whereabouts or to the girl's; and how he could have induced her to go with him remained a mystery.

Then Ned, who had obtained only temporary employment in the neighbourhood, took a sudden hatred towards his native district, and a rumour reaching his ears through the police that a somewhat similar man and child had been seen at a fair near London, he playing a violin, she dancing on stilts, a new interest in the capital took possession of Hipcroft with an intensity which would scarcely allow him time to pack before returning thither. He did not, however, find the lost one, though he made it the entire business of his over-hours to stand about in by-streets in the hope of discovering her, and would start up in the night, saying, "That rascal's torturing her to maintain him!" To which his wife would answer peevishly, "Don't 'ee raft yourself so, Ned! You prevent my getting a bit o' rest! He won't hurt her!" and fall asleep again.

That Carry and her father had emigrated to America was the general opinion; Mop, no doubt, finding the girl a highly desirable companion when he had trained her to keep him by her earnings as a dancer. There, for that matter, they may be performing in some capacity now, though he must be an old scamp verging on three-score-and-ten, and she a woman of four-and-forty.

May 1893.

A FEW CRUSTED CHARACTERS

Introduction

IT is a Saturday afternoon of blue and yellow autumn-time, and the scene is the high street of a well-known market-town. A large carrier's van stands in the quadrangular fore-court of the White Hart Inn, upon the sides of its spacious tilt being painted, in weather-beaten letters: "Burthen, Carrier to Longpuddle." These vans, so numerous hereabout, are a respectable, if somewhat lumbering, class of conveyance, much resorted to by decent travellers not overstocked with money, the better among them roughly corresponding to the old French *diligences*.

The present one is timed to leave the town at four in the afternoon precisely, and it is now half-past three by the clock in the turret at the top of the street. In a few seconds errand-boys from the shops begin to arrive with packages, which they fling into the vehicle, and turn away whistling, and care for the packages no more. At twenty minutes to four an elderly woman places her basket upon the shafts, slowly mounts, takes up a seat inside, and folds her hands and her lips. She has secured her corner for the journey, though there is as yet no sign of a horse being put in, nor of a carrier. At the three-quarters, two other women arrive, in whom the first recognizes the postmistress of Upper Longpuddle and the registrar's wife, they recognizing her as the aged groceress of the same village. At five minutes to the hour there approach Mr Profitt, the schoolmaster, in a soft felt hat, and Christopher Twink, the master-thatcher; and as the hour strikes there rapidly drop in the parish clerk and his wife, the seedsman and his aged father, the registrar; also Mr Day, the world-ignored local landscape-painter, an elderly man who resides in his native place, and has never sold a picture outside it, though his pretensions to art have been nobly supported by his fellow-villagers, whose confidence in his genius has been as remarkable as the outer neglect of it, leading them to buy his paintings so extensively (at the price of a few shillings each, it is true) that every dwelling in the parish exhibits three or four of those admired productions on its walls.

Burthen, the carrier, is by this time seen bustling round the vehicle; the horses are put in, the proprietor arranges the reins and springs up into his seat as if he were used to it—which he is.

"Is everybody here?" he asks preparatorily over his shoulder to the passengers within.

As those who were not there did not reply in the negative the muster was assumed to be complete, and after a few hitches and hindrances the van with its human freight was got under way. It jogged on at an easy pace till it reached the bridge which formed the last outpost of the town. The carrier pulled up suddenly.

"Bless my soul!" he said, "I've forgot the curate!"

All who could do so gazed from the little back window of the van, but the curate was not in sight.

"Now I wonder where that there man is?" continued the carrier.

"Poor man, he ought to have a living at his time of life."

"And he ought to be punctual," said the carrier. "'Four o'clock sharp is my time for starting,' I said to 'en. And he said, 'I'll be there.' Now he's not here; and as a serious old church minister he ought to be as good as his word. Perhaps Mr Flaxton knows, being in the same line of life?" He turned to the parish clerk.

"I was talking an immense deal with him, that's true, half an hour ago," replied that ecclesiastic, as one of whom it was no erroneous supposition that he should be on intimate terms with another of the cloth. "But he didn't say he would be late."

The discussion was cut off by the appearance round the corner of the van of rays from the curate's spectacles, followed hastily by his face and a few white whiskers, and the swinging tails of his long gaunt coat. Nobody reproached him, seeing how he was reproaching himself; and he entered breathlessly and took his seat.

"Now be we all here?" said the carrier again. They started a second time, and moved on till they were about three hundred yards out of the town, and had nearly reached the second bridge, behind which, as every native remembers, the road takes a turn and travellers by this highway disappear finally from the view of gazing burghers.

"Well, as I'm alive!" cried the postmistress from the interior of the conveyance, peering through the little square back-window along the road townward.

"What?" said the carrier.

"A man hailing us!"

Another sudden stoppage. "Somebody else?" the carrier asked.

"Ay, sure!" All waited silently, while those who could gaze out did so.

"Now, who can that be?" Burthen continued. "I just put it to ye, neighbours, can any man keep time with such hindrances? Bain't we full a'ready? Who in the world can the man be?"

"He's a sort of gentleman," said the schoolmaster, his position commanding the road more comfortably than that of his comrades.

The stranger, who had been holding up his umbrella to attract their notice, was walking forward leisurely enough, now that he found, by their stopping, that it had been secured. His clothes were decidedly not of a local cut, though it was difficult to point out any particular mark of difference. In his left hand he carried a small leather travelling bag. As soon as he had overtaken the van he glanced at the inscription on its side, as if to assure himself that he had hailed the right conveyance, and asked if they had room.

The carrier replied that though they were pretty well laden he supposed they could carry one more, whereupon the stranger mounted, and took the seat cleared for him within. And then the horses made another move, this time for good, and swung along with their burden of fourteen souls all told.

"You bain't one of these parts, sir?" said the carrier. "I could tell that as far as I could see 'ee."

"Yes, I am one of these parts," said the stranger.

"Oh? H'm."

The silence which followed seemed to imply a doubt of the truth of the new-comer's assertion. "I was speaking of Upper Longpuddle more particular," continued the carrier hardily, "and I think I know most faces of that valley."

"I was born at Longpuddle, and nursed at Longpuddle, and my father and grandfather before me," said the passenger quietly.

"Why, to be sure," said the aged groceress in the background, "it isn't John Lackland's son—never—it can't be he who went to foreign parts five-and-thirty years ago with his wife and family? Yet—what do I hear?—that's his father's voice!"

"That's the man," replied the stranger. "John Lackland was my father, and I am John Lackland's son. Five-and-thirty years ago, when I was a boy of eleven, my parents emigrated across the seas, taking me and my sister with them. Kytes's boy Tony was the one who drove us and our belongings to Casterbridge on the morning we left; and his was the last Longpuddle face I saw. We sailed the same week across the ocean, and there we've been ever since, and there I've left those I went with— all three."

"Alive or dead?"

"Dead," he replied in a low voice. "And I have come back to the old place, having nourished a thought—not a definite intention, but just a thought—that I should like to return here in a year or two, to spend the remainder of my days."

"Married man, Mr Lackland?"

"No."

"And have the world used 'ee well, sir—or rather John, knowing 'ee as a child? In these rich new countries that we hear of so much, you've got rich with the rest?"

"I am not very rich," Mr Lackland said. "Even in new countries, you know, there are failures. The race is not always to the swift, nor the battle to the strong; and even if it sometimes is, you may be neither swift nor strong. However, that's enough about me. Now, having answered your inquiries, you must answer mine; for being in London, I have come down here entirely to discover what Longpuddle is looking like, and who are living there. That was why I preferred a seat in your van to hiring a carriage for driving across."

"Well, as for Longpuddle, we rub on there much as usual. Old figures have dropped out o' their frames, so to speak it, and new ones have been put in their places. You mentioned Tony Kytes as having been the one to drive your family and your goods to Casterbridge in his father's waggon when you left. Tony is, I believe, living still, but not at Longpuddle. He went away and settled at Lewgate, near Mellstock, after his marriage. Ah, Tony was a sort o' man!"

"His character had hardly come out when I knew him."

"No. But 'twas well enough, as far as that goes—except as to women. I shall never forget his courting—never!"

The returned villager waited silently, and the carrier went on:—

Tony Kytes, the Arch-Deceiver

"I SHALL never forget Tony's face. 'Twas a little, round, firm, tight face, with a seam here and there left by the smallpox, but not enough to hurt his looks in a woman's eye, though he'd had it badish when he was a boy. So very serious looking and unsmiling 'a was, that young man, that it really seemed as if he couldn't laugh at all without great pain to his conscience. He looked very hard at a small speck in your eye when talking to 'ee. And there was no more sign of a whisker or beard on Tony Kytes's face than on the palm of my hand. He used to sing 'The Tailor's Breeches' with a religious manner, as if it were a hymn:—

" 'O the petticoats went off, and the breeches they went on!'

and all the rest of the scandalous stuff. He was quite the women's favourite, and in return for their likings he loved 'em in shoals.

"But in course of time Tony got fixed down to one in particular, Milly Richards, a nice, light, small, tender little thing; and it was soon said that they were engaged to be married. One Saturday he had been to market to do business for his father, and was driving home the waggon in the afternoon. When he reached the foot of the very hill we shall be going over in ten minutes, who should he see waiting for him at the top but Unity Sallet, a handsome girl, one of the young women he'd been very tender towards before he'd got engaged to Milly.

"As soon as Tony came up to her she said, 'My dear Tony, will you give me a lift home?'

" 'That I will, darling,' said Tony. 'You don't suppose I could refuse 'ee?'

"She smiled a smile, and up she hopped, and on drove Tony.

" 'Tony,' she says, in a sort of tender chide, 'why did ye desert me for that other one? In what is she better than I? I should have made 'ee a finer wife, and a more loving one too. 'Tisn't girls that are so easily won at first that are the best. Think how long we've known each other—ever since we were children almost—now haven't we, Tony?'

" 'Yes, that we have,' says Tony, a-struck with the truth o't.

" 'And you've never seen anything in me to complain of, have ye, Tony? Now tell the truth to me.'

" 'I never have, upon my life,' says Tony.

" 'And—can you say I'm not pretty, Tony? Now look at me!'

"He let his eyes light upon her for a long while. 'I really can't,' says he. 'In fact, I never knowed you was so pretty before!'

" 'Prettier than she?'

"What Tony would have said to that nobody knows, for before he could speak, what should he see ahead, over the hedge past the turning, but a feather he knew well—the feather in Milly's hat—she to whom he had been thinking of putting the question as to giving out the banns that very week.

"'Unity,' says he, as mild as he could, 'here's Milly coming. Now I shall catch it mightily if she sees 'ee riding here with me; and if you get down she'll be turning the corner in a moment, and, seeing 'ee in the road, she'll know we've been coming on together. Now, dearest Unity, will ye, to avoid all unpleasantness, which I know ye can't bear any more than I, will ye lie down in the back part of the waggon, and let me cover you over with the tarpaulin till Milly has passed? It will all be done in a minute. Do!—and I'll think over what we've said; and perhaps I shall put a loving question to you after all, instead of to Milly. 'Tisn't true that it is all settled between her and me.'

"Well, Unity Sallet agreed, and lay down at the back end of the waggon, and Tony covered her over, so that the waggon seemed to be empty but for the loose tarpaulin; and then he drove on to meet Milly.

"'My dear Tony!' cries Milly, looking up with a little pout at him as he came near. 'How long you've been coming home! Just as if I didn't live at Upper Longpuddle at all! And I've come to meet you as you asked me to do, and to ride back with you, and talk over our future home—since you asked me, and I promised. But I shouldn't have come else, Mr Tony!'

"'Ay, my dear, I did ask 'ee—to be sure I did, now I think of it—but I had quite forgot it. To ride back with me, did you say, dear Milly?'

"'Well, of course! What can I do else? Surely you don't want me to walk, now I've come all this way?'

"'O no, no! I was thinking you might be going on to town to meet your mother. I saw her there—and she looked as if she might be expecting 'ee.'

"'O no; she's just home. She came across the fields, and so got back before you.'

"'Ah! I didn't know that,' says Tony. And there was no help for it but to take her up beside him.

"They talked on very pleasantly, and looked at the trees and beasts, and birds and insects, and at the ploughmen at work in the fields, till presently who should they see looking out of the upper window of a house that stood beside the road they were following but Hannah Jolliver, another young beauty of the place at that time, and the very first woman that Tony had fallen in love with—before Milly and before Unity, in fact—the one that he had almost arranged to marry instead of Milly. She was a much more dashing girl than Milly Richards, though he'd not thought much of her of late. The house Hannah was looking from was her aunt's.

"'My dear Milly—my coming wife, as I may call 'ee,' says Tony in his modest way, and not so loud that Unity could overhear, 'I see a young woman a-looking out of window, who I think may accost me. The fact is, Milly, she had a notion that I was wishing to marry her, and since she's discovered I've promised another, and a prettier than she, I'm rather afeard of her temper if she sees us together. Now, Milly, would you do me a favour—my coming wife, as I may say?'

"'Certainly, dearest Tony,' says she.

"'Then would ye creep under the empty sacks just here in the front of the waggon, and hide there out of sight till we've passed the house? She hasn't seen us yet. You see, we ought to live in peace and good-will since 'tis almost Christmas, and 'twill prevent angry passions rising, which we always should do.'

"'I don't mind, to oblige you, Tony,' Milly said; and though she didn't care much about doing it, she crept under, and crouched down just behind the seat, Unity being snug at the other end. So they drove on till they got near the road-side cottage. Hannah had soon seen him coming, and waited at the window, looking down upon him. She tossed her head a little disdainful and smiled off-hand.

"'Well, aren't you going to be civil enough to ask me to ride home with you?' she says, seeing that he was for driving past with a nod and a smile.

"'Ah, to be sure! What was I thinking of?' said Tony, in a flutter. 'But you seem as if you was staying at your aunt's?'

"'No, I am not,' she said. 'Don't you see I have my bonnet and jacket on? I have only called to see her on my way home. How can you be so stupid, Tony?'

"'In that case—ah—of course you must come along wi' me,' says Tony, feeling a dim sort of sweat rising up inside his clothes. And he reined in the horse, and waited till she'd come downstairs, and then helped her up beside him, her feet outside. He drove on again, his face as long as a face that was a round one by nature well could be.

"Hannah looked round sideways into his eyes. 'This is nice, isn't it, Tony?' she says. 'I like riding with you.'

"Tony looked back into her eyes. 'And I with you,' he said after a while. In short, having considered her, he warmed up, and the more he looked at her the more he liked her, till he couldn't for the life of him think why he had ever said a word about marriage to Milly or Unity while Hannah Jolliver was in question. So they sat a little closer and closer, their feet upon the footboard and their shoulders touching, and Tony thought over and over again how handsome Hannah was. He spoke tenderer and tenderer, and called her 'dear Hannah' in a whisper at last.

"'You've settled it with Milly by this time, I suppose,' said she.

"'N—no, not exactly.'

"'What? How low you talk, Tony.'

"'Yes—I've a kind of hoarseness. I said, not exactly.'

"'I suppose you mean to?'

"'Well, as to that—' His eyes rested on her face, and hers on his. He wondered how he could have been such a fool as not to follow up Hannah. 'My sweet Hannah!' he bursts out, taking her hand, not being really able to help it, and forgetting Milly and Unity and all the world besides. 'Settled it? I don't think I have!'

"'Hark!' says Hannah.

"'What?' says Tony, letting go her hand.

"'Surely I heard a sort of little screaming squeak under those sacks? Why, you've been carrying corn, and there's mice in this waggon, I declare!' She began to haul up the tails of her gown.

"'O no; 'tis the axle,' said Tony in an assuring way. 'It do go like that sometimes in dry weather.'

"'Perhaps it was. . . . Well, now, to be quite honest, dear

Tony, do you like her better than me? Because—because, although I've held off so independent, I'll own at last that I do like 'ee, Tony, to tell the truth; and I wouldn't say no if you asked me—you know what.'

"Tony was so won over by this pretty offering mood of a girl who had been quite the reverse (Hannah had a backward way with her at times, if you can mind) that he just glanced behind, and then whispered very soft, 'I haven't quite promised her, and I think I can get out of it, and ask you that question you speak of.'

"'Throw over Milly?—all to marry me! How delightful!' broke out Hannah, quite loud, clapping her hands.

"At this there was a real squeak—an angry, spiteful squeak, and afterwards a long moan, as if something had broke its heart, and a movement of the empty sacks.

"'Something's there!' said Hannah, starting up.

"'It's nothing, really,' says Tony in a soothing voice, and praying inwardly for a way out of this. 'I wouldn't tell 'ee at first, because I wouldn't frighten 'ee. But, Hannah, I've really a couple of ferrets in a bag under there, for rabbiting, and they quarrel sometimes. I don't wish it knowed, as 'twould be called poaching. Oh, they can't get out, bless 'ee—you are quite safe! And—and—what a fine day it is, isn't it, Hannah, for this time of year? Be you going to market next Saturday? How is your aunt now?' And so on, says Tony, to keep her from talking any more about love in Milly's hearing.

"But he found his work cut out for him, and wondering again how he should get out of this ticklish business, he looked about for a chance. Nearing home he saw his father in a field not far off, holding up his hand as if he wished to speak to Tony.

"'Would you mind taking the reins a moment, Hannah,' he said, much relieved, 'while I go and find out what father wants?'

"She consented, and away he hastened into the field, only too glad to get breathing time. He found that his father was looking at him with rather a stern eye.

"'Come, come, Tony,' says old Mr Kytes, as soon as his son was alongside him, 'this won't do, you know.'

"'What?' says Tony.

"'Why, if you mean to marry Milly Richards, do it, and there's an end o't. But don't go driving about the country with Jolliver's daughter and making a scandal. I won't have such things done.'

"'I only asked her—that is, she asked me—to ride home.'

"'She? Why, now, if it had been Milly, 'twould have been quite proper; but you and Hannah Jolliver going about by yourselves—'

"'Milly's there too, father.'

"'Milly? Where?'

"'Under the corn-sacks! Yes, the truth is, father, I've got rather into a nunny-watch, I'm afeard! Unity Sallet is there too—yes, at the other end, under the tarpaulin. All three are in that waggon, and what to do with 'em I know no more than the dead! The best plan is, as I'm thinking, to speak out loud and plain to one of 'em before the rest, and that will settle it; not but what 'twill cause 'em to kick up a bit of a miff, for certain. Now which would you marry, father, if you was in my place?'

"'Whichever of 'em did *not* ask to ride with thee.'

"'That was Milly, I'm bound to say, as she only mounted by my invitation. But Milly—'

"'Then stick to Milly, she's the best. . . . But look at that!'

"His father pointed towards the waggon. 'She can't hold that horse in. You shouldn't have left the reins in her hands. Run on and take the horse's head, or there'll be some accident to them maids!'

"Tony's horse, in fact, in spite of Hannah's tugging at the reins, had started on his way at a brisk walking pace, being very anxious to get back to the stable, for he had had a long day out. Without another word, Tony rushed away from his father to overtake the horse.

"Now of all things that could have happened to wean him from Milly, there was nothing so powerful as his father's recommending her. No; it could not be Milly, after all. Hannah must be the one, since he could not marry all three as he longed to do. This he thought while running after the waggon. But queer things were happening inside it.

"It was, of course, Milly who had screamed under the sackbags, being obliged to let off her bitter rage and shame in that way at what Tony was saying, and never daring to show, for very pride and dread o' being laughed at, that she was in hiding. She became more and more restless, and in twisting herself about, what did she see but another woman's foot and white stocking close to her head. It quite frightened her, not knowing that Unity Sallet was in the waggon likewise. But after the fright was over she determined to get to the bottom of all this, and she crept and crept along the bed of the waggon, under the tarpaulin, like a snake, when lo and behold she came face to face with Unity.

"'Well, if this isn't disgraceful!' says Milly in a raging whisper to Unity.

"''Tis,' says Unity, 'to see you hiding in a young man's waggon like this, and no great character belonging to either of ye!'

"'Mind what you are saying!' replied Milly, getting louder. 'I am engaged to be married to him, and haven't I a right to be here? What right have you, I should like to know? What has he been promising you? A pretty lot of nonsense, I expect! But what Tony says to other women is all mere wind, and no concern to me!'

"'Don't you be too sure!' says Unity. 'He's going to have Hannah, and not you, nor me either; I could hear that.'

"Now at these strange voices sounding from under the cloth Hannah was thunderstruck a'most into a swound; and it was just at this time that the horse moved on. Hannah tugged away wildly, not knowing what she was doing; and as the quarrel rose louder and louder Hannah got so horrified that she let go the reins altogether. The horse went on at his own pace, and coming to the corner where we turn round to drop down the hill to Lower Longpuddle he turned too quick, the off wheels went up the bank, the waggon rose sideways till it was quite on edge upon the near axles, and out rolled the three maidens into the road in a heap. The horse looked round and stood still.

"When Tony came up, frightened and breathless, he was relieved enough to see that neither of his darlings was hurt, beyond a few scratches from the brambles of the hedge. But he was rather alarmed when he heard how they were going on at one another.

"'Don't ye quarrel, my dears—don't ye!' says he, taking off his hat out of respect to 'em. And then he would have kissed them all round, as fair and square as a man could, but they were in too much of a taking to let him, and screeched and sobbed till they was quite spent.

"'Now I'll speak out honest, because I ought to,' says Tony, as soon as he could get heard. 'And this is the truth,' says he. 'I've asked Hannah to be mine, and she is willing, and we are going to put up the banns next—'

"Tony had not noticed that Hannah's father was coming up behind, nor had he noticed that Hannah's face was beginning to bleed from the scratch of a bramble. Hannah had seen her father, and had run to him, crying worse than ever.

"'My daughter is *not* willing, sir,' says Mr Jolliver, hot and strong. 'Be you willing, Hannah? I ask ye to have spirit enough to refuse him, if yer virtue is left to 'ee and you run no risk?'

"'She's as sound as a bell for me, that I'll swear!' says Tony, flaring up. 'And so's the others, come to that, though you may think it an onusual thing in me!'

"'I have spirit, and I do refuse him!' says Hannah, partly because her father was there, and partly, too, in a tantrum because of the discovery and the scar that might be left on her face. 'Little did I think when I was so soft with him just now that I was talking to such a false deceiver!'

"'What, you won't have me, Hannah?' says Tony, his jaw hanging down like a dead man's.

"'Never—I would sooner marry no—nobody at all!' she gasped out, though with her heart in her throat, for she would not have refused Tony if he had asked her quietly, and her father had not been there, and her face had not been scratched by the bramble. And having said that, away she walked upon her father's arm, thinking and hoping he would ask her again.

"Tony didn't know what to say next. Milly was sobbing her heart out; but as his father had strongly recommended her he couldn't feel inclined that way. So he turned to Unity.

"'Well, will you, Unity dear, be mine?' he says.

"'Take her leavings? Not I!' says Unity. 'I'd scorn it!' And away walks Unity Sallet likewise, though she looked back when she'd gone some way, to see if he was following her.

"So there at last were left Milly and Tony by themselves, she crying in watery streams, and Tony looking like a tree struck by lightning.

"'Well, Milly,' he says at last, going up to her, 'it do seem as if fate had ordained that it should be you and I, or nobody. And what must be must be, I suppose. Hey, Milly?'

"'If you like, Tony. You didn't really mean what you said to them?'

"'Not a word of it,' declares Tony, bringing down his fist upon his palm.

"And then he kissed her, and put the waggon to rights, and they mounted together; and their banns were put up the very next Sunday. I was not able to go to their wedding, but it was a rare party they had, by all account. Everybody in Longpuddle was there almost; you among the rest, I think, Mr Flaxton?" The speaker turned to the parish clerk.

"I was," said Mr Flaxton. "And that party was the cause of a very curious change in some other people's affairs; I mean in Steve Hardcome's and his cousin James's."

"Ah! the Hardcomes," said the stranger. "How familiar that name is to me! What of them?"

The clerk cleared his throat and began:—

The History of the Hardcomes

"YES, Tony's was the very best wedding-randy that ever I was at; and I've been at a good many, as you may suppose"—turning to the newly-arrived one—"having as a Church officer, the privilege to attend all christening, wedding, and funeral parties—such being our Wessex custom.

"'Twas on a frosty night in Christmas week, and among the folk invited were the said Hardcomes o' Climmerston—Steve and James—first cousins, both of them small farmers, just entering into business on their own account. With them came, as a matter of course, their intended wives, two young women of the neighbourhood, both very pretty and sprightly maidens, and numbers of friends from Abbot's-Cernel, and

Weatherbury, and Mellstock, and I don't know where—a regular houseful.

"The kitchen was cleared of furniture for dancing, and the old folk played at 'Put' and 'All-fours' in the parlour, though at last they gave that up to join in the dance. The top of the figure was by the large front window of the room, and there were so many couples that the lower part of the figure reached through the door at the back, and into the darkness of the out-house; in fact, you couldn't see the end of the row at all, and 'twas never known exactly how long that dance was, the lowest couples being lost among the faggots and brushwood in the out-house.

"When we had danced a few hours, and the crowns of we taller men were swelling into lumps with bumping the beams of the ceiling, the first fiddler laid down his fiddle-bow, and said he should play no more, for he wished to dance. And in another hour the second fiddler laid down his, and said he wanted to dance too; so there was only the third fiddler left, and he was a' old, veteran man, very weak in the wrist. However, he managed to keep up a faltering tweedle-dee; but there being no chair in the room, and his knees being as weak as his wrists, he was obliged to sit upon as much of the little corner-table as projected beyond the corner cupboard fixed over it, which was not a very wide seat for a man advanced in years.

"Among those who danced most continually were the two engaged couples, as was natural to their situation. Each pair was very well matched, and very unlike the other. James Hardcome's intended was called Emily Darth, and both she and James were gentle, nice-minded, in-door people, fond of a quiet life. Steve and his chosen, named Olive Pawle, were different; they were of a more bustling nature, fond of racketing about and seeing what was going on in the world. The two couples had arranged to get married on the same day, and that not long thence; Tony's wedding being a sort of stimulant, as is often the case; I've noticed it professionally many times.

"They danced with such a will as only young people in that stage of courtship can dance; and it happened that as the evening wore on James had for his partner Stephen's plighted one, Olive, at the same time that Stephen was dancing with James's Emily. It was noticed that in spite o' the exchange the young men seemed to enjoy the dance no less than before. By-and-by they were treading another tune in the same changed order as we had noticed earlier, and though at first each one had held the other's mistress strictly at half-arm's length, lest there should be shown any objection to too close quarters by the lady's proper man, as time passed there was a little more closeness between 'em; and presently a little more closeness still.

"The later it got the more did each of the two cousins dance with the wrong young girl, and the tighter did he hold her to his side as he whirled her round; and, what was very re-markable, neither seemed to mind what the other was doing. The party began to draw towards its end, and I saw no more that night, being one of the first to leave, on account of my morning's business. But I learnt the rest of it from those that knew.

"After finishing a particularly warming dance with the changed partners, as I've mentioned, the two young men looked at one another, and in a moment or two went out into the porch together.

"'James,' says Steve, 'what were you thinking of when you were dancing with my Olive?'

"'Well,' said James, 'perhaps what you were thinking of when you were dancing with my Emily.'

"'I was thinking,' said Steve, with some hesitation, 'that I wouldn't mind changing for good and all!'

"'It was what I was feeling likewise,' said James.

"'I willingly agree to it, if you think we could manage it.'

"'So do I. But what would the girls say?'

"''Tis my belief,' said Steve, 'that they wouldn't particularly object. Your Emily clung as close to me as if she already belonged to me, dear girl.'

"'And your Olive to me,' says James. 'I could feel her heart beating like a clock.'

"Well, they agreed to put it to the girls when they were all four walking home together. And they did so. When they parted that night the exchange was decided on—all having been done under the hot excitement of that evening's dancing. Thus it happened that on the following Sunday morning, when the people were sitting in church with mouths wide open to hear the names published as they had expected, there was no small amazement to hear them coupled the wrong way, as it seemed. The congregation whispered, and thought the parson had made a mistake; till they discovered that his reading of the names was verily the true way. As they had decided, so they were married, each one to the other's original property.

"Well, the two couples lived on for a year or two ordinarily enough, till the time came when these young people began to grow a little less warm to their respective spouses, as is the rule of married life; and the two cousins wondered more and more in their hearts what had made 'em so mad at the last moment to marry crosswise as they did, when they might have married straight, as was planned by nature, and as they had fallen in love. 'Twas Tony's party that had done it, plain enough, and they half wished they had never gone there. James, being a quiet, fireside, perusing man, felt at times a wide gap between himself and Olive, his wife, who loved riding and driving and out-door jaunts to a degree; while Steve, who was always knocking about hither and thither, had a very domestic wife, who worked samplers, and made hearth-rugs, scarcely ever wished to cross the threshold, and only drove out with him to please him.

"However, they said very little about this mismating to any of their acquaintances, though sometimes Steve would look at James's wife and sigh, and James would look at Steve's wife and do the same. Indeed, at last the two men were frank enough towards each other not to mind mentioning it quietly to themselves, in a long-faced, sorry-smiling, whimsical sort of way, and would shake their heads together over their foolishness in upsetting a well-considered choice on the strength of an hour's fancy in the whirl and wildness of a dance. Still, they were sensible and honest young fellows enough, and did their best to make shift with their lot as they had arranged it, and not to repine at what could not now be altered or mended.

"So things remained till one fine summer day they went for their yearly little outing together, as they had made it their custom to do for a long while past. This year they chose Budmouth-Regis as the place to spend their holiday in; and off they went in their best clothes at nine o'clock in the morning.

"When they had reached Budmouth-Regis they walked two and two along the shore—their new boots going squeakity-squash upon the clammy velvet sands. I can seem to see 'em now! Then they looked at the ships in the harbour; and then went up to the Look-out; and then had dinner at an inn; and then again walked two and two, squeakity-squash, upon the velvet sands. As evening drew on they sat on one of the public seats upon the Esplanade, and listened to the band; and then they said 'What shall we do next?'

"'Of all things,' said Olive (Mrs James Hardcome, that is), 'I should like to row in the bay! We could listen to the music from the water as well as from here, and have the fun of rowing besides.'

"'The very thing; so should I,' says Stephen, his tastes being always like hers."

Here the clerk turned to the curate.

"But you, sir, know the rest of the strange particulars of that strange evening of their lives better than anybody else, having had much of it from their own lips, which I had not; and perhaps you'll oblige the gentleman?"

"Certainly, if it is wished," said the curate. And he took up the clerk's tale:—

"Stephen's wife hated the sea, except from land, and couldn't bear the thought of going into a boat. James, too, disliked the water, and said that for his part he would much sooner stay on and listen to the band in the seat they occupied, though he did not wish to stand in his wife's way if she desired a row. The end of the discussion was that James and his cousin's wife Emily agreed to remain where they were sitting and enjoy the music, while they watched the other two hire a boat just beneath, and take their water-excursion of half an hour or so, till they should choose to come back and join the sitters on the Esplanade; when they would all start homeward together.

"Nothing could have pleased the other two restless ones better than this arrangement; and Emily and James watched them go down to the boatman below and choose one of the little yellow skiffs, and walk carefully out upon the little plank that was laid on trestles to enable them to get alongside the craft. They saw Stephen hand Olive in, and take his seat facing her; when they were settled they waved their hands to the couple watching them, and then Stephen took the pair of sculls and pulled off to the tune beat by the band, she steering through the other boats skimming about, for the sea was as smooth as glass that evening, and pleasure-seekers were rowing everywhere.

"'How pretty they look moving on, don't they?' said Emily to James (as I've been assured). 'They both enjoy it equally. In everything their likings are the same.'

"'That's true,' said James.

"'They would have made a handsome pair if they had married,' said she.

"'Yes,' said he. ''Tis a pity we should have parted 'em.'

"'Don't talk of that, James,' said she. 'For better or for worse we decided to do as we did, and there's an end of it.'

"They sat on after that without speaking, side by side, and the band played as before; the people strolled up and down; and Stephen and Olive shrank smaller and smaller as they shot straight out to sea. The two on shore used to relate how they saw Stephen stop rowing a moment, and take off his coat to get at his work better; but James's wife sat quite still in the stern, holding the tiller-ropes by which she steered the boat. When they had got very small indeed she turned her head to shore.

"'She is waving her handkerchief to us,' said Stephen's wife, who thereupon pulled out her own, and waved it as a return signal.

"The boat's course had been a little awry while Mrs James

neglected her steering to wave her handkerchief to her husband and Mrs Stephen; but now the light skiff went straight onward again, and they could soon see nothing more of the two figures it contained than Olive's light mantle and Stephen's white shirt sleeves behind.

"The two on the shore talked on. ' 'Twas very curious—our changing partners at Tony Kytes's wedding,' Emily declared. 'Tony was of a fickle nature by all account, and it really seemed as if his character had infected us that night. Which of you two was it that first proposed not to marry as we were engaged?'

"'H'm—I can't remember at this moment,' says James. 'We talked it over, you know; and no sooner said than done.'

"' 'Twas the dancing,' said she. 'People get quite crazy sometimes in a dance.'

"'They do,' he owned.

"'James—do you think they care for one another still?' asks Mrs Stephen.

"James Hardcome mused, and admitted that perhaps a little tender feeling might flicker up in their hearts for a moment now and then. 'Still, nothing of any account,' he said.

"'I sometimes think that Olive is in Steve's mind a good deal,' murmurs Mrs Stephen; 'particularly when she pleases his fancy by riding past our window at a gallop on one of the draught-horses. . . . I never could do anything of that sort; I could never get over my fear of a horse.'

"'And I am no horseman, though I pretend to be on her account,' murmured James Hardcome. 'But isn't it almost time for them to turn and sweep round to the shore, as the other boating folk have done? I wonder what Olive means by steering away straight to the horizon like that? She has hardly swerved from a direct line seaward since they started.'

"'No doubt they are talking, and don't think of where they are going,' suggests Stephen's wife.

"'Perhaps so,' said James. 'I didn't know Steve could row like that.'

"'O yes,' says she. 'He often comes here on business, and generally has a pull round the bay.'

" 'I can hardly see the boat or them,' says James again; 'and it is getting dark.'

"The heedless pair afloat now formed a mere speck in the films of the coming night, which thickened apace, till it completely swallowed up their distant shapes. They had disappeared while still following the same straight course away from the world of land-livers, as if they were intending to drop over the sea-edge into space, and never return to earth again.

"The two on the shore continued to sit on, punctually abiding by their agreement to remain on the same spot till the others returned. The Esplanade lamps were lit one by one, the bandsmen folded up their stands and departed, the yachts in the bay hung out their riding lights, and the little boats came back to shore one after another, their hirers walking on to the sands by the plank they had climbed to go afloat; but among these Stephen and Olive did not appear.

" 'What a time they are!' said Emily. 'I am getting quite chilly. I did not expect to have to sit so long in the evening air.'

"Thereupon James Hardcome said that he did not require his overcoat, and insisted on lending it to her.

"He wrapped it round Emily's shoulders.

" 'Thank you, James,' she said. 'How cold Olive must be in that thin jacket!'

"He said he was thinking so, too. 'Well, they are sure to be quite close at hand by this time, though we can't see 'em. The boats are not all in yet. Some of the rowers are fond of paddling along the shore to finish out their hour of hiring.'

" 'Shall we walk by the edge of the water,' said she, 'to see if we can discover them?'

"He assented, reminding her that they must not lose sight of the seat, lest the belated pair should return and miss them, and be vexed that they had not kept the appointment.

"They walked a sentry beat up and down the sands immediately opposite the seat; and still the others did not come. James Hardcome at last went to the boatman, thinking that after all his wife and cousin might have come in under shadow of the dusk without being perceived, and might have forgotten the appointment at the bench.

" 'All in?' asked James.

" 'All but one boat,' said the lessor. 'I can't think where that couple is keeping to. They might run foul of something or other in the dark.'

"Again Stephen's wife and Olive's husband waited, with more and more anxiety. But no little yellow boat returned. Was it possible they could have landed further down the Esplanade?

" 'It may have been done to escape paying,' said the boat-owner. 'But they didn't look like people who would do that.'

"James Hardcome knew that he could found no hope on such a reason as that. But now, remembering what had been casually discussed between Steve and himself about their wives from time to time, he admitted for the first time the possibility that their old tenderness had been revived by their face-to-face position more strongly than either had anticipated at starting—the excursion having been so obviously undertaken for the pleasure of the performance only—and that they had landed at some steps he knew of further down towards the pier, to be longer alone together.

"Still he disliked to harbour the thought, and would not mention its existence to his companion. He merely said to her, 'Let us walk further on.'

"They did so, and lingered between the boat-stage and the pier till Stephen Hardcome's wife was uneasy, and was obliged to accept James's offered arm. Thus the night advanced. Emily was presently so worn out by fatigue that James felt it necessary to conduct her home; there was, too, a remote chance that the truants had landed in the harbour on the other side of the town, or elsewhere, and hastened home in some unexpected way, in the belief that their consorts would not have waited so long.

"However, he left a direction in the town that a look-out should be kept, though this was arranged privately, the bare possibility of an elopement being enough to make him reticent; and, full of misgivings, the two remaining ones hastened to catch the last train out of Budmouth-Regis; and when they got to Casterbridge drove back to Upper Longpuddle."

"Along this very road as we do now," remarked the parish clerk.

"To be sure—along this very road," said the curate. "However, Stephen and Olive were not at their homes; neither had entered the village since leaving it in the morning. Emily and James Hardcome went to their respective dwellings to snatch a hasty night's rest, and at daylight the next morning they drove again to Casterbridge and entered the Budmouth train, the line being just opened.

"Nothing had been heard of the couple there during this brief absence. In the course of a few hours some young men testified to having seen such a man and woman rowing in a frail hired craft, the head of the boat kept straight to sea; they had sat looking in each other's faces as if they were in a dream, with no consciousness of what they were doing, or whither they were steering. It was not till late that day that more tidings reached James's ears. The boat had been found drifting bottom upward a long way from land. In the evening the sea rose somewhat, and a cry spread through the town that two bodies were cast ashore in Lullwind Bay, several miles to the eastward. They were brought to Budmouth, and inspection revealed them to be the missing pair. It was said that they had been found tightly locked in each other's arms, his lips upon hers, their features still wrapt in the same calm and dream-like repose which had been observed in their demeanour as they had glided along.

"Neither James nor Emily questioned the original motives of the unfortunate man and woman in putting to sea. They were both above suspicion as to intention. Whatever their mutual feelings might have led them on to, underhand behaviour at starting was foreign to the nature of either. Conjecture pictured that they might have fallen into tender reverie while gazing each into a pair of eyes that had formerly flashed for him and her alone, and, unwilling to avow what their mutual sentiments were, they had done no more than continue thus, oblivious of time and space, till darkness suddenly overtook them far from land. But nothing was truly known. It had been their destiny to die thus. The two halves, intended by Nature to make the perfect whole, had failed in that result during their lives, though 'in their death they were not divided.' Their bodies were brought home, and buried on one day. I remember that, on looking round the churchyard while reading the service, I observed nearly all the parish at their funeral."

"It was so, sir," said the clerk.

"The remaining two," continued the curate (whose voice had grown husky while relating the lovers' sad fate), "were a more thoughtful and far-seeing, though less romantic, couple than the first. They were now mutually bereft of a companion, and found themselves by this accident in a position to fulfil their destiny according to Nature's plan and their own original and calmly-formed intention. James Hardcome took Emily to wife in the course of a year and a half; and the marriage proved in every respect a happy one. I solemnized the service, Hardcome having told me, when he came to give notice of the proposed wedding, the story of his first wife's loss almost word for word as I have told it to you."

"And are they living in Longpuddle still?" asked the newcomer.

"O no, sir," interposed the clerk. "James has been dead these dozen years, and his mis'ess about six or seven. They had no children. William Privett used to be their odd man till he died."

"Ah—William Privett! He, dead too?—dear me!" said the other. "All passed away!"

"Yes, sir. William was much older than I. He'd ha' been over eighty if he had lived till now."

"There was something very strange about William's death— very strange indeed!" sighed a melancholy man in the back of the van. It was the seedsman's father, who had hitherto kept silence.

"And what might that have been?" asked Mr Lackland.

The Superstitious Man's Story

"WILLIAM, as you may know, was a curious, silent man; you could feel when he came near 'ee; and if he was in the house or anywhere behind your back without your seeing him, there seemed to be something clammy in the air, as if a cellar door was opened close by your elbow. Well, one Sunday, at a time that William was in very good health to all appearance, the bell that was ringing for church went very heavy all of a sudden; the sexton, who told me o't, said he'd not known the bell go so heavy in his hand for years—and he feared it meant a death in the parish. That was on the Sunday, as I say. During the week after, it chanced that William's wife was staying up late one night to finish her ironing, she doing the washing for Mr and Mrs Hardcome. Her husband had finished his supper and gone to bed as usual some hour or two before. While she ironed she heard him coming down stairs; he stopped to put on his boots at the stair-foot, where he always left them, and then came on into the living-room where she was ironing, passing through it towards the door, this being the only way from the staircase to the outside of the house. No word was said on either side, William not being a man given to much speaking, and his wife being occupied with her work. He went out and closed the door behind him. As her husband had now and then gone out in this way at night before when unwell, or unable to sleep for want of a pipe, she took no particular notice, and continued at her ironing. This she finished shortly after, and as he had not come in she waited awhile for him, putting away the irons and things, and preparing the table for his breakfast in the morning. Still he did not return, but supposing him not far off, and wanting to get to bed herself, tired as she was, she left the door unbarred and went to the stairs, after writing on the back of the door with chalk: *Mind and do the door* (because he was a forgetful man).

"To her great surprise, and I might say alarm, on reaching the foot of the stairs his boots were standing there as they always stood when he had gone to rest; going up to their chamber she found him in bed sleeping as sound as a rock. How he could have got back again without her seeing or hearing him was beyond her comprehension. It could only have been by passing behind her very quietly while she was bumping with the iron. But this notion did not satisfy her: it was surely impossible that she should not have seen him come in through a room so small. She could not unravel the mystery, and felt very queer and uncomfortable about it. However, she would not disturb him to question him then, and went to bed herself.

"He rose and left for his work very early the next morning, before she was awake, and she waited his return to breakfast with much anxiety for an explanation, for thinking over the matter by daylight made it seem only the more startling. When he came in to the meal he said, before she could put her question, 'What's the meaning of them words chalked on the door?'

"She told him, and asked him about his going out the night before. William declared that he had never left the bedroom after entering it, having in fact undressed, lain down, and fallen asleep directly, never once waking till the clock struck five, and he rose up to go to his labour.

"Betty Privett was as certain in her own mind that he did go out as she was of her own existence, and was little less certain that he did not return. She felt too disturbed to argue with him, and let the subject drop as though she must have been mistaken. When she was walking down Longpuddle street later in the day she met Jim Weedle's daughter Nancy, and said, 'Well, Nancy, you do look sleepy to-day!'

"'Yes, Mrs Privett,' says Nancy. 'Now don't tell anybody, but I don't mind letting you know what the reason o't is. Last night, being Old Midsummer Eve, some of us went to church porch, and didn't get home till near one.'

"'Did ye?' says Mrs Privett. 'Old Midsummer yesterday was it? Faith I didn't think whe'r 'twas Midsummer or Michaelmas; I'd too much work to do.'

"'Yes. And we were frightened enough, I can tell 'ee, by what we saw.'

"'What did ye see?'

"'(You may not remember, sir, having gone off to foreign parts so young, that on Midsummer Night it is believed hereabout that the faint shapes of all the folk in the parish who are going to be at death's door within the year can be seen entering the church. Those who get over their illness come out again after a while; those that are doomed to die do not return.)'

"'What did you see?' asked William's wife.

"'Well,' says Nancy, backwardly—'we needn't tell what we saw, or who we saw.'

"'You saw my husband,' says Betty Privett, in a quiet way.

"'Well, since you put it so,' says Nancy, hanging fire, 'we— thought we did see him; but it was darkish, and we was frightened, and of course it might not have been he.'

"'Nancy, you needn't mind letting it out, though 'tis kept back in kindness. And he didn't come out of church again: I know it as well as you.'

"Nancy did not answer yes or no to that, and no more was said. But three days after, William Privett was mowing with John Chiles in Mr Hardcome's meadow, and in the heat of the day they sat down to eat their bit o' nunch under a tree, and empty their flagon. Afterwards both of 'em fell asleep as they sat. John Chiles was the first to wake, and as he looked towards his fellow-mower he saw one of those great white miller's-souls as we call 'em—that is to say, a miller-moth— come from William's open mouth while he slept, and fly straight away. John thought it odd enough, as William had worked in a mill for several years when he was a boy. He then looked at the sun, and found by the place o't that they had slept a long while, and as William did not wake, John called to him and said it was high time to begin work again. He took no notice, and then John went up and shook him, and found he was dead.

"Now on that very day old Philip Hookhorn was down at Longpuddle Spring dipping up a pitcher of water; and as he turned away, who should he see coming down to the spring on the other side but William, looking very pale and odd. This surprised Philip Hookhorn very much, for years before that time William's little son—his only child—had been drowned in that spring while at play there, and this had so preyed upon William's mind that he'd never been seen near the spring afterwards, and had been known to go half a mile out of his way to avoid the place. On inquiry, it was found that William in body could not have stood by the spring, being in the mead two miles off; and it also came out that the time at which he was seen at the spring was the very time when he died."

"A rather melancholy story," observed the emigrant, after a minute's silence.

"Yes, yes. Well, we must take ups and downs together," said the seedsman's father.

"You don't know, Mr Lackland, I suppose, what a rum start that was between Andrey Satchel and Jane Vallens and the pa'son and clerk o' Scrimpton?" said the master-thatcher, a man with a spark of subdued liveliness in his eye, who had hitherto kept his attention mainly upon small objects a long way ahead, as he sat in front of the van with his feet outside. "Theirs was a queerer experience of a pa'son and clerk than some folks get, and may cheer 'ee up a little after this damp-ness that's been flung over yer soul."

The returned one replied that he knew nothing of the history, and should be happy to hear it, quite recollecting the personality of the man Satchel.

"Ah no; this Andrey Satchel is the son of the Satchel that you knew; this one has not been married more than two or three years, and 'twas at the time o' the wedding that the accident happened that I could tell 'ee of, or anybody else here, for that matter."

"No, no; you must tell it, neighbour, if anybody," said several; a request in which Mr Lackland joined, adding that the Satchel family was one he had known well before leaving home.

"I'll just mention, as you be a stranger," whispered the carrier to Lackland, "that Christopher's stories will bear pruning."

The emigrant nodded.

"Well, I can soon tell it," said the master-thatcher, school-ing himself to a tone of actuality. "Though as it has more to do with the pa'son and clerk than with Andrey himself, it ought to be told by a better church-man than I."

Andrey Satchel and the Parson and Clerk

"IT all arose, you must know, from Andrey being fond of a drop of drink at that time—though he's a sober enough man now by all account, so much the better for him. Jane, his bride, you see, was somewhat older than Andrey; how much older I don't pretend to say; she was not one of our parish, and the register alone may be able to tell that. But, at any rate, her being a little ahead of her young man in mortal years, coupled with other bodily circumstances owing to that young man—"

("Ah, poor thing!" sighed the women.)

"—made her very anxious to get the thing done before he changed his mind; and 'twas with a joyful countenance (they say) that she, with Andrey and his brother and sister-in-law, marched off to church one November morning as soon as 'twas day a'most, to be made one with Andrey for the rest of her life. He had left our place long before it was light, and the folks that were up all waved their lanterns at him, and flung up their hats as he went.

"The church of her parish was a mile and more from where she lived, and, as it was a wonderful fine day for the time of year, the plan was that as soon as they were married they would make out a holiday by driving straight off to Port Bredy, to see the ships and the sea and the sojers, instead of coming back to a meal at the house of the distant relation she lived wi', and moping about there all the afternoon.

"Well, some folks noticed that Andrey walked with rather wambling steps to church that morning; the truth o't was that his nearest neighbour's child had been christened the day before, and Andrey, having stood godfather, had stayed all night keeping up the christening, for he had said to himself, 'Not if I live to be a thousand shall I again be made a godfather one day, and a husband the next, and perhaps a father the next, and therefore I'll make the most of the blessing.' So that when he started from home in the morning he had not been in bed at all. The result was, as I say, that when he and his bride-to-be walked up the church to get married, the pa'son (who was a very strict man inside the church, whatever he was outside) looked hard at Andrey, and said, very sharp:

"'How's this, my man? You are in liquor. And so early, too. I'm ashamed of you!'

"'Well, that's true, sir,' says Andrey. 'But I can walk straight enough for practical purposes. I can walk a chalk line,' he says (meaning no offence), 'as well as some other folk: and—' (getting hotter)—'I reckon that if you, Pa'son Billy Toogood, had kept up a christening all night so thoroughly as I have done, you wouldn't be able to stand at all; damn me if you would!'

"This answer made Pa'son Billy—as they used to call him—rather spitish, not to say hot, for he was a warm-tempered man if provoked, and he said, very decidedly: 'Well, I cannot marry you in this state; and I will not! Go home and get sober!' And he slapped the book together like a rat-trap.

"Then the bride burst out crying as if her heart would break, for very fear that she would lose Andrey after all her hard work to get him, and begged and implored the pa'son to go on with the ceremony. But no.

"'I won't be a party to your solemnizing matrimony with a tipsy man,' says Mr Toogood. 'It is not right and decent. I am sorry for you, my young woman, seeing the condition you are in, but you'd better go home again. I wonder how you could think of bringing him here drunk like this!'

"'But if—if he don't come drunk he won't come at all, sir!' she says, through her sobs.

"'I can't help that,' says the pa'son; and plead as she might, it did not move him. Then she tried him another way.

"'Well, then, if you'll go home, sir, and leave us here, and come back to the church in an hour or two, I'll undertake to say that he shall be as sober as a judge,' she cries. 'We'll bide here, with your permission; for if he once goes out of this here church unmarried, all Van Amburgh's horses won't drag him back again!'

"'Very well,' says the parson. 'I'll give you two hours, and then I'll return.'

"'And please, sir, lock the door, so that we can't escape!' says she.

"'Yes,' says the parson.

"'And let nobody know that we are here.'

"The pa'son then took off his clane white surplice, and went away; and the others consulted upon the best means for keeping the matter a secret, which it was not a very hard thing to do, the place being so lonely, and the hour so early. The witnesses, Andrey's brother and brother's wife, neither one o' which cared about Andrey's marrying Jane, and had come rather against their will, said they couldn't wait two hours in that hole of a place, wishing to get home to Longpuddle before dinner-time. They were altogether so crusty that the clerk said there was no difficulty in their doing as they wished. They could go home as if their brother's wedding had actually taken place and the married couple had gone onward for their day's pleasure jaunt to Port Bredy as intended. He, the clerk, and any casual passer-by would act as witnesses when the pa'son came back.

"This was agreed to, and away Andrey's relations went, nothing loath, and the clerk shut the church door and prepared to lock in the couple. The bride went up and whispered to him, with her eyes a-streaming still.

"'My dear good clerk,' she says, 'if we bide here in the church, folk may see us through the winders, and find out what has happened; and 'twould cause such a talk and scandal that I never should get over it: and perhaps, too, dear Andrey might try to get out and leave me! Will ye lock us up in the tower, my dear good clerk?' she says. 'I'll tole him in there if you will.'

"The clerk had no objection to do this to oblige the poor young woman, and they toled Andrey into the tower, and the clerk locked 'em both up straightway, and then went home, to return at the end of the two hours.

"Pa'son Toogood had not been long in his house after leaving the church when he saw a gentleman in pink and top-boots ride past his windows, and with a sudden flash of heat he called to mind that the hounds met that day just on the edge of his parish. The pa'son was one who dearly loved sport, and much he longed to be there.

"In short, except o' Sundays and at tide-times in the week,

Pa'son Billy was the life o' the Hunt. 'Tis true that he was poor, and that he rode all of a heap, and that his black mare was rat-tailed and old, and his tops older, and all over of one colour, whitey-brown, and full o' cracks. But he'd been in at the death of three thousand foxes. And—being a bachelor man—every time he went to bed in summer he used to open the bed at bottom and crawl up head foremost, to mind en of the coming winter and the good sport he'd have, and the foxes going to earth. And whenever there was a christening at the Squire's, and he had dinner there afterwards, as he always did, he never failed to christen the chiel over again in a bottle of port wine.

"Now the clerk was the parson's groom and gardener and jineral manager, and had just got back to his work in the garden when he, too, saw the hunting man pass, and presently saw lots more of 'em, noblemen and gentry, and then he saw the hounds, the huntsman, Jim Treadhedge, the whipper-in, and I don't know who besides. The clerk loved going to cover as frantical as the pa'son, so much so that whenever he saw or heard the pack he could no more rule his feelings than if they were the winds of heaven. He might be bedding, or he might be sowing—all was forgot. So he throws down his spade and rushes in to the pa'son, who was by this time as frantical to go as he.

"'That there mare of yours, sir, do want exercise bad, very bad, this morning!' the clerk says, all of a tremble. 'Don't ye think I'd better trot her round the downs for an hour, sir?'

"'To be sure, she does want exercise badly. I'll trot her round myself,' says the parson.

"'Oh—you'll trot her yerself? Well, there's the cob, sir. Really that cob is getting oncontrollable through biding in a stable so long! If you wouldn't mind my putting on the saddle—'

"'Very well. Take him out, certainly,' says the pa'son, never caring what the clerk did so long as he himself could get off immediately. So, scrambling into his riding-boots and breeches as quick as he could, he rode off towards the meet, intending to be back in an hour. No sooner was he gone than the clerk mounted the cob, and was off after him. When the pa'son got to the meet he found a lot of friends, and was as jolly as he could be: the hounds found a'most as soon as they threw off, and there was great excitement. So, forgetting that he had meant to go back at once, away rides the pa'son with the rest o' the hunt, all across the fallow ground that lies between Lippet Wood and Green's Copse; and as he galloped he looked behind for a moment, and there was the clerk close to his heels.

"'Ha, ha, clerk—you here?' he says.

"'Yes, sir, here be I,' says t'other.

"'Fine exercise for the horses!'

"'Ay, sir—hee, hee!' says the clerk.

"So they went on and on, into Green's Copse, then across to Higher Jirton; then on across this very turnpike-road to Waterston Ridge, then away towards Yalbury Wood: up hill and down dale, like the very wind, the clerk close to the pa'son, and the pa'son not far from the hounds. Never was there a finer run knowed with that pack than they had that day; and neither pa'son nor clerk thought one word about the unmarried couple locked up in the church tower waiting to get j'ined.

"'These hosses of yours, sir, will be much improved by this!' says the clerk as he rode along, just a neck behind the pa'son. ''Twas a happy thought of your reverent mind to bring 'em out to-day. Why, it may be frosty and slippery in a day or two, and then the poor things mid not be able to leave the stable for weeks.'

"'They may not, they may not, it is true. A merciful man is merciful to his beast,' says the pa'son.

"'Hee, hee!' says the clerk, glancing sly into the pa'son's eye.

"'Ha, ha!' says the pa'son, a-glancing back into the clerk's. 'Halloo!' he shouts, as he sees the fox break cover at that moment.

"'Halloo!' cries the clerk. 'There he goes! Why, dammy, there's two foxes—'

"'Hush, clerk, hush! Don't let me hear that word again! Remember our calling.'

"'True, sir, true. But really, good sport do carry away a man so, that he's apt to forget his high persuasion!' And the next minute the corner of the clerk's eye shot again into the corner of the pa'son's, and the pa'son's back again to the clerk's. 'Hee, hee!' said the clerk.

"'Ha, ha!' said Pa'son Toogood.

"'Ah, sir,' says the clerk again, 'this is better than crying Amen to your Ever-and-ever on a winter's morning!'

"'Yes, indeed, clerk! To everything there's a season,' says Pa'son Toogood, quite pat, for he was a learned Christian man when he liked, and had chapter and ve'se at his tongue's end, as a pa'son should.

"At last, late in the day, the hunting came to an end by the fox running into a' old woman's cottage, under her table, and up the clock-case. The pa'son and clerk were among the first in at the death, their faces a-staring in at the old woman's winder, and the clock striking as he'd never been heard to strik' before. Then came the question of finding their way home.

"Neither the pa'son nor the clerk knowed how they were going to do this, for their beasts were wellnigh tired down to the ground. But they started back-along as well as they could, though they were so done up that they could only drag along at a' amble, and not much of that at a time.

"'We shall never, never get there!' groaned Mr Toogood, quite bowed down.

"'Never!' groans the clerk. ''Tis a judgment upon us for our iniquities!'

"'I fear it is,' murmurs the pa'son.

"Well, 'twas quite dark afore they entered the pa'sonage gate, having crept into the parish as quiet as if they'd stole a hammer, little wishing their congregation to know what they'd been up to all day long. And as they were so dog-tired, and so anxious about the horses, never once did they think of the unmarried couple. As soon as ever the horses had been stabled and fed, and the pa'son and clerk had had a bit and a sup theirselves, they went to bed.

"Next morning when Pa'son Toogood was at breakfast, thinking of the glorious sport he'd had the day before, the clerk came in a hurry to the door and asked to see him.

"'It has just come into my mind, sir, that we've forgot all about the couple that we was to have married yesterday!'

"The half-chawed victuals dropped from the pa'son's mouth as if he'd been shot. 'Bless my soul,' says he, 'so we have! How very awkward!'

"'It is, sir; very. Perhaps we've ruined the 'ooman!'

"'Ah—to be sure—I remember! She ought to have been married before.'

"'If anything has happened to her up in that there tower, and no doctor or nuss—'

("Ah—poor thing!" sighed the women.)

"'—'twill be a quarter-sessions matter for us, not to speak of the disgrace to the Church!'

"'Good God, clerk, don't drive me wild!' says the pa'son. 'Why the hell didn't I marry 'em, drunk or sober!' (Pa'sons used to cuss in them days like plain honest men.) 'Have you been to the church to see what happened to them, or inquired in the village?'

"'Not I, sir! It only came into my head a moment ago, and I always like to be second to you in church matters. You could have knocked me down with a sparrer's feather when I thought o't, sir; I assure 'ee you could!'

"Well, the pa'son jumped up from his breakfast, and together they went off to the church.

"'It is not at all likely that they are there now,' says Mr Toogood, as they went; 'and indeed I hope they are not. They be pretty sure to have 'scaped and gone home.'

"However, they opened the church-hatch, entered the churchyard, and looking up at the tower, there they seed a little small white face at the belfry-winder, and a little small hand waving. 'Twas the bride.

"'God my life, clerk,' says Mr Toogood, 'I don't know how to face 'em!' And he sank down upon a tombstone. 'How I wish I hadn't been so cussed particular!'

"'Yes—'twas a pity we didn't finish it when we'd begun,' the clerk said. 'Still, since the feelings of your holy priestcraft wouldn't let ye, the couple must put up with it.'

"'True, clerk, true! Does she look as if anything premature had took place?'

"'I can't see her no lower down than her arm-pits, sir.'

"'Well—how do her face look?'

"'It do look mighty white!'

"'Well, we must know the worst! Dear me, how the small of my back do ache from that ride yesterday! . . . But to more godly business!'

"They went on into the church, and unlocked the tower stairs, and immediately poor Jane and Andrey busted out like starved mice from a cupboard, Andrey limp and sober enough now, and his bride pale and cold, but otherwise as usual.

"'What,' says the pa'son, with a great breath of relief, 'you haven't been here ever since?'

"'Yes, we have, sir!' says the bride, sinking down upon a seat in her weakness. 'Not a morsel, wet or dry, have we had since! It was impossible to get out without help, and here we've stayed!'

"'But why didn't you shout, good souls?' said the pa'son.

"'She wouldn't let me,' says Andrey.

"'Because we were so ashamed at what had led to it,' sobs Jane. 'We felt that if it were noised abroad it would cling to us all our lives! Once or twice Andrey had a good mind to toll the bell, but then he said: "No; I'll starve first. I won't bring disgrace on my name and yours, my dear." And so we waited and waited, and walked round and round; but never did you come till now!'

"'To my regret!' says the parson. 'Now, then, we will soon get it over.'

"'I—I should like some victuals,' said Andrey; ' 'twould gie me courage to do it, if it is only a crust o' bread and a' onion; for I am that leery that I can feel my stomach rubbing against my backbone.'

"'I think we had better get it done,' said the bride, a bit anxious in manner; 'since we are all here convenient, too!'

"Andrey gave way about the victuals, and the clerk called in a second witness who wouldn't be likely to gossip about it, and soon the knot was tied, and the bride looked smiling and calm forthwith, and Andrey limper than ever.

"'Now,' said Pa'son Toogood, 'you two must come to my

house, and have a good lining put to your insides before you
go a step further.'

"They were very glad of the offer, and went out of the
churchyard by one path while the pa'son and clerk went out
by the other, and so did not attract notice, it being still early.
They entered the rectory as if they'd just come back from
their trip to Port Bredy; and then they knocked in the victuals
and drink till they could hold no more.

"It was a long while before the story of what they had gone
through was known, but it was talked of in time, and they
themselves laugh over it now; though what Jane got for her
pains was no great bargain after all. 'Tis true she saved her
name."

"Was that the same Andrey who went to the Squire's house as
one of the Christmas fiddlers?" asked the seedsman.

"No, no," replied Mr Profitt, the schoolmaster. "It was his
father did that. Ay, it was all owing to his being such a man for
eating and drinking." Finding that he had the ear of the
audience, the schoolmaster continued without delay:—

Old Andrey's Experience as a Musician

"I was one of the choir-boys at that time, and we and the
players were to appear at the manor-house as usual that
Christmas week, to play and sing in the hall to the Squire's
people and visitors (among 'em being the archdeacon, Lord
and Lady Baxby, and I don't know who); afterwards going, as
we always did, to have a good supper in the servants' hall.
Andrew knew this was the custom, and meeting us when we
were starting to go, he said to us: 'Lord, how I should like to
join in that meal of beef, and turkey, and plum-pudding, and
ale, that you happy ones be going to just now! One more or
less will make no difference to the Squire. I am too old to pass
as a singing boy, and too bearded to pass as a singing girl; can
ye lend me a fiddle, neighbours, that I may come with ye as a
bandsman?'

"Well, we didn't like to be hard upon him, and lent him an
old one, though Andrew knew no more of music than the

Giant o' Cernel; and armed with the instrument he walked up
to the Squire's house with the others of us at the time appointed, and went in boldly, his fiddle under his arm. He
made himself as natural as he could in opening the music-
books and moving the candles to the best points for throwing
light upon the notes; and all went well till we had played and
sung 'While shepherds watch,' and 'Star, arise,' and 'Hark the
glad sound.' Then the Squire's mother, a tall gruff old lady,
who was much interested in church-music, said quite unexpectedly to Andrew: 'My man, I see you don't play your instrument with the rest. How is that?'

"Every one of the choir was ready to sink into the earth with
concern at the fix Andrew was in. We could see that he had
fallen into a cold sweat, and how he would get out of it we did
not know.

" 'I've had a misfortune, mem,' he says, bowing as meek as
a child. 'Coming along the road I fell down and broke my
bow.'

" 'O, I am sorry to hear that,' says she. 'Can't it be mended?'

" 'O no, mem,' says Andrew. ' 'Twas broke all to splinters.'

" 'I'll see what I can do for you,' says she.

"And then it seemed all over, and we played 'Rejoice, ye
drowsy mortals all,' in D and two sharps. But no sooner had
we got through it than she says to Andrew,

" 'I've sent up into the attic, where we have some old musical instruments, and found a bow for you.' And she hands the
bow to poor wretched Andrew, who didn't even know which
end to take hold of. 'Now we shall have the full accompaniment,' says she.

"Andrew's face looked as if it were made of rotten apple as
he stood in the circle of players in front of his book; for if
there was one person in the parish that everybody was afraid
of, 'twas this hook-nosed old lady. However, by keeping a little
behind the next man he managed to make pretence of beginning, sawing away with his bow without letting it touch the
strings, so that it looked as if he were driving into the tune
with heart and soul. 'Tis a question if he wouldn't have got
through all right if one of the Squire's visitors (no other than
the archdeacon) hadn't noticed that he held the fiddle up-

side down, the nut under his chin, and the tail-piece in his hand; and they began to crowd round him, thinking 'twas some new way of performing.

"This revealed everything; the Squire's mother had Andrew turned out of the house as a vile impostor, and there was great interruption to the harmony of the proceedings, the Squire declaring he should have notice to leave his cottage that day fortnight. However, when we got to the servants' hall there sat Andrew, who had been let in at the back door by the orders of the Squire's wife, after being turned out at the front by the orders of the Squire, and nothing more was heard about his leaving his cottage. But Andrew never performed in public as a musician after that night; and now he's dead and gone, poor man, as we all shall be!"

"I had quite forgotten the old choir, with their fiddles and bass-viols," said the home-comer, musingly. "Are they still going on the same as of old?"

"Bless the man!" said Christopher Twink, the master-thatcher; "why, they've been done away with these twenty year. A young teetotaler plays the organ in church now, and plays it very well; though 'tis not quite such good music as in old times, because the organ is one of them that go with a winch, and the young teetotaler says he can't always throw the proper feeling into the tune without wellnigh working his arms off."

"Why did they make the change, then?"

"Well, partly because of fashion, partly because the old musicians got into a sort of scrape. A terrible scrape 'twas too—wasn't it, John? I shall never forget it—never! They lost their character as officers of the church as complete as if they'd never had any character at all."

"That was very bad for them."

"Yes." The master-thatcher attentively regarded past times as if they lay about a mile off, and went on:—

Absent-Mindedness in a Parish Choir

"It happened on Sunday after Christmas—the last Sunday ever they played in Longpuddle church gallery, as it turned out, though they didn't know it then. As you may know, sir, the players formed a very good band—almost as good as the Mellstock parish players that were led by the Dewys; and that's saying a great deal. There was Nicholas Puddingcome, the leader, with the first fiddle; there was Timothy Thomas, the bass-viol man; John Biles, the tenor fiddler; Dan'l Hornhead, with the serpent; Robert Dowdle, with the clarionet; and Mr Nicks, with the oboe—all sound and powerful musicians, and strong-winded men—they that blowed. For that reason they were very much in demand Christmas week for little reels and dancing parties; for they could turn a jig or a hornpipe out of hand as well as ever they could turn out a psalm, and perhaps better, not to speak irreverent. In short, one half-hour they could be playing a Christmas carol in the Squire's hall to the ladies and gentlemen, and drinking tay and coffee with 'em as modest as saints; and the next, at The Tinker's Arms, blazing away like wild horses with the 'Dashing White Sergeant' to nine couple of dancers and more, and swallowing rum-and-cider hot as flame.

"Well, this Christmas they'd been out to one rattling randy after another every night, and had got next to no sleep at all. Then came the Sunday after Christmas, their fatal day. 'Twas so mortal cold that year that they could hardly sit in the gallery; for though the congregation down in the body of the church had a stove to keep off the frost, the players in the gallery had nothing at all. So Nicholas said at morning service, when 'twas freezing an inch an hour, 'Please the Lord I won't stand this numbing weather no longer: this afternoon we'll have something in our insides to make us warm, if it cost a king's ransom.'

"So he brought a gallon of hot brandy and beer, ready mixed, to church with him in the afternoon, and by keeping the jar well wrapped up in Timothy Thomas's bass-viol bag it kept drinkably warm till they wanted it, which was just a thimbleful in the Absolution, and another after the Creed, and the remainder at the beginning o' the sermon. When they'd had the last pull they felt quite comfortable and warm, and as the sermon went on—most unfortunately for 'em it was a long one that afternoon—they fell asleep, every man jack of 'em; and there they slept on as sound as rocks.

" 'Twas a very dark afternoon, and by the end of the sermon all you could see of the inside of the church were the pa'son's two candles alongside of him in the pulpit, and his spaking face behind 'em. The sermon being ended at last, the pa'son gie'd out the Evening Hymn. But no choir set about sounding up the tune, and the people began to turn their heads to learn the reason why, and then Levi Limpet, a boy who sat in the gallery, nudged Timothy and Nicholas, and said, 'Begin! begin!'

" 'Hey? what?' says Nicholas, starting up; and the church being so dark and his head so muddled he thought he was at the party they had played at all the night before, and away he went, bow and fiddle, at 'The Devil among the Tailors,' the favourite jig of our neighbourhood at that time. The rest of the band, being in the same state of mind and nothing doubting, followed their leader with all their strength, according to custom. They poured out that there tune till the lower bass notes of 'The Devil among the Tailors' made the cobwebs in the roof shiver like ghosts; then Nicholas, seeing nobody moved, shouted out as he scraped (in his usual commanding way at dances when the folk didn't know the figures), 'Top couples cross hands! And when I make the fiddle squeak at the end, every man kiss his pardner under the mistletoe!'

"The boy Levi was so frightened that he bolted down the gallery stairs and out homeward like lightning. The pa'son's hair fairly stood on end when he heard the evil tune raging through the church, and thinking the choir had gone crazy, he held up his hand and said: 'Stop, stop, stop! Stop, stop! What's this?' But they didn't hear'n for the noise of their own playing, and the more he called the louder they played.

"Then the folks came out of their pews, wondering down to the ground, and saying: 'What do they mean by such wickedness! We shall be consumed like Sodom and Gomorrah!'

"And the Squire, too, came out of his pew lined wi' green baize, where lots of lords and ladies visiting at the house were worshipping along with him, and went and stood in front of the gallery, and shook his fist in the musicians' faces, saying, 'What! In this reverent edifice! What!'

"And at last they heard'n through their playing, and stopped.

"'Never such an insulting, disgraceful thing—never!' says the Squire, who couldn't rule his passion.

"'Never!' says the pa'son, who had come down and stood beside him.

"'Not if the Angels of Heaven,' says the Squire (he was a wickedish man, the Squire was, though now for once he happened to be on the Lord's side)—'not if the Angels of Heaven come down,' he says, 'shall one of you villainous players ever sound a note in this church again; for the insult to me, and my family, and my visitors, and the parson, and God Almighty, that you've a-perpetrated this afternoon!'

"Then the unfortunate church band came to their senses, and remembered where they were; and 'twas a sight to see Nicholas Puddingcome and Timothy Thomas and John Biles creep down the gallery stairs with their fiddles under their arms, and poor Dan'l Hornhead with his serpent, and Robert Dowdle with his clarionet, all looking as little as ninepins; and out they went. The pa'son might have forgi'ed 'em when he learned the truth o't, but the Squire would not. That very week he sent for a barrel-organ that would play two-and-twenty new psalm-tunes, so exact and particular that, however sinful inclined you was, you could play nothing but psalm-tunes whatsomever. He had a really respectable man to turn the winch, as I said, and the old players played no more."

"And, of course, my old acquaintance, the annuitant, Mrs Winter, who always seemed to have something on her mind, is dead and gone?" said the home-comer, after a long silence.

Nobody in the van seemed to recollect the name.

"O yes, she must be dead long since: she was seventy when I as a child knew her," he added.

"I can recollect Mrs Winter very well, if nobody else can," said the aged groceress. "Yes, she's been dead these five-and-twenty year at least. You knew what it was upon her mind, sir, that gave her that hollow-eyed look, I suppose?"

"It had something to do with a son of hers, I think I once was told. But I was too young to know particulars."

The groceress sighed as she conjured up a vision of days long past. "Yes," she murmured, "it had all to do with a son." Finding that the van was still in a listening mood, she spoke on:—

The Winters and the Palmleys

"To go back to the beginning—if one must—there were two women in the parish when I was a child, who were to a certain extent rivals in good looks. Never mind particulars, but in consequence of this they were at daggers-drawn, and they did not love each other any better when one of them tempted the other's lover away from her and married him. He was a young man of the name of Winter, and in due time they had a son.

"The other woman did not marry for many years; but when she was about thirty a quiet man named Palmley asked her to be his wife, and she accepted him. You don't mind when the Palmleys were Longpuddle folk, but I do well. She had a son also, who was, of course, nine or ten years younger than the son of the first. The child proved to be of rather weak intellect, though his mother loved him as the apple of her eye.

"This woman's husband died when the child was eight years old, and left his widow and boy in poverty. Her former rival, also a widow now, but fairly well provided for, offered for pity's sake to take the child as errand-boy, small as he was, her own son, Jack, being hard upon seventeen. Her poor neighbour could do no better than let the child go there. And to the richer woman's house little Palmley straightway went.

"Well, in some way or other—how, it was never exactly known—the thriving woman, Mrs Winter, sent the little boy with a message to the next village one December day, much against his will. It was getting dark, and the child prayed to be allowed not to go, because he would be afraid coming home. But the mistress insisted, more out of thoughtlessness than cruelty, and the child went. On his way back he had to pass through Yalbury Wood, and something came out from behind a tree and frightened him into fits. The child was quite ruined by it; he became quite a drivelling idiot, and soon afterwards died.

"Then the other woman had nothing left to live for, and vowed vengeance against that rival who had first won away her lover, and now had been the cause of her bereavement. This last affliction was certainly not intended by her thriving acquaintance, though it must be owned that when it was done she seemed but little concerned. Whatever vengeance poor Mrs Palmley felt, she had no opportunity of carrying it out, and time might have softened her feelings into forgetfulness of her supposed wrongs as she dragged on her lonely life. So matters stood when, a year after the death of the child, Mrs Palmley's niece, who had been born and bred in the city of Exonbury, came to live with her.

"This young woman—Miss Harriet Palmley—was a proud and handsome girl, very well brought up, and more stylish and genteel than the people of our village, as was natural, considering where she came from. She regarded herself as much above Mrs Winter and her son in position as Mrs Winter and her son considered themselves above poor Mrs Palmley. But love is an unceremonious thing, and what in the world should happen but that young Jack Winter must fall woefully and wildly in love with Harriet Palmley almost as soon as he saw her.

"She, being better educated than he, and caring nothing for the village notion of his mother's superiority to her aunt, did not give him much encouragement. But Longpuddle being no very large world, the two could not help seeing a good deal of each other while she was staying there, and, disdainful young woman as she was, she did seem to take a little pleasure in his attentions and advances.

"One day when they were picking apples together, he asked her to marry him. She had not expected anything so practical as that at so early a time, and was led by her surprise into a half-promise; at any rate she did not absolutely refuse him, and accepted some little presents that he made her.

"But he saw that her view of him was rather as a simple village lad than as a young man to look up to, and he felt that he must do something bold to secure her. So he said one day, 'I am going away, to try to get into a better position than I can get here.' In two or three weeks he wished her good-bye, and went away to Monksbury, to superintend a farm, with a view to start as a farmer himself; and from there he wrote regularly to her, as if their marriage were an understood thing.

"Now Harriet liked the young man's presents and the admiration of his eyes; but on paper he was less attractive to her. Her mother had been a school-mistress, and Harriet had besides a natural aptitude for pen-and-ink work, in days when to be a ready writer was not such a common thing as it is now, and when actual handwriting was valued as an accomplishment in itself. Jack Winter's performances in the shape of love-letters quite jarred her city nerves and her finer taste, and when she answered one of them, in the lovely running hand that she took such pride in, she very strictly and loftily bade him to practise with a pen and spelling-book if he wished to please her. Whether he listened to her request or not nobody knows, but his letters did not improve. He ventured to tell her in his clumsy way that if her heart were more warm towards him she would not be so nice about his handwriting and spelling; which indeed was true enough.

"Well, in Jack's absence the weak flame that had been set alight in Harriet's heart soon sank low, and at last went out altogether. He wrote and wrote, and begged and prayed her to give a reason for her coldness; and then she told him plainly that she was town born, and he was not sufficiently well educated to please her.

"Jack Winter's want of pen-and-ink training did not make him less thin-skinned than others; in fact, he was terribly tender and touchy about anything. This reason that she gave for finally throwing him over grieved him, shamed him, and mortified him more than can be told in these times, the pride of that day in being able to write with beautiful flourishes, and the sorrow at not being able to do so, raging so high. Jack replied to her with an angry note, and then she hit back with smart little stings, telling him how many words he had misspelt in his last letter, and declaring again that this alone was sufficient justification for any woman to put an end to an understanding with him. Her husband must be a better scholar.

"He bore her rejection of him in silence, but his suffering was sharp—all the sharper in being untold. She communicated with Jack no more; and as his reason for going out into the world had been only to provide a home worthy of her, he had no further object in planning such a home now that she was lost to him. He therefore gave up the farming occupation by which he had hoped to make himself a master-farmer, and left the spot to return to his mother.

"As soon as he got back to Longpuddle he found that Harriet had already looked wi' favour upon another lover. He was a young road-contractor, and Jack could not but admit that his rival was both in manners and scholarship much ahead of him. Indeed, a more sensible match for the beauty who had been dropped into the village by fate could hardly have been found than this man, who could offer her so much better a chance than Jack could have done, with his uncertain future and narrow abilities for grappling with the world. The fact was so clear to him that he could hardly blame her.

"One day by accident Jack saw on a scrap of paper the handwriting of Harriet's new beloved. It was flowing like a stream, well spelt, the work of a man accustomed to the inkbottle and the dictionary, of a man already called in the parish a good scholar. And then it struck all of a sudden into Jack's mind what a contrast the letters of this young man must make to his own miserable old letters, and how ridiculous they must make his lines appear. He groaned and wished he had never written to her, and wondered if she had ever kept his poor performances. Possibly she had kept them, for women are in the habit of doing that, he thought, and whilst they were in her hands there was always a chance of his honest, stupid love-assurances to her being joked over by

Harriet with her present lover, or by anybody who should accidentally uncover them.

"The nervous, moody young man could not bear the thought of it, and at length decided to ask her to return them, as was proper when engagements were broken off. He was some hours in framing, copying, and recopying the short note in which he made his request, and having finished it he sent it to her house. His messenger came back with the answer, by word of mouth, that Miss Palmley bade him say she should not part with what was hers, and wondered at his boldness in troubling her.

"Jack was much affronted at this, and determined to go for his letters himself. He chose a time when he knew she was at home, and knocked and went in without much ceremony; for though Harriet was so high and mighty, Jack had small respect for her aunt, Mrs Palmley, whose little child had been his boot-cleaner in earlier days. Harriet was in the room, this being the first time they had met since she had jilted him. He asked for his letters with a stern and bitter look at her.

"At first she said he might have them for all that she cared, and took them out of the bureau where she kept them. Then she glanced over the outside one of the packet, and suddenly altering her mind, she told him shortly that his request was a silly one, and slipped the letters into her aunt's work-box, which stood open on the table, locking it, and saying with a bantering laugh that of course she thought it best to keep 'em, since they might be useful to produce as evidence that she had good cause for declining to marry him.

"He blazed up hot. 'Give me those letters!' he said. 'They are mine!'

"'No, they are not,' she replied; 'they are mine.'

"'Whos'ever they are I want them back,' says he. 'I don't want to be made sport of for my penmanship: you've another young man now! He has your confidence, and you pour all your tales into his ear. You'll be showing them to him!'

"'Perhaps,' said my lady Harriet, with calm coolness, like the heartless woman that she was.

"Her manner so maddened him that he made a step towards the work-box, but she snatched it up, locked it in the bureau, and turned upon him triumphant. For a moment he seemed to be going to wrench the key of the bureau out of her hand; but he stopped himself, and swung round upon his heel and went away.

"When he was out-of-doors alone, and it got night, he walked about restless, and stinging with the sense of being beaten at all points by her. He could not help fancying her telling her new lover or her acquaintances of this scene with himself, and laughing with them over those poor blotted, crooked lines of his that he had been so anxious to obtain. As the evening passed on he worked himself into a dogged resolution to have them back at any price, come what might.

"At the dead of night he came out of his mother's house by the back door, and creeping through the garden hedge went along the field adjoining till he reached the back of her aunt's dwelling. The moon struck bright and flat upon the walls, 'twas said, and every shiny leaf of the creepers was like a little looking-glass in the rays. From long acquaintance Jack knew the arrangement and position of everything in Mrs Palmley's house as well as in his own mother's. The back window close to him was a casement with little leaded squares, as it is to this day, and was, as now, one of two lighting the sitting-room. The other, being in front, was closed up with shutters, but this back one had not even a blind, and the moonlight as it streamed in showed every article of the furniture to him outside. To the right of the room is the fireplace, as you may remember; to the left was the bureau at that time; inside the bureau was Harriet's work-box, as he supposed (though it was really her aunt's), and inside the work-box were his letters. Well, he took out his pocket-knife, and without noise lifted the leading of one of the panes, so that he could take out the glass, and putting his hand through the hole he unfastened the casement, and climbed in through the opening. All the household—that is to say, Mrs Palmley, Harriet, and the little maidservant—were asleep. Jack went straight to the bureau, so he said, hoping it might have been unfastened again—it not being kept locked in ordinary—but Harriet had never unfastened it since she secured her letters there the day before. Jack told afterwards how he thought of her asleep upstairs, caring nothing for him, and of the way she had made sport of him and of his letters; and having advanced so far, he was not to be hindered now. By forcing the large blade of his knife under the flap of the bureau, he burst the weak lock; within was the rosewood work-box just as she had placed it in her hurry to keep it from him. There being no time to spare for getting the letters out of it then, he took it under his arm, shut the bureau, and made the best of his way out of the house, latching the casement behind him, and refixing the pane of glass in its place.

"Winter found his way back to his mother's as he had come, and being dog-tired, crept upstairs to bed, hiding the box till he could destroy its contents. The next morning early he set about doing this, and carried it to the linhay at the back of his mother's dwelling. Here by the hearth he opened the box, and began burning one by one the letters that had cost him so much labour to write and shame to think of, meaning to return the box to Harriet, after repairing the slight damage he had caused it by opening it without a key, with a note— the last she would ever receive from him—telling her triumphantly that in refusing to return what he had asked for she had calculated too surely upon his submission to her whims.

"But on removing the last letter from the box he received a shock; for underneath it, at the very bottom, lay money— several golden guineas—'Doubtless Harriet's pocket-money,' he said to himself; though it was not, but Mrs Palmley's. Before he had got over his qualms at this discovery he heard footsteps coming through the house-passage to where he was. In haste he pushed the box and what was in it under some brushwood which lay in the linhay; but Jack had been already seen. Two constables entered the out-house, and seized him as he knelt before the fireplace, securing the work-box and all it contained at the same moment. They had come to appre-hend him on a charge of breaking into the dwelling-house of

Mrs Palmley on the night preceding; and almost before the lad knew what had happened to him they were leading him along the lane that connects that end of the village with this turnpike-road, and along they marched him between 'em all the way to Casterbridge gaol.

"Jack's act amounted to night burglary—though he had never thought of it—and burglary was felony, and a capital offence in those days. His figure had been seen by some one against the bright wall as he came away from Mrs Palmley's back window, and the box and money were found in his possession, while the evidence of the broken bureau-lock and tinkered window-pane was more than enough for circumstantial detail. Whether his protestation that he went only for his letters, which he believed to be wrongfully kept from him, would have availed him anything if supported by other evidence I do not know; but the one person who could have borne it out was Harriet, and she acted entirely under the sway of her aunt. That aunt was deadly towards Jack Winter. Mrs Palmley's time had come. Here was her revenge upon the woman who had first won away her lover, and next ruined and deprived her of her heart's treasure—her little son. When the assize week drew on, and Jack had to stand his trial, Harriet did not appear in the case at all, which was allowed to take its course, Mrs Palmley testifying to the general facts of the burglary. Whether Harriet would have come forward if Jack had appealed to her is not known; possibly she would have done it for pity's sake; but Jack was too proud to ask a single favour of a girl who had jilted him; and he let her alone. The trial was a short one, and the death sentence was passed.

"The day o' young Jack's execution was a cold dusty Saturday in March. He was so boyish and slim that they were obliged in mercy to hang him in the heaviest fetters kept in the gaol, lest his heft should not break his neck, and they weighed so upon him that he could hardly drag himself up to the drop. At that time the gover'ment was not strict about burying the body of an executed person within the precincts of the prison, and at the earnest prayer of his poor mother his body was allowed to be brought home. All the parish waited at their cottage doors in the evening for its arrival: I remember how, as a very little girl, I stood by my mother's side. About eight o'clock, as we hearkened on our door-stones in the cold bright starlight, we could hear the faint crackle of a waggon from the direction of the turnpike-road. The noise was lost as the waggon dropped into a hollow, then it was plain again as it lumbered down the next long incline, and presently it entered Longpuddle. The coffin was laid in the belfry for the night, and the next day, Sunday, between the services, we buried him. A funeral sermon was preached the same afternoon, the text chosen being, 'He was the only son of his mother, and she was a widow.' . . . Yes, they were cruel times!

"As for Harriet, she and her lover were married in due time; but by all account her life was no jocund one. She and her good-man found that they could not live comfortably at Longpuddle, by reason of her connection with Jack's misfortunes, and they settled in a distant town, and were no more heard of by us; Mrs Palmley, too, found it advisable to join 'em shortly after. The dark-eyed, gaunt old Mrs Winter, remembered by the emigrant gentleman here, was, as you will have foreseen, the Mrs Winter of this story; and I can well call to mind how lonely she was, how afraid the children were of her, and how she kept herself as a stranger among us, though she lived so long."

"Longpuddle has had her sad experiences as well as her sunny ones," said Mr Lackland.

"Yes, yes. But I am thankful to say not many like that, though good and bad have lived among us."

"There was Georgy Crookhill—he was one of the shady sort, as I have reason to know," observed the registrar, with the manner of a man who would like to have his say also.

"I used to hear what he was as a boy at school."

"Well, as he began so he went on. It never got so far as a hanging matter with him, to be sure; but he had some narrow escapes of penal servitude; and once it was a case of the biter bit."

Incident in the Life of Mr George Crookhill

"ONE day," the registrar continued, "Georgy was ambling out of Melchester on a miserable screw, the fair being just over, when he saw in front of him a fine-looking young farmer riding out of the town in the same direction. He was mounted on a good strong handsome animal, worth fifty guineas if worth a crown. When they were going up Bissett Hill, Georgy made it his business to overtake the young farmer. They passed the time o' day to one another; Georgy spoke of the state of the roads, and jogged alongside the well-mounted stranger in very friendly conversation. The farmer had not been inclined to say much to Georgy at first, but by degrees he grew quite affable too—as friendly as Georgy was towards him. He told Crookhill that he had been doing business at Melchester fair, and was going on as far as Shottsford-Forum that night, so as to reach Casterbridge market the next day. When they came to Woodyates Inn they stopped to bait their horses, and agreed to drink together; with this they got more friendly than ever, and on they went again. Before they had nearly reached Shottsford it came on to rain, and as they were now passing through the village of Trantridge, and it was quite dark, Georgy persuaded the young farmer to go no further that night; the rain would most likely give them a chill. For his part he had heard that the little inn here was comfortable, and he meant to stay. At last the young farmer agreed to put up there also; and they dismounted, and entered, and had a good supper together, and talked over their affairs like men who had known and proved each other a long time. When it was the hour for retiring they went upstairs to a double-bedded room which Georgy Crookhill had asked the landlord to let them share, so sociable were they.

"Before they fell asleep they talked across the room about one thing and another, running from this to that till the conversation turned upon disguises, and changing clothes for particular ends. The farmer told Georgy that he had often heard tales of people doing it; but Crookhill professed to be very ignorant of all such tricks; and soon the young farmer sank into slumber.

"Early in the morning, while the tall young farmer was still asleep (I tell the story as 'twas told me), honest Georgy crept out of his bed by stealth, and dressed himself in the farmer's clothes, in the pockets of the said clothes being the farmer's money. Now though Georgy particularly wanted the farmer's nice clothes and nice horse, owing to a little transaction at the fair which made it desirable that he should not be too easily recognized, his desires had their bounds: he did not wish to take his young friend's money, at any rate more of it than was necessary for paying his bill. This he abstracted, and leaving the farmer's purse containing the rest on the bedroom table, went downstairs. The inn folks had not particularly noticed the faces of their customers, and the one or two who were up at this hour had no thought but that Georgy was the farmer; so when he had paid the bill very liberally, and said he must be off, no objection was made to his getting the farmer's horse saddled for himself; and he rode away upon it as if it were his own.

"About half an hour after the young farmer awoke, and looking across the room saw that his friend Georgy had gone away in clothes which didn't belong to him, and had kindly left for himself the seedy ones worn by Georgy. At this he sat up in a deep thought for some time, instead of hastening to give an alarm. 'The money, the money is gone,' he said to himself, 'and that's bad. But so are the clothes.'

"He then looked upon the table and saw that the money, or most of it, had been left behind.

"'Ha, ha, ha!' he cried, and began to dance about the room. 'Ha, ha, ha!' he said again, and made beautiful smiles to himself in the shaving glass and in the brass candlestick; and then swung about his arms for all the world as if he were going through the sword exercise.

"When he had dressed himself in Georgy's clothes and gone downstairs, he did not seem to mind at all that they took him for the other; and even when he saw that he had been left a bad horse for a good one, he was not inclined to cry out.

They told him his friend had paid the bill, at which he seemed much pleased, and without waiting for breakfast he mounted Georgy's horse and rode away likewise, choosing the nearest by-lane in preference to the high-road, without knowing that Georgy had chosen that by-lane also.

"He had not trotted more than two miles in the personal character of Georgy Crookhill when, suddenly rounding a bend that the lane made thereabout, he came upon a man struggling in the hands of two village constables. It was his friend Georgy, the borrower of his clothes and horse. But so far was the young farmer from showing any alacrity in rushing forward to claim his property that he would have turned the poor beast he rode into the wood adjoining, if he had not been already perceived.

"'Help, help, help!' cried the constables. 'Assistance in the name of the Crown!'

"The young farmer could do nothing but ride forward. 'What's the matter?' he inquired, as coolly as he could.

"'A deserter—a deserter!' said they. 'One who's to be tried by court-martial and shot without parley. He deserted from the Dragoons at Cheltenham some days ago, and was tracked; but the search-party can't find him anywhere, and we told 'em if we met him we'd hand him on to 'em forthwith. The day after he left the barracks the rascal met a respectable farmer and made him drunk at an inn, and told him what a fine soldier he would make, and coaxed him to change clothes, to see how well a military uniform would become him. This the simple farmer did; when our deserter said that for a joke he would leave the room and go to the landlady, to see if she would know him in that dress. He never came back, and Farmer Jollice found himself in soldier's clothes, the money in his pockets gone, and, when he got to the stable, his horse gone too.'

"'A scoundrel!' says the young man in Georgy's clothes. 'And is this the wretched caitiff?' (pointing to Georgy).

"'No, no!' cries Georgy, as innocent as a babe of this matter of the soldier's desertion. 'He's the man! He was wearing Farmer Jollice's suit o' clothes, and he slept in the same room wi' me, and brought up the subject of changing clothes, which put it into my head to dress myself in his suit before he was awake. He's got on mine!'

"'D'ye hear the villain?' groans the tall young man to the constables. 'Trying to get out of his crime by charging the first innocent man with it that he sees! No, master soldier—that won't do!'

"'No, no! That won't do!' the constables chimed in. 'To have the impudence to say such as that, when we caught him in the act almost! But, thank God, we've got the handcuffs on him at last.'

"'We have, thank God,' said the tall young man. 'Well, I must move on. Good luck to ye with your prisoner!' And off he went, as fast as his poor jade would carry him.

"The constables then, with Georgy handcuffed between 'em, and leading the horse, marched off in the other direction, towards the village where they had been accosted by the escort of soldiers sent to bring the deserter back, Georgy groaning: 'I shall be shot, I shall be shot!' They had not gone more than a mile before they met them.

"'Hoi, there!' says the head constable.

"'Hoi, yerself!' says the corporal in charge.

"'We've got your man,' says the constable.

"'Where?' says the corporal.

"'Here, between us,' said the constable. 'Only you don't recognize him out o' uniform.'

"The corporal looked at Georgy hard enough; then shook his head and said he was not the absconder.

"'But the absconder changed clothes with Farmer Jollice, and took his horse; and this man has 'em, d'ye see!'

"''Tis not our man,' said the soldiers. 'He's a tall young fellow with a mole on his right cheek, and a military bearing, which this man decidedly has not.'

"'I told the two officers of justice that 'twas the other!' pleaded Georgy. 'But they wouldn't believe me.'

"And so it became clear that the missing dragoon was the tall young farmer, and not Georgy Crookhill—a fact which Farmer Jollice himself corroborated when he arrived on the scene. As Georgy had only robbed the robber, his sentence was comparatively light. The deserter from the Dragoons was never traced: his double shift of clothing having been of the greatest advantage to him in getting off; though he left Georgy's horse behind him a few miles ahead, having found the poor creature more hindrance than aid."

The man from abroad seemed to be less interested in the questionable characters of Longpuddle and their strange adventures than in the ordinary inhabitants and the ordinary events, though his local fellow-travellers preferred the former as subjects of discussion. He now for the first time asked concerning young persons of the opposite sex—or rather those who had been young when he left his native land. His informants, adhering to their own opinion that the remarkable was better worth telling than the ordinary, would not allow him to dwell upon the simple chronicles of those who had merely come and gone. They asked him if he remembered Netty Sargent.

"Netty Sargent—I do, just remember her. She was a young woman living with her uncle when I left, if my childish recollection may be trusted."

"That was the maid. She was a oneyer, if you like, sir. Not any harm in her, you know, but up to everything. You ought to hear how she got the copyhold of her house extended. Oughtn't he, Mr Day?"

"He ought," replied the world-ignored old painter.

"Tell him, Mr Day. Nobody can do it better than you, and you know the legal part better than some of us."

Day apologized, and began:—

Netty Sargent's Copyhold

"SHE continued to live with her uncle, in the lonely house by the copse, just as at the time you knew her; a tall spry young woman. Ah, how well one can remember her black hair and dancing eyes at that time, and her sly way of screwing up her mouth when she meant to tease ye! Well, she was hardly out of short frocks before the chaps were after her, and by long and by late she was courted by a young man whom perhaps you did not know—Jasper Cliff was his name—and, though she might have had many a better fellow, he so greatly took her fancy that 'twas Jasper or nobody for her. He was a selfish customer, always thinking less of what he was going to do than of what he was going to gain by his doings. Jasper's eyes might have been fixed upon Netty, but his mind was upon her uncle's house; though he was fond of her in his way—I admit that.

"This house, built by her great-great-grandfather, with its garden and little field, was copyhold—granted upon lives in the old way, and had been so granted for generations. Her uncle's was the last life upon the property; so that at his death, if there was no admittance of new lives, it would all fall into the hands of the lord of the manor. But 'twas easy to admit— a slight 'fine,' as 'twas called, of a few pounds, was enough to entitle him to a new deed o' grant by the custom of the manor; and the lord could not hinder it.

"Now there could be no better provision for his niece and only relative than a sure house over her head, and Netty's uncle should have seen to the renewal in time, owing to the peculiar custom of forfeiture by the dropping of the last life before the new fine was paid; for the Squire was very anxious to get hold of the house and land; and every Sunday when the old man came into the church and passed the Squire's pew, the Squire would say, 'A little weaker in his knees, a little crookeder in his back—and the readmittance not applied for: ha! ha! I shall be able to make a complete clearing of that corner of the manor some day!'

" 'Twas extraordinary, now we look back upon it, that old Sargent should have been so dilatory; yet some people are like it; and he put off calling at the Squire's agent's office with the fine week after week, saying to himself, 'I shall have more time next market-day than I have now.' One unfortunate hindrance was that he didn't very well like Jasper Cliff, and as Jasper kept urging Netty, and Netty on that account kept urging her uncle, the old man was inclined to postpone the re-liveing as long as he could, to spite the selfish young lover. At last old Mr Sargent fell ill, and then Jasper could bear it no longer: he produced the fine-money himself, and handed it to Netty, and spoke to her plainly.

"'You and your uncle ought to know better. You should press him more. There's the money. If you let the house and ground slip between ye, I won't marry; hang me if I will! For folks won't deserve a husband that can do such things.'

"The worried girl took the money and went home, and told her uncle that it was no house no husband for her. Old Mr Sargent pooh-poohed the money, for the amount was not worth consideration, but he did now bestir himself, for he saw she was bent upon marrying Jasper, and he did not wish to make her unhappy, since she was so determined. It was much to the Squire's annoyance that he found Sargent had moved in the matter at last; but he could not gainsay it, and the documents were prepared (for on this manor the copyholders had writings with their holdings, though on some manors they had none). Old Sargent being now too feeble to go to the agent's house, the deed was to be brought to his house signed, and handed over as a receipt for the money; the counterpart to be signed by Sargent, and sent back to the Squire.

"The agent had promised to call on old Sargent for this purpose at five o'clock, and Netty put the money into her desk to have it close at hand. While doing this she heard a slight cry from her uncle, and turning round, saw that he had fallen forward in his chair. She went and lifted him, but he was unconscious; and unconscious he remained. Neither medicine nor stimulants would bring him to himself. She had been told that he might possibly go off in that way, and it seemed as if the end had come. Before she had started for the doctor his face and extremities grew quite cold and white, and she saw that help would be useless. He was stone-dead.

"Netty's situation rose upon her distracted mind in all its seriousness. The house, garden, and field were lost—by a few hours—and with them a home for herself and her lover. She would not think so meanly of Jasper as to suppose that he would adhere to the resolution declared in a moment of impatience; but she trembled, nevertheless. Why could not her uncle have lived a couple of hours longer, since he had lived so long? It was now past three o'clock; at five the agent was to call, and, if all had gone well, by ten minutes past five the house and holding would have been securely hers for

her own and Jasper's lives, these being two of the three proposed to be added by paying the fine. How that wretched old
Squire would rejoice at getting the little tenancy into his
hands! He did not really require it, but constitutionally hated
these tiny copyholds and leaseholds and freeholds, which
made islands of independence in the fair, smooth ocean of
his estates.

"Then an idea struck into the head of Netty how to accom-
plish her object in spite of her uncle's negligence. It was a dull
December afternoon: and the first step in her scheme—so the
story goes, and I see no reason to doubt it—"

"'Tis true as the light," affirmed Christopher Twink. "I was
just passing by."

"The first step in her scheme was to fasten the outer door,
to make sure of not being interrupted. Then she set to work
by placing her uncle's small, heavy oak table before the fire;
then she went to her uncle's corpse, sitting in the chair as he
had died—a stuffed arm-chair, on castors, and rather high in
the seat, so it was told me—and wheeled the chair, uncle and
all, to the table, placing him with his back towards the window, in the attitude of bending over the said oak table, which
I knew as a boy as well as I know any piece of furniture in my
own house. On the table she laid the large family Bible open
before him, and placed his forefinger on the page; and then
she opened his eyelids a bit, and put on him his spectacles, so
that from behind he appeared for all the world as if he were
reading the Scriptures. Then she unfastened the door and sat
down, and when it grew dark she lit a candle, and put it on the
table beside her uncle's book.

"Folk may well guess how the time passed with her till the
agent came, and how, when his knock sounded upon the
door, she nearly started out of her skin—at least that's as it
was told me. Netty promptly went to the door.

"'I am sorry, sir,' she says, under her breath; 'my uncle is
not so well to-night, and I'm afraid he can't see you.'

"'H'm!—that's a pretty tale,' says the steward. 'So I've come
all this way about this trumpery little job for nothing!'

"'O no, sir—I hope not,' says Netty. 'I suppose the business
of granting the new deed can be done just the same?'

"'Done? Certainly not. He must pay the renewal money, and sign the parchment in my presence.'

"She looked dubious. 'Uncle is so dreadful nervous about law business,' says she, 'that, as you know, he's put it off and put it off for years; and now to-day really I've feared it would verily drive him out of his mind. His poor three teeth quite chattered when I said to him that you would be here soon with the parchment writing. He always was afraid of agents, and folks that come for rent, and such like.'

"'Poor old fellow—I'm sorry for him. Well, the thing can't be done unless I see him and witness his signature.'

"'Suppose, sir, that you see him sign, and he don't see you looking at him? I'd soothe his nerves by saying you weren't strict about the form of witnessing, and didn't wish to come in. So that it was done in your bare presence it would be sufficient, would it not? As he's such an old, shrinking, shivering man, it would be a great considerateness on your part if that would do?'

"'In my bare presence would do, of course—that's all I come for. But how can I be a witness without his seeing me?'

"'Why, in this way, sir; if you'll oblige me by just stepping here.' She conducted him a few yards to the left, till they were opposite the parlour window. The blind had been left up purposely, and the candle-light shone out upon the garden bushes. Within the agent could see, at the other end of the room, the back and side of the old man's head, and his shoulders and arm, sitting with the book and candle before him, and his spectacles on his nose, as she had placed him.

"'He's reading his Bible, as you see, sir,' she says, quite in her meekest way.

"'Yes. I thought he was a careless sort of man in matters of religion?'

"'He always was fond of his Bible,' Netty assured him. 'Though I think he's nodding over it just at this moment. However, that's natural in an old man, and unwell. Now you could stand here and see him sign, couldn't you, sir, as he's such an invalid?'

"'Very well,' said the agent, lighting a cigar. 'You have

ready by you the merely nominal sum you'll have to pay for the admittance, of course?'

"'Yes,' said Netty. 'I'll bring it out.' She fetched the cash, wrapped in paper, and handed it to him, and when he had counted it the steward took from his breast pocket the precious parchments and gave one to her to be signed.

"'Uncle's hand is a little paralyzed,' she said. 'And what with his being half asleep, too, really I don't know what sort of a signature he'll be able to make.'

"'Doesn't matter, so that he signs.'

"'Might I hold his hand?'

"'Ay, hold his hand, my young woman—that will be near enough.'

"Netty re-entered the house, and the agent continued smoking outside the window. Now came the ticklish part of Netty's performance. The steward saw her put the inkhorn— 'horn,' says I in my oldfashioned way—the inkstand, before her uncle, and touch his elbow as if to arouse him, and speak to him, and spread out the deed; when she had pointed to show him where to sign she dipped the pen and put it into his hand. To hold his hand she artfully stepped behind him, so that the agent could only see a little bit of his head, and the hand she held; but he saw the old man's hand trace his name on the document. As soon as 'twas done she came out to the steward with the parchment in her hand, and the steward signed as witness by the light from the parlour window. Then he gave her the deed signed by the Squire, and left; and next morning Netty told the neighbours that her uncle was dead in his bed."

"She must have undressed him and put him there."

"She must. O, that girl had a nerve, I can tell ye! Well, to cut a long story short, that's how she got back the house and field that were, strictly speaking, gone from her; and by getting them, got her a husband.

"Every virtue has its reward, they say. Netty had hers for her ingenious contrivance to gain Jasper. Two years after they were married he took to beating her—not hard, you know; just a smack or two, enough to set her in a temper, and let out to the neighbours what she had done to win him, and how she repented of her pains. When the old Squire was dead, and his son came into the property, this confession of hers began to be whispered about. But Netty was a pretty young woman, and the Squire's son was a pretty young man at that time, and wider-minded than his father, having no objection to little holdings; and he never took any proceedings against her."

There was now a lull in the discourse, and soon the van descended the hill leading into the long straggling village. When the houses were reached the passengers dropped off one by one, each at his or her own door. Arrived at the inn, the returned emigrant secured a bed, and having eaten a light meal, sallied forth upon the scene he had known so well in his early days. Though flooded with the light of the rising moon, none of the objects wore the attractiveness in this their real presentation that had ever accompanied their images in the field of his imagination when he was more than two thousand miles removed from them. The peculiar charm attaching to an old village in an old country, as seen by the eyes of an absolute foreigner, was lowered in his case by magnified expectations from infantine memories. He walked on, looking at this chimney and that old wall, till he came to the churchyard, which he entered.

The head-stones, whitened by the moon, were easily decipherable; and now for the first time Lackland began to feel himself amid the village community that he had left behind him five-and-thirty years before. Here, besides the Sallets, the Darths, the Pawles, the Privetts, the Sargents, and others of whom he had just heard, were names he remembered even better than those: the Jickses, and the Crosses, and the Knights, and the Olds. Doubtless representatives of these families, or some of them, were yet among the living; but to him they would all be as strangers. Far from finding his heart ready-supplied with roots and tendrils here, he perceived that in returning to this spot it would be incumbent upon him to re-establish himself from the beginning, precisely as though he had never known the place, nor it him. Time had not condescended to wait his pleasure, nor local life his greeting.

The figure of Mr Lackland was seen at the inn, and in the village street, and in the fields and lanes about Upper Longpuddle, for a few days after his arrival, and then, ghost-like, it silently disappeared. He had told some of the villagers that his immediate purpose in coming had been fulfilled by a sight of the place, and by conversation with its inhabitants: but that his ulterior purpose—of coming to spend his latter days among them—would probably never be carried out. It is now a dozen or fifteen years since his visit was paid, and his face has not again been seen.

March 1891.

[THE END]

APPENDIX A

THE 1896 PREFACE

The preface Hardy wrote for *Life's Little Ironies* when it appeared as Volume XIV of the 1896 Osgood, McIlvaine collected edition of The Wessex Novels was replaced in later editions because of the changes he made to the volume's contents for the 1912 Wessex Edition. It is nevertheless of interest for what it tells us of the relationship between his art and "real life".

A story-teller's interest in his own stories is usually independent of any merits or demerits they may show as specimens of narrative art; turning on something behind the scenes, something real in their history, which may have no attraction for a reader even if known to him—a condition by no means likely. In the present collection "The Melancholy Hussar of the German Legion" has just such a hold upon myself for the technically inadmissible reasons that the old people who gave me their recollections of its incidents did so in circumstances that linger pathetically in the memory; that she who, at the age of ninety, pointed out the unmarked resting-place of the two soldiers of the tale, was probably the last remaining eyewitness of their death and interment; that the extract from the register of burials is literal, to be read any day in the original by the curious who recognize the village.

Several of the other stories are true in their main facts, if there should be anybody who cares to know it. In respect of the tale of "Andrey Satchel," some persons still living may discern in Parson Toogood one to whom they, or at least their fathers, were not altogether strangers. To present that truly delightful personage as he entirely was, is beyond the power of my uncertain pen. One would like to tell of the second baptisms in old port which he used to perform on the squire's children at the christening dinner; of the bishop's descent one day upon the parsonage to convict Toogood of absenteeism, the latter's breakneck ride across country from a cocking party in consequence, and his breathless entry by his back door just in time to open his front to his visitor, whom he meekly received with a quill behind his ear, and a sermon outspread. He had several imitators in his composite calling of sportsman and divine, but no rival.

T. H.

June 1896.

APPENDIX B

TEXTUAL VARIATION IN "ON THE WESTERN CIRCUIT"

Hardy bowdlerized "On the Western Circuit" for magazine publication and, instead of simply reverting to the text of the manuscript, revised the story thoroughly for the first edition of *Life's Little Ironies*. Below are the manuscript and *The English Illustrated Magazine* versions of two passages that received much attention. Comparison of the texts in each case, and with the edited text in parts IV and V of the story (the words of which will be close to those of the first edition), will give the reader some idea of what Hardy was doing. In the manuscript transcriptions deletions are given within angle brackets and insertions are within vertical lines (insertions within insertions are within double vertical lines).

PASSAGE 1

MS fo. 17

Now, from some ambiguous expressions in Raye's letter, which Mrs Harnham had looked over again, she was led to <as[k]> put <some> |certain| questions to Anna as to her actual relations with the young man. The answers she received <led to> gave her a sad suspicion, & she looked very grave. Anna's mien ultimately resolved itself into a flood of tears, & sinking down at Edith's knees she made a full confession of the extent of her trust in her |too winning| lover, notwithstanding the shortness of their acquaintance.

<Mrs Harnham was deeply concerned, &>|Deep concern filled Mrs Harnham's eyes: she| blamed herself much for not interfering, though at the time of seeing the<m> |pair| together she had a feeling that it was hardly within her province to nip young affection in the bud. |However, transposed from after "done"|| what was done<,> could not be undone; & it behoved her now, as Anna's only protector, to help her as much as she could|.|<; &> |To| Anna's eager request that she, Mrs Harnham, should compose & write the answer to this young <fellow's>|London man's| letter, she felt seriously bound to accede, |to keep alive his attachment to the girl if possible;| though in other circumstances she might have suggested the cook as an amanuensis.

The English Illustrated Magazine (p. 282)

Deep concern filled Mrs. Harnham's eyes at perceiving how the girl's happiness hung on this quickly matured attachment. She blamed herself much for not interfering in a flirtation which had so unsettled the pretty little creature, though at the time of seeing the pair together she had a feeling that it was hardly within her province to nip young affection in the bud. However what was done could not be undone, and it behoved her now, as Anna's only protector, to help her as much as she could. To Anna's eager request that she, Mrs. Harnham, should compose and write the answer to this young London man's letter, she felt seriously bound to accede, to keep alive his passion for the girl if possible; though in other circumstances she might have suggested the cook as an amanuensis.

PASSAGE 2

MS fos. 19–22

The letter-writing of that day Anna never discovered, but Mrs Harnham did not venture to repeat the luxury of not consulting her. A few weeks later the girl came to her mistress's room with a strange anxiety of manner. <The result of> Her relations with her lover <it> would soon <be necessary to> disclose themselves[.]

Mrs Harnham was <much |deeply| grieved> |distressed|; but she had feared as much, [*possibly mended from a full-stop*] |& was generous enough not to cut Anna adrift. No true woman thinks of doing so from a personal point of view, however prompt in such measures she may be to safeguard <those> ||innocent ones|| dear to her. One thing was imperative: to keep the young man faithful.| By Mrs Harnham's advice Anna was to <ref> refrain from appeals, reproaches or bitterness on account of this <upshot> |contretemps|, a course of conduct less difficult in |the| real life |of such| than in the assumed state of mind of young women so <situated> overtaken.

Hinting therefore very delicately the actual state of affairs Edith, in the name of her maid, requested him on no account to be alarmed, <at the new situation,> or to be distressed at all about it. She <wished> |desired| above everything to be no weight upon him <on the> |in his career,| no clog upon his high activities. She had <desired> wished him to know the news, but he was to dismiss it again from his mind. He must write tenderly as ever, & when he should come again on the Spring circuit it would be soon enough to discuss what had better be done.

Anna's own feelings had been quite in accord |with these expressions.| "What I want is, that niceness you can so well put into your words, my dear dear mistress, & that I can't make up out of my own head; though I mean it & feel it exactly when you've written it down."

When the letter <was> containing the information <was> |had been marked "Private," &| sent off, & <M>Edith Harnham was left alone, she bowed herself on the back of the chair & wept.

"I wish it was mine—I wish it was!" she murmured. "Yet how can I say such a wicked thing!"

V

The news moved Raye considerably when it reached him, though perhaps the intelligence itself was not so moving as her manner of conveying it. Her avoidance of every word of reproach, her devotion to his interests, her self-sacrifice, made up in his eyes a nobility of character which he had never anticipated as |among| the |good| gift|s| of woman.

"God forgive me!" he said tremulously. "I have been a wicked wretch. I did not know that she was such a treasure as this!"

He wrote a hasty assurance that he would not desert her, and would provide a home of some sort for her if necessary; though she was to stay where she was as long as possible, if her mistress was kind.

This the young girl did, till misfortune supervened. An inkling of the truth reached the knowledge of Mr. Harnham by some means or other, & despite his wife's entreaties Anna had to leave the house at somewhat short notice. By her own choice she went to the cottage on the Plain awhile, to await the arrival of her lover in the spring. This arrangement led to a consultation with her mistress as to how the correspondence should be carried on; & in the girl's sheer inability to continue personally what had been begun in her name, & in the difficulty of their acting in collaboration as heretofore, she requested Mrs Harnham—the only friend she had in the world—to receive the letters & reply to them |off hand,| sending them on afterwards to herself on the Plain, where she might get some friend to read them to her |at least,| though disqualified from replying because of the handwriting. Anna & her box then departed for the Plain.

Thus it befel that Edith Harnham found herself in the strange position of having to correspond with a man not her husband in terms which were virtually those of a wife at a touching period of her existence; the man being one for whom, |mainly| from the fact of <her> |the sympathies involved in| playing this |<pathetic>| part, she |secretly| cherished a predilection, subtle & imaginative truly, but strong & absorbing.

The English Illustrated Magazine (pp. 283–4)

The letter-writing of that day Anna never discovered; but Mrs. Harnham did not venture to repeat the luxury of not consulting her. On Anna's return the next morning she declared she wished to see her lover about something, and begged Mrs. Harnham to ask him to come. This Mrs. Harnham did, although she had written but such a short time previously; and the result was that Raye sent a hasty note to say how much he was won by her sweetness; it made him feel that he must run down for a day to see her as requested.

But a week later the girl came to her mistress's room with another note, which, on being read, informed her that after all he could not find time for the journey. Anna was grieved, but by Mrs. Harnham's advice strictly refrained from reproaches or bitterness on account of this disappointment; one thing being imperative—to keep the young man's romantic interest in Anna alive. Rather, therefore, did Edith in the name of her *protégée*, request him on no account to be distressed at all about his inability to come. She desired above everything to be no weight upon him in his career, no clog upon his high activities. He must write tenderly as ever, and when he should come again on the Spring circuit it would be soon enough to see him.

Anna's own feelings had not been quite in accord with these expressions, but the young widow's judgment had ruled, and Anna had acquiesced. "All I want is, that niceness you can so well put into your words, my dear, dear mistress, and that I can't make up out of my own head, though I mean it and feel it exactly when you've written it down."

Occasionally, when one of these letters had been sent off, and Edith Harnham was left alone, she would bow herself on the back of her chair and weep.

"I wish he was mine—I wish he was!" she murmured. "Yet how can I say such a wicked thing!"

V

The damps of winter, aggravated, perhaps, by her secret heart-sickness at her lover's non-appearance, made Anna unwell ["ill" *Harper's Weekly*], and by her own choice she went for a while to the cottage on the Plain. This arrangement led to a consultation with her mistress as to how the correspondence should be carried on; and in the girl's sheer inability to continue personally what had been begun in her name, and in the difficulty of their acting in collaboration as heretofore, she requested Mrs. Harnham—the only friend she had in the world—to receive the letters and reply to them off-hand, sending them on afterwards to herself on the Plain, where she might get some friend to read them to her at least, though disqualified from replying because of the handwriting. Anna and her box then departed for the Plain.

Thus it befel that Edith Harnham found herself in the strange position of having to correspond, under no supervision, with a man not her lover, in terms which were those of a devoted sweetheart, the man being one for whom, mainly through the sympathies involved in playing this part, she secretly cherished a predilection, subtle and imaginative truly, but strong and absorbing.

APPENDIX C

THE FIRST DRAFT OF "TONY KYTES, THE ARCH-DECEIVER"

The writing in this first draft is often tentative, so full of contractions as to be in virtual note-form, has marginalia concerning possible developments, and is extremely skeletal when compared to the finished story. However, the germ of the story is here, as are some of the strengths of the finished version, such as the vivid imagery in the description of Tony in the first paragraph (some interestingly in the hand of Hardy's wife). Deletions are shown within angled brackets, insertions are within vertical lines, and words interlined above undeleted material are within slashes.

fo. 3a

<Tobias> |Tony| Kytes, the arch deceiver.
I shall never forget Tobe Kytes's face—Twas a little round firm tight face |with a| seam<ed with> |here & there| left by the small pox, <here & there> |though not engh to hurt his looks|; for he had it hard after you left./when he was a boy./ So very serious looking & unsmiling he was |that young man| that it really seemed as if he couldnt laugh to save his life. He looked very hard (at a small speck in your eye when talking to ye. There was no more sign of a whisker or beard on TK's face than on the palm of my hand. He used to sing with a religious face as if it were a hymn:) [*Hardy's note:*] ( ) in Emma's handwriting

I've lost my love & I care not. &c
He was quite the women's favourite, & he loved them |in shoals| in return. But in course of time he got fixed down to one in particular |Milly Roberts.| & it was soon sd. engagd. to be md. One day had been to market, doing business for his father; & was comg home in afternoon with his father's waggon. When he got to this very hill we're coming to who shd. he see waiting for him ahead but Unity Sallet, one of the /a handsome/ young women he'd <been> <|grown|> |been| very tender towards <at one> <since> |before| he'd got engaged to Milly (so that he almost wished he hadn't made up his mind so soon) As soon as he came up to her she sd. My dear Tobe, will ye give me a lift home? That I will darling said Tobe. You don't suppose I cd. refuse ye? And up she got. T: she sd. Why did you desert me for

that other one. I shd. have made you a more loving wife than
she. . . . |You deceived me T. &c| Well they talked on, when what shd.
T. see over the hedge past the turning but the feather he knew so well
<th> in the hat of Milly

fo. 4

the young woman with whom he was going to put up the banns of
marriage that next—

Unity, says he. There's Milly. Now I shall catch it mightily if she sees
you riding here with me: & if you get down she'll turn the corner in
a moment & see you in the road, & know we've been coming on
together. Now darling Unity, will ye<t> lie down in the |back part of
the| waggon & let me cover ye over with the tarpaulin till Milly's
passed? Do—& I'll think over what we've said, & perhaps I shall ask
you a question after all instead of Milly. Well Unity agreed, & lay
down in the waggon & T. covered her over: & then drove on to meet
Milly. My dear T. says Milly, looking up with a pout at him when he
got near, how long you've been coming home: & I've <been> come
to meet you as you asked me, to ride home with ye: & talk over our
future home. Ay my dear: I did ask ye—now I think of it—thgh I'd
quite forgot. To ride back with me, dear Milly.   ¶ Yes, of course.
Surely you don't wish me to walk, now I've come all this way.   ¶ O
no no. I thought you might be going on to town to meet your
mother: I saw her there; & I think she's expecting ye.   ¶ She's
home. She came across the fields, & has got before ye.   ¶ O. I didn't
know that, says T. And there<'s> was no help for it but to take her up
beside him.

Talked very lovingly. . . .
Presently who shd. they see crossing a path that led towards the
road they were following but Anna Jolliver—the last one he had
fallen love with—& the one he'd <promised secretly to marry> |al-
most wished he'd arranged| to marry instead of Milly—as she was
much finer & dashing girl than Milly.

My dear Milly—my coming wife, as I may call ye, says T. in his
modest way. I see a young woman comg who I think will accost me—
The fact is Milly she thought I was free to marry her. <When> |&
since| she found out I've promised you, I'm rather afeard of her
temper if she sees us together. Now M. would you do me a favour—
my comg wife, as I may say?   ¶ Certainly darling T. says she. Then
would ye creep under the tarpaulin just here <at> |in| the front of the

fo. 5

waggon |behind the seat,| & hide there out of sight till Anna has
passed? You see we ought to live in peace <& U> |& amity| & |perhaps|

twill prevent angry passions rising? says he—which we shd. do. <My>
With all my heart, dear T. says she, & crope under & crouched down
in the lspot inl front—Unity being safe at the other end.

And then he overtook Anna. She tossed her head a little disdainful, & looked sly . . .

Well—are n't you going to lbe civil enough tol ask me to ride? says
she, seeing he was for driving on.

Ah—To be sure to be sure! says T. What was I a thinking of But you
was going another way Anna?   ¶ No, says she . . .

She was up in a moment & T. with a face as long as a round face by
nater cd. in reason be drove on. She looked round sideways into his
eyes. This is nice, T. isn't it, she sd. I like riding with you. . . .

T. the more he looked at her the more he liked her, & he cdn't for
the life of him think why he'd ever said a word about marrying to
Milly while Anna was in question. So they sat a little closer & closer.
& he thought how pretty Anna was. & he spoke tenderer &
tenderer . . . "You've settled it with Milly I suppose, sd. A.

<No> N—no. Not exactly. says T.   ¶ I suppose you mean to? . . .
She looked in his face, & he looked in hers . . . How cd. he have been
such a fool. "My sweet A. he <says> bursts out not being really able to
help it, & forgetting M. & the other. I don't quite know about having
settled it—.

Hark, sd. A. all of a sudden. Surely I heard a sort of a little screamy
squeak under that tarpaulin? Why there's rats in this waggon, I'll
declare—or what can it be?

Oh, tis the axle," sd. T. It do go like that sometimes, in dry
weather.

Ah pps it was that, sd. A. Well, now—to be quite honest, dear T. Do
you like her better than me—Because—because—although I've held
off so independently I do like ye, T. to tell the truth—& I <won't>
lwould n'tl say no, if you asked me.

T. was so won over by her pretty way (A. had a pretty way with her,
if you can mind) that he just glanced behind, & then whispered very
softly: I <think I really> lhaven't quitel promised her, & I think I can
get out it, & marry you.

And throw over Milly l—all to marry mel l—how delightful! bursts
out A. clapping her hands.

fo. 6

At this there was another squeak—an angry, spitish squeak—& a
movement of the tarpaulin.   ¶ Something's there! sd. A quickly.

It's nothing really, says T. in a soothing tone, & looking <round>
laboutl for a way out of this. I wouldn't tell ye at first because I
wouldn't frighten ye, but I've <two>[*stet*] ferrets in a bag <just> under

there—& they quarrel sometimes. Oh—they can't get out, bless ye.
Tis a fine day, isn't it. Be you going to—Fair Anna. How's your
brother now. & so on, says T. to keep her from saying any more about
love. But he found his work cut out for him: & wondering how he
shd. get out of this he looked round again. Presently he |pretends he
sees—he| saw his /Anna's/ |<or Unity's>| father in a field, holding
up his hand, as if he wanted to speak to him. [*in margin:* Anna's
father—for sake of sequel] Wd. you mind taking the reins a moment
Anna, he sd <tho[?] he> while <he> I go & see what father wants?
<&> |He| handed them to her, & went into the field |glad to escape—
| saying as he went—How <I> shall I get out of this!

He found that his father was looking at him with rather a stern eye.
"Come Come, T. says his f. as soon as T. was alongside him. This
won't do you know.   ¶ What says T.   ¶ Why—if you mean to
marry Milly Roberts, do it, & there's an end o't—but don't go driving
about the country with Anna Jolliver /my daughter/, & making a
scandal. I won't have such things done.   ¶ I only asked her—she
asked me—to ride f.

She—Why now if 't had been M. <It[?]> twould have been quite
proper. You & Anna J. going about by yourselves—   ¶ Milly's there
too, father.   ¶ <What> |M? Where|?   ¶ <Well> |Under the tar-
paulin. Yes—| the fact is father, I've got rather into a quag.
<Newn[?]> Unity S. is there too—|Yes—under the tarpaulin.| All
three is in that waggon. & what to do with "em I don't know. |Perhaps
you've been in such quags in yr. time fr. & can tell me what to do.|
The best plan, I'm thinking is to speak out plain to one, before the
rest—& that will settle it. <But> Now which wd. you marry, if you were
in my place?   ¶ Whichever of 'em did <u>not</u> /has never/ ask|ed| <ye>
to ride with ye.   ¶ Well, Anna |often| asked/s/. & U. |often| asked/
s/—but M. never. I ask her.   ¶ Then stick to M. She's the best.
[*transposed from higher up leaf, from end of previous paragraph:*]   ¶ Now
look at that sd. his father |pointing towds the waggon|. She can't hold
that horse in—You shdn't have left the reins in her hands. |—Just run
on & take the horse's head—or there'll be some accident.| The
horse, in spite of A. had started on at a brisk walking pace, being very
anxious to get home to the stable, for he'd had a long day out. T.
hastened away from his fr. to overtake the waggon witht |stopping
for| another word. [*end of transposed material*] Making up his mind
that |since he cd. not marry them all| he cd. not marry M. but that it
must be A. <since he>

Now all this while queer things had |been| happen<ed>|ing| in that
waggon. As you'll have guessed, it was M. who had screamed under
the tarpaulin, being obliged to let

fo. 7

to let off her bitter rage that way, at what T. was saying: & not daring to show that she was in hiding, for very pride |& shame|. <Well> She <was very> |became more & more| restless—& in twisting herself what did she see but another woman's foot & white stocking |close to her head;|: & it quite frightened her, not knowing that Unity was in the waggon likewise. <Milly> But after her fright she was determined to get to the bottom of this: & she crept & crept along the bottom of the waggon |under the cloth| like a snake: & lo & behold she came face to face with U.

Well—if this isn't disgraceful! says M.   ¶ 'Tis, says U. to see you hiding in a |young| man's waggon like this: & no great character belonging to either of ye.   ¶ Mind what you are saying! sd. Milly |getting louder—| I am engaged to be married to him: & have n't I a right to be here, I shd. like to know? What's he been promising you? A pretty lot of nonsense, I expect. But what h[*possibly mended to a* T]im says to other women is all wind.   ¶ Don't you be too sure, says U. He's going to have Anna: & neither you nor me either: I can see that!" Now at <this h> these strange |quarrelling| voices coming from under the cloth Anna <sat> |was| thunderstruck: & <the way she held> |just then the h. moved on. Anna| tugged away wildly at the reins, not knowing what she was doing. But the horse took no notice & as the quarrel got louder & louder she let go the reins altogether: on went the horse, & coming to the corner where we go round to get down the hill to Lewgate turned too quickly; the off wheels went up the bank, the waggon rose sideways, till it was quite on edge upon the near axles—& out rolled all three girls into the road one upon the other.

When T. came up, frightened & breathless, he was relieved enough to see that <nobody> |neither of his darlings| was hurt— but[*over* &] he was rather alarmed again when he heard how they were going on at one another. Don't 'ee[*mended to* ye] quarrel, my dears—don't ye! he says, taking off his hat out of respect to 'em |& then he kissed 'em all <roug> round, as fair as a man could.| Now I'll speak out honest, because I ought to. And this is the truth. I've asked Anna to be mine: & she's willing: |& we are going to put up the banns next—| & I hope—

|Now T. hadn't seen that A's father come up behind . . . hated T . . . | She is <u>not</u> willing, sir! says Anna /'s father—(registrar (Mr Cox))/ hot & strong, for she was the one of the three that had most spirit. [*In margin:* Modify to A's fr. takes him [*sic*] away. <u>She</u> wd. have accepted him. (She is Betsy C.)] Little did I think when I was soft with

you just now that I was talking to such a false deceiver. <No, n>   ¶
What—you won't have me, A? says T. his <chops> |jaw| hanging down
like a dead man's.   ¶ Never. I'd sooner marry a scarecrow /
mormon/. |And away she walked with her head in the clouds.| T. did
n't know what to say. Milly was sobbing away: but as his father had
recommended her he couldn't feel inclined that way. So he turned
to U.   ¶ Well, will you, U. he says.   ¶ What |take| her leavings—
I shd. think not! says U. & walked away likewise. So

fo. 8

there at last were left M. & T. by themselves, <But T. cdn't> she crying
|in streams,| <bucketfuls> & T.like a tree struck by lightning. Well, M.
he says at last. It do seem as if fate had ordained that it shd. be you
& I, or nobody. & what must be must be, I suppose. So he kissed her:
& put the waggon right. & they mounted together: & their banns was
put up the very next Sunday.

I was<n't> at their wedding. But I was at Unity's: she married
Jolliver, the farmer . . . [*previous sentence was deleted in pencil which was
then erased:* "still"[?] *written in erased pencil above* "farmer"] And a very
good wedding it was—a regular rattler. She bore T. no ill will; for he
& his wife Milly were asked to the party. |¶ Yes—sd.—| And 'twas the
cause of <a> |that| very awkward meeting: which nearly <ruined>
|spoilt| /which you can. . . . / the <party> evening

Oh—what was that? sd. . . .

EXPLANATORY NOTES

THERE is no one manuscript for *Life's Little Ironies*. In these notes 'MS' refers to the individual extant manuscripts. These are as follows: 'An Imaginative Woman' in Aberdeen University Library; 'The Son's Veto' in Bibliotheca Bodmeriana, Geneva; 'For Conscience' Sake' and 'A Tragedy of Two Ambitions', both in John Rylands University Library of Manchester; 'On the Western Circuit' in Manchester Central Public Library; 'A Few Crusted Characters' ['Wessex Folk'] in the Berg Collection, New York Public Library [also one leaf of a later manuscript of 'Wessex Folk' reproduced in *Harper's Monthly Magazine*, July 1925, p. 241].

The following sigla are used here for particular editions of *Life's Little Ironies*:

A1   American first edition.
E1   English first edition.
WE Wessex Edition.

The following abbreviations for source material are also used in the notes:

Brady	Kristin Brady, *The Short Stories of Thomas Hardy* (1982).
Kay-Robinson	Denys Kay-Robinson, *Hardy's Wessex Re-appraised* (1972).
Letters	Richard Little Purdy and Michael Millgate (eds.), *The Collected Letters of Thomas Hardy*, 7 vols. (Oxford, 1978–88).
Life	Florence Emily Hardy, *The Life of Thomas Hardy 1840–1928* (1962).
Pinion	F. B. Pinion, *A Thomas Hardy Dictionary* (1989).
Purdy	Richard Little Purdy, *Thomas Hardy: A Bibliographical Study* (1954).

An Imaginative Woman

Hardy refers to payment of £100 'for world serial rights in a story of 6000 words' in letters of 26 March and 14 April 1893 (letters to

W. M. Colles; *Letters*, ii. 5, 7), and on 13 July he promises to start on
the story 'as soon as possible; but not till after next week, when I have
to be in London' (*Letters*, ii. 22). The story was ready by 14 September (letter to W. M. Colles; *Letters*, ii. 32), although Hardy noted in
Life (p. 260) that he 'Found and touched up a short story called "An
Imaginative Woman"' in December 1893. The story was first published in *The Pall Mall Magazine* for April 1894 in a slightly
bowdlerized version (but with Hardy's permission—see letter to the
editor, Sir Douglas Straight, 20 January 1894) and was collected into
Wessex Tales in 1896 before being transferred to *Life's Little Ironies* in
the 1912 Wessex Edition. According to Pinion the story is 'based on
a psychological fantasy Hardy found in Weisman's *Essays on Heredity*,
i. 457–61. . . . Undoubtedly its imaginings were fanned by Hardy's
love of Mrs Henniker, who lived at Southsea'. Pinion also points out
that Robert Trewe [Crewe in MS] is 'drawn considerably from the
poet Dante Gabriel Rossetti [1828–82], and the idealization of his
lady in *The House of Life*.'

7 *Solentsea in Upper Wessex*: Southsea, Hampshire.

　"a votary of the muse": cf. 'the votaries of the northern Muses', Dr
　Johnson.

8 *mentally walked round it*: cf. 'she had mentally walked round love':
　written of Eustacia Vye (*The Return of the Native*, part 1, ch. 7).

10 *the Island opposite*: the Isle of Wight which is across the Solent
　from Southsea.

11 *embayed*: shut in.

　symboliste nor décadent: Hardy had read an article on Symbolists
　and Décadents in contemporary French literature in *Revue des
　Deux Mondes*, 1 November 1881 (Pinion).

12 *afflatus*: inspiration; overmastering poetic impulse.

13 *jerry-built*: unsubstantially built of poor materials.

14 *cheap-trippers*: a cheap-trip is an excursion.

15 *The mantle of Elijah*: Elijah puts his cloak on Elisha who then
　becomes his disciple (1 Kings 19).

16 *"Severed Lives"*: cf. D. G. Rossetti's 'Severed Selves'.

18 *Budmouth*: Weymouth.

　black moustache and imperial . . . slouched hat: Pinion suggests that
　Hardy bases his description of Trewe on Holman Hunt's por-
　trait of D. G. Rossetti 'and the "slouched hat" of his later years'.
　An imperial is a small tuft of hair growing beneath the lower lip,
　so called because the Emperor Napoleon III wore one. A

slouched hat is one of soft material, with a broad brim which hangs down over the face.

19 *bouts-rimés*: rhymed endings, that a poet might use.

Shelley's scraps: poetic fragments left in note-books by Shelley at his death.

Forms more real . . . immortality: Shelley's 'Prometheus Unbound', i. 748–9.

20 *sleeping on a poet's lips*: cf. 'On a poet's lips I slept | Dreaming like a love-adept', Shelley's 'Prometheus Unbound', i. 737–8.

if I can. . . .: MS includes the following passage, removed for *The Pall Mall Magazine*:

He passed through into the dressing-room communicating, and she could hear him pulling off his clothes. She wondered which of the rooms he was going to occupy, and finding that he showed no sign of withdrawing she said,
'That is a comfortable little bed in the upper room, isn't it?'
'O yes,' he replied. 'Well no, it isn't. It is so beastly narrow.'

What the devil's: bowdlerized in *The Pall Mall Magazine* to 'What the deuce'.

22 *the fashionable town on the Island opposite*: identified by Kay-Robinson (p. 187) as Ryde, Isle of Wight.

packet: packet-boat, a vessel plying at regular intervals between two ports, carrying mail, goods, and passengers.

permanent way: the railway.

24 *Behold he standeth . . . heard in our land*: Song of Solomon 2: 9, 11–12. [verse 8, 'leaping upon the mountains, skipping upon the hills', is deleted in MS].

chiton: the ancient Greek tunic.

25 *tremolo stop*: a mechanical contrivance in an organ to produce a vibrating effect.

turnpike-road: a main road with toll-gates.

28 *God is a jealous God*: Exodus 20: 5.

The hour which might . . . life was barren: D. G. Rossetti, Sonnet XXVIII, 'Stillborn Love'.

29 *flys*: a fly is a one-horse, covered carriage.

32 *Then she did play . . . yes . . .*: these lines were omitted from *The Pall Mall Magazine*. Brady (p. 210) suggests that the idea here 'may have been suggested to Hardy by Ibsen's *The Lady from*

the Sea, in which a child's eyes uncannily resemble those of his mother's former lover, whom she had seen while she was pregnant'.

The Son's Veto

First published in the Christmas Number of *The Illustrated London News*, 1891 (1 December) and collected into the first edition of *Life's Little Ironies*. Hardy had written to his wife on 16 April 1891, 'I think we must settle down in a quiet lodging, where I can work, for I am quite indifferent to society at present: & am engrossed in the matter of a story which shall have its scene in London—I am going out looking about on that account now' (*Letters*, i. 232). Before E1 Sam is called Ned (probably altered because 'Ned' is also used in 'The Fiddler of the Reels').

33 *black beaver hat*: a hat made of beaver fur.

  poll: the top of the head, or, more likely here, the nape of the neck.

35 *North Wessex*: an area approximating to Berkshire and south-west Oxfordshire.

  Aldbrickham: Reading (Oldbrickham before E1).

  Gaymead: identified as Theale, WSW of Reading (Pinion).

37 *tie-beams*: horizontal beams connecting rafters in a roof.

38 *glebe*: a portion of land assigned to a clergyman as part of his benefice.

40 *milieu*: environment; here specifically Sophy's social circle.

  Covent Garden market: cf. *Life*, p. 210: '*July* 7 [1888]. One o'clock A.M. I got out of bed, attracted by the never-ending procession [of market-carts to Covent Garden] as seen from our bedroom windows, Phillimore Place. Chains rattle, and each cart cracks under its weighty pyramid of vegetables.' The description was greatly expanded for E1.

  howdahs: a howdah is a seat for riding on an elephant.

45 *débris of luxurious luncheons*: the detail of these luncheons was added for E1.

47 *dropped for months*: originally 'dropped for three years': the addition of more attempts by Sophy to plead with her son was made for E1.

For Conscience' Sake

First published as 'For Conscience Sake' in the *Fortnightly Review*, March 1891, for which Hardy received £17 (letter to H. Blanchamp 6 March 1891; *Letters*, i. 230). The three parts were originally called respectively: 'Sherton-Street, W.'; 'High Street, Exonbury'; and 'London again'. The origin of the story may owe something to a tale Hardy was told in December 1882 'of a girl . . . who had been betrayed and deserted by a lover. She kept her child by her own exertions, and lived bravely and throve. After a time the man returned poorer than she, and wanted to marry her; but she refused . . . The eminently modern idea embodied in this example— of a woman's not becoming necessarily the chattel and slave of her seducer—impressed Hardy as being one of the first glimmers of woman's enfranchisement' (*Life*, p. 157).

49 *utilitarian or the intuitive theory of the moral sense*: the utilitarian theory would regard the greatest good or happiness of the greatest number as the chief consideration; the intuitive would be guided by intuition.

50 *Toneborough, in Outer Wessex*: Taunton, Devon.

51 *Exonbury*: Exeter.

58 *Ivell*: Yeovil.

59 *in the Island*: before E1, 'at Cowes'.

60 *Nausea in such circumstances*: for comment by Hardy on facial change cf. 'Cold weather brings out upon the faces of people the written marks of their habits, vices, passions, and memories . . .' (*Life*, p. 177). Brady (p. 210) suggests that 'this incident may have been suggested by Harrison Ainsworth's *Old St Paul's* . . . , in which the heroine and her mother are described as suddenly resembling each other while they are parting, "for intense emotion, whether of grief or joy, will bring out lines in the features that lie hidden at other times".' Cf. also 'In sleep there come to the surface buried genealogical facts, ancestral curves, dead men's traits, which the mobility of daytime animation screens and overwhelms.' (*The Mayor of Casterbridge*, ch. 19).

62 *apple of discord*: the apple of discord was the golden apple thrown by Eris, the personification of discord, into the assembly of Gods. The strife it caused among Hera, Athene, and Aphrodite as to which goddess was the fairest led to the 'Judgement of Paris' which was in favour of Aphrodite because she could prom-

ise Paris the most beautiful woman. His abduction of the beautiful Helen caused the Trojan War.

63 *feast of Hymen*: marriage celebration, Hymen being the god of marriage.

66 *Antigone*: Sophocles' *Antigone*, 'by burying her brother she obeys the unwritten law of Heaven, but breaks the law of the state and forfeits her life' (Pinion).

The reference to Antigone was added to the text for the *Fortnightly Review*. In MS Millborne was at first 'burdened with weariness of life', but 'life' is deleted and replaced by an insertion which did not appear in print: 'his fellow creatures—ever answering negatively, as he sat and smoked among men, the inquiry in the *Hippolytus*: "What reserved person is not hateful?—And in the sociable is there any charm?"'

the Cercle: social club.

A Tragedy of Two Ambitions

First published in *The Universal Review*, December 1888. An alternative title in MS was 'The Shame of the Halboroughs'. In a letter to Harry Quilter, editor of *The Universal Review*, Hardy wrote: 'I have in my head a story of a different character [i.e. different from "The Melancholy Hussar"]—embodying present day aspirations—i.e., concerning the ambitions of two men, their struggles for education, a position in the Church, & so on, ending tragically . . . it exists only in the form of half a dozen notes' (24 July 1888; *Letters*, i. 178). A week later he described himself as 'at present up to the elbows in a cold blooded murder which I hope to get finished in a day or two' (letter to Edmund Gosse, 1 August 1888; *Letters*, i. 179). He sent the story to Quilter on 19 August 1888 (*Life*, p. 213).

67 *Homeric blows . . . Argonautic voyaging . . . Theban family woe*: 'Homeric blows and knocks' refer to the fighting between Greeks and Trojans in the *Iliad*; 'Argonautic voyaging' refers to Jason and his voyage in the Argo in search of the golden fleece; 'Theban family woe' refers to the disasters of Oedipus and his family.

Dog-day sun: the hottest period in England (early July to mid-August).

an old-fashioned country tradesman: in MS Halborough's occupation is changed from miller to millwright.

68 *float-boards*: the boards of a water-wheel.

Donnegan's Lexicon: *New Greek and English Lexicon* by James Donnegan (1826).

mother's nine hundred pound: a revision made in page proofs for E1; in earlier texts (and A1) the sum is seven hundred.

national schoolmasters: a National School was a school organized by the National Society (founded 1811, to promote education of the poor according to Church of England principles).

licentiates: those licensed to preach but not yet appointed to a church.

without a hood: i.e. not having a university degree.

69 *semi-clerical dress*: in the dress of a cleric, with a dog-collar, but without a cassock.

70 *"heard his days before him"*: cf. Tennyson, 'Locksley Hall', 110.

71 *construing*: translating.

a title: a guarantee of support required by the bishop from a candidate for ordination.

Sandbourne: Bournemouth (see letter to B. Windle, 28 September 1896, *Letters* ii).

72 *Paley's Evidences*: *Evidences of Christianity* (1794), by William Paley, English theologian (1743–1805).

Pusey's Library of the Fathers: Edward B. Pusey (1800–82), English theologian and leader of the Oxford Movement. He began the *Oxford Library of the Fathers* in 1836.

Archbishop Tillotson . . . Clare College: John Tillotson (1630–94). He studied at Clare Hall, Cambridge, becoming a fellow in 1651. Archbishop of Canterbury 1691–4.

73 *alma mater*: the university attended (literally, 'bounteous mother'—Latin).

73 *Fountall Theological College*: Fountall is Wells. In a letter to Walter Tyndale (16 November 1904) Hardy wrote that 'Wells Cathedral and Close came a good deal into "A Tragedy of Two Ambitions".'

75 *Binegar Fair*: in the Mendip Hills not far from Wells (Pinion).

drop of Old Tom: a kind of strong gin.

secondly . . . gentleman: this passage was added for E1 to heighten the satire aimed at Joshua's concept of his vocation.

76 *Narrobourne*: one of the Coker villages, south of Yeovil.

76 *Lord . . . helper!*: Psalms 30: 10.

   indifferentism: an indifferentist is one who lacks religious zeal.

78 *désinvolture*: ease of manner (French).

79 *a Dorcas, or Martha, or Rhoda*: meaning a plain, industrious, homely girl. The story of Dorcas (or Tabitha) says: 'this woman was full of good works and almsdeeds which she did' (Acts 9: 36–43). See also Luke 10: 38–42 and Acts 12: 12–13.

80 *the cloud no bigger than a man's hand*: 'There ariseth a little cloud out of the sea, like a man's hand' (1 Kings 18: 44). Thus, the precursor of a storm.

84 *Hendford Hill*: in Yeovil, on the main road south.

87 *In their pause . . . save him twice over*: added in WE.

   kerseymere: fine, twilled woollen cloth.

89 *hatches had to be drawn*: the floodgates in the weir had to be opened.

91 *To tell the truth, the Church*: in MS Joshua first said 'Damn the Church', which Hardy wisely decided against.

92 *a straight little silver-poplar*: Pinion comments, 'the stick turned tree (an external sign of implanted and undying guilt) was suggested by the Bockhampton tradition of a carter's whip-handle which grew into a willow tree after he had been drowned in Heedless William's Pond.' In MS Joshua had picked up his father's walking-stick and 'thrust it into the sedge', but the detail of it taking root was not introduced until E1.

   Hebrews: 'Jesus . . . who for the joy that was set before him endured the cross, despising the shame' (Hebrews 12: 2).

On the Western Circuit

Magazine publication was arranged by A. P. Watt simultaneously in *The English Illustrated Magazine*, December 1891, and *Harper's Weekly*, 28 November 1891. Hardy had sent the story to Watt at the beginning of September 1891 (see *Letters*, i. 243). It was collected in the first edition of *Life's Little Ironies*. The title refers to the practice of having a court that moved around the West Country to hear cases; there is a reference to 'the two judges on the Western Circuit' in *Far from the Madding Crowd* (ch. 55). In MS the title is written over pencil and above two deleted ink titles, 'The Writer of the Letters' and 'The Amanuensis'. The magazine versions are considerably bowdlerized, so that Edith Harnham is a widow, her husband is metamorphosed into an uncle, Anna's physical relations with Raye are played down, and her pregnancy is glossed over (see Appendix B, which reproduces the longer passages of textual variants).

93 *Melchester*: Salisbury. 'Old Melchester', mentioned later in the story, is Old Sarum, the earthworks outside Salisbury.

  the Close: the precinct of the Cathedral.

  steam barrel-organs: musical instruments (whose cylinder revolved to create the sound), driven by steam-engines.

  the eighth chasm of the Inferno: 'Malebolge, all of stone, and iron-coloured (Dante, *Inferno* xviii, 1–2)' (Pinion, p. 144).

  the Homeric heaven: as merry as the gods in Homer's Heaven—see end of *Iliad* Bk 1 (Pinion).

  naphtha lamps: lamps lit by naphtha oil, distilled from coal, shale, and petroleum.

94 *spring . . . pitch*: rise and fall.

95 *rococo-work*: lavish decoration, with ornate features such as shell- and scroll-work.

  sparkish: having the manner of a spark or gallant.

  journeyman-carpenters: a journeyman is one who has served his apprenticeship but is not yet a master-craftsman.

96 *the Great Plain*: Salisbury Plain.

  Mrs Harnham: according to Pinion (pp. 200–1), Mrs Harnham's name comes from Harnham Bridge at Salisbury and Constable's picture of Salisbury from Harnham Hill. There are villages just south of Salisbury named West and East Harnham.

  Wintoncester: Winchester.

97 *rough pea-jacket and wideawake*: a pea-jacket is a short overcoat of heavy wool; a wideawake is a soft, wide-brimmed, felt hat.

  stuff-gownsman: a junior counsel, wearing a gown made from cloth (as distinct from the silk of a Queen's Counsel).

100 *a black-coated man*: a man from the professional classes.

101 *calendar*: a list of prisoners for trial at the assizes.

  Casterbridge: Dorchester.

  Assyrian bas-reliefs: like the conventionally sculptured hair in the bas-reliefs of ancient Assyria, which Hardy was familiar with in the British Museum (Pinion).

102 *won her, body and soul*: a revision for E1: MS has 'won her en-
      tirely'; the bowdlerized magazine texts have 'won her heart
      entirely'.

104 *ensemble*: all the parts taken together as a whole.

107 *pis aller*: last resort.

      That he had . . . she-animal: this sentence was added in the page
      proofs for E1.

108 *protégée*: one under the care or protection of another.

110 *rough copies . . . many letters . . . not sent on at all*: before E1 the
      copies were 'exact' and the abridged copies 'consisted of heads
      rather than of details': that many letters were not sent is an E1
      addition.

      fairly educated . . . elementary schools: before E1 Miss Raye de-
      scribes Anna as 'fairly ladylike', 'And bright-minded'. Their as-
      sessment of how Anna expresses herself and writes was added to
      the printer's copy for E1, and the references to 'educated' and
      elementary schools were added in the galley proofs.

111 *don't bear his child*: 'have no child' MS; 'have no lover' *Harper's
      Weekly*; 'have neither lover nor child' *English Illustrated Magazine*.

      the woolsack: the seat of the Lord Chancellor in the House of
      Lords, and thus referring to the office of Lord Chancellor.

114 *or rather ratification of a previous union*: this aside is suppressed in
      the magazine texts.

      Knollsea: Swanage; 'Tunbridge Wells' in MS and magazines, and
      'Solentsea' in E1 before galley revisions.

115 *She slid . . . face against him*: the sentence is not in MS; 'She
      passionately clasped his waist and laid her face against him' in
      magazines; E1 is as the edited text ('abjectly' replacing 'passion-
      ately' in the galley proof revisions).

117 *Simultaneously with Edith's journey* . . . : the final scene of the story
      was an afterthought in the MS.

To Please his Wife

First published in *Black and White*, 27 June 1891; collected in first
edition of *Life's Little Ironies*. Hardy had sold the right 'to make use of
the story how, when, & as long as you please' to S. S. McClure for £50
(letter to S. S. McClure, 13 September 1890; *Letters*, i. 216). It
appeared also (with only styling variants) in *Stories from 'Black and*

White' (London 1892/3), *Stories from Black and White* (New York 1893), and reprints by Croome & Co., Richard Butterworth & Co., and others.

Hardy uses the end of the story in 'The Sailor's Mother' (*Late Lyrics and Earlier*):

"O whence do you come,
Figure in the night-fog that chills me numb?"

"I come to you across from my house up there,
And I don't mind the brine-mist clinging to me
    That blows from the quay,
For I heard him in my chamber, and thought you unaware."

    "But what did you hear,
That brought you blindly knocking in this middle-watch so drear?"

"My sailor son's voice as 'twere calling at your door,
And I don't mind my bare feet clammy on the stones,
    And the blight to my bones,
For he knows only of *this* house I lived in before."

"Nobody's nigh,
Woman like a skeleton, with socket-sunk eye."

"Ah—nobody's nigh! And my life is drearisome,
And this is the old home we loved in many a day
    Before he went away;
And the salt fog mops me. And nobody's come!"

119 *St James's Church, in Havenpool Town*: Havenpool was identified as
    Poole by Hardy (letter to B. Windle). The name 'Jolliffe' is that
    of a famous citizen of Poole who captured a French privateer in
    1694; all four surnames are from memorial tablets in St James's
    Church (John Hutchins, *The History and Antiquities of the County
    of Dorset* (1861), pp. 47–9).

125 *Town Hall*: identified by Kay-Robinson as the Old Guildhall,
    Poole.

127 *The way to wealth . . . this route*: sentence added in WE.

129 *sovereigns and guineas*: gold coins worth respectively twenty shil-
    lings (a pound) and twenty-one shillings (the latter not minted
    since 1813).

133 *the University . . . for them*: an addition made in E1 galleys to point
    up further the difference between the fortunes and status of the
    two families.

135 *Town Cellar*: the Town Cellar is on the quay in Poole.

136 *gone to the bottom*: WE revision, much blunter than 'could not return'.

The Fiddler of the Reels

First published in *Scribner's Magazine*, May 1893. 'This was a special "Exhibition Number" for the Chicago World's Fair, which accounts for Hardy's opening lines and his use of the Great Exhibition of 1851' (Purdy, p. 82). Hardy's fascination with such exhibitions is evident when he mentions that the fact that the Great Exhibition of 1862 was about to be opened 'perhaps influenced him in the choice of a date for his migration [to London]' (*Life*, p. 35). Scribner wrote to commission a story on 28 October 1892 (see *Letters*, i. 289): *The Fiddler of the Reels* was posted to the publisher on 13 January 1893. It was collected in the first edition of *Life's Little Ironies*.

137 *South Wessex*: Dorset.

   geological "fault": a break in continuity of the strata, which would bring together rocks of different ages.

   the Conquest: the Battle of Hastings (1066) when the Normans conquered Britain.

   Stickleford, Mellstock, and Egdon: the area which is the setting for several of Hardy's works, particularly *The Return of the Native*. Mellstock is based on Stinsford and Bockhampton where Hardy was born and brought up. Stickleford is based on Tincleton, 4 miles east of Stinsford.

138 *Greenhill Fair*: Woodbury Hill near Bere Regis. Hardy wrote of himself: 'While thus in the seclusion of Bockhampton, writing *Far from the Madding Crowd*, we find him on September 21 [1873], walking to Woodbury-Hill Fair, approximately described in the novel as "Greenhill Fair"' (*Life*, p. 96).

   "*boys'-love*" (*southernwood*): an aromatic shrub.

   Paganini: Niccolo Paganini, an Italian violinist (1782–1840).

   lingual character: as though formed by the tongue.

139 *Mellstock quire-band . . . Dewys, Mail*: the Mellstock Quire appears in several of Hardy's novels and poems (particularly *Under the Greenwood Tree*), and is based upon the group of church musicians of the Stinsford parish in which his father and grand-

father played in the early nineteenth century (see *Life*, pp. 8–12).

tranter: a carrier of goods or passengers.

the Wold Hundredth: 'Old Hundredth' is a musical setting of Psalm 100, 'All people that on earth do dwell', dating from the mid-sixteenth century and retained for the metrical form of the psalm by Nahum Tate and Nicholas Brady (1696). It is mentioned as one of the staple tunes of the Stinsford choir (*Life*, p. 10).

brazen serpent: a serpent was a bass wind instrument about 8 feet long, formed with three U-shaped turns, usually made of wood covered with leather (although 'brazen' indicates brass).

Lower Mellstock: Lower Bockhampton.

140 *Moreford*: Moreton, in the Frome valley; in *Scribner's Magazine* it was 'six miles eastward'.

galvanic: electric.

141 *serious lovemakings*: before WE these were less explicitly 'serious performances'.

withywind: bindweed.

142 *railway to South Wessex*: the railway between Dorchester and Waterloo, opened by the time the story has moved on below by four years.

145 *But who's the father? . . . courted me*: added in WE.

146 *catched the first time he took advantage o' me*: 'catched' (*Scribner's Magazine*); 'catched the first time' (E1); the final and most explicit version is from WE.

148 *Heedless-William's Pond . . . Bloom's End . . . Quiet Woman . . . Egdon Heath*: the area of *The Return of the Native*, in which the Quiet Woman's sign is described as 'the figure of a matron carrying her head under her arm, beneath which gruesome design was written the couplet so well known to frequenters of the inn:—/SINCE THE WOMAN'S QUIET /LET NO MAN BREED A RIOT' (Wessex Edition, p. 46)

150 *saltatory*: leaping or dancing.

Lewgate: according to Pinion (p. 164), the upper end of Higher Bockhampton, near the heath, the name being suggested for the Hardy's home there.

My Fancy-Lad . . . The Fairy Dance: these are listed among the airs that Hardy's father played and which moved the young Hardy to tears (*Life*, p. 15). They are also both mentioned in Hardy's poem 'The Dance at the Phoenix', in which music and dance prove the fatal undoing of an old woman who had reformed after a wild youth.

151 *foods of love*: cf. 'If music be the food of love . . .' (*Twelfth Night*, I. i. 1).

153 *Blast him!*: revised in E1 galleys from 'Curse him!'

Yalbury coppices: Yellowham Wood.

Dantesque gloom: like scenes in Dante's *Inferno*.

154 *She's throwed up the sperrits*: E1 galley revision of 'The drink's gone out o' her', itself an addition for the E1 text.

distracted by his passionate . . . not his own: before WE, Ned was merely 'distracted'.

and how he could . . . mystery: added for E1.

A Few Crusted Characters

The extant MS not only has several leaves missing, but is largely first draft. The Introduction, for example, is often merely notes, is full of contracted word-forms, and has several alternative readings (e.g. three versions of Flaxton's name, none of which is eventually used); in the left-hand margin Hardy keeps count of the number of passengers in the carrier's van; whilst interlined above the first line is the question 'winter or summer?' (in the printed texts Hardy decides on autumn). The group of stories was first published in four monthly parts as 'Wessex Folk' in *Harper's New Monthly Magazine*, March–June 1891, and collected as part of the first edition of *Life's Little Ironies*. 'Absentmindedness in a Parish Choir' appeared also in *The One and All Reciter*, ed. Marshall Steele (published J. Lane, 1909).

156 *high street . . . market-town . . . White Hart Inn*: the well-known market-town is Casterbridge (Dorchester), where the White Hart Inn stands at the bottom of High East Street. The Inn features in other of Hardy's work, including *Far from the Madding Crowd*.

Longpuddle: Hardy identifies Longpuddle as Piddlehinton and Piddletrenthide (*Letters*, ii, 28 September 1896). MS has 'Upper Joggingford', and gives the journey as 7 miles (fo. 1).

diligences: public stage-coaches in France.

157 *the bridge . . . last outpost of town*: Grey's Bridge, Dorchester.

159 *Lackland*: for someone returning to their native place after being absent a long time cf. 'Welcome Home' (*Late Lyrics and Earlier*). In MS his name is given as Trent and Trantwell.

160 *the race . . . battle to the strong*: Ecclesiastes. 2: 'The race is not to the swift . . .'

Tony Kytes, the Arch-Deceiver

MS has the main character's name as Tobias or Tobe. The section where Tony goes to talk to his father in the field is as originally intended in MS, but MS also contains a note in the margin that it needs to be 'Anna[i.e. Hannah]'s father for sake of sequel', and the text is marked with alternatives consistent with that (e.g. 'my daughter' interlined above 'Anna Jolliver'). The sequel referred to is Hardy's decision to have Anna's father arrive at the point where Tony is announcing that he has proposed to Anna. Originally she herself says 'she is *not* willing', but Hardy interlines the arrival of her father and that he should say these words. In the margin Hardy notes: 'Modify to A[nna]'s f[athe]r takes him [*sic*] away. *She* w[oul]d have accepted him.'

160 *"The Tailor's Breeches"*: this replaces for E1 a verse, 'I've lost my love, and I care not' etc., which Hardy had already used in *Far from the Madding Crowd* (ch. 23).

167 *Lower Longpuddle*: 'Lewgate' in MS.

The History of the Hardcomes

In the MS this was titled 'Incident at a wedding party', which, in the preamble to the tale (fo. 8), was not Tony's but that of Unity to Jolliver the farmer, although it is later referred to as 'T.K.'s wedding' (fo. 12). James is 'Jose' in the MS, for which sections are missing.

169 *Climmerston*: Higher Waterston in the Piddle Valley, NE of Dorchester.

170 *Abbot's-Cernel, and Weatherbury, and Mellstock*: Cerne Abbas, Puddletown, and Bockhampton respectively.

"Put" and "All-fours": two card games.

173 *Budmouth-Regis*: Weymouth. Where the train is mentioned below, the phrase 'the line being just opened' was added in E1.

clerk turned to the curate: in MS the story-telling is not passed to the curate at this point.

178 *Lullwind Bay*: Lulworth Cove; 'Lullstead Bay' before WE.

"*in their death they were not divided*": referring to Saul and Jonathan (2 Samuel 1: 23).

179 *living in Longpuddle still*: in MS 'the American gent[le]m[an]' asks 'And are they living?' As well as the answer surviving in printed texts there is also the alternative: 'I don't know. They went off to Australia.'

The Superstitious Man's Story

In MS the melancholy man who narrates this story is 'the master thatcher'. Longpuddle is Lewgate in MS and a couple of minor characters' names are slightly different. The incident in which Betsy Privett encounters Nancy Weedle and the superstition attached to Old Midsummer Eve is added on a verso in MS. Hardy wrote concerning this story:

"The incident of the 'miller moth' flying out of a man's mouth at the moment of his death—supposed to be his soul—is or was a belief of this county.

"The spot whereon the particular instance of it that I had in mind is assumed to have occurred was a place called 'Buttock's Spring' [so named in MS for Longpuddle Spring] in the parish of Melbury Osmond.

"How old the superstition may be I do not know. The old lady who told it me [possibly Hardy's mother] said it happened in her childhood, & that would have been about 1820.

"The common white moth is still called a 'miller's soul' by the peasantry, for obvious reasons." (Letter to E. B. Poulton, 20 May 1924). See also the letter to Edward Clodd (*Letters*, ii, 1 April 1894).

180 *bell that was ringing for church*: cf. 'Premonitions' (*Human Shows*): 'The bell went heavy to-day I At afternoon service, they say . . .' The addition 'he feared it meant a death in the parish' (which gives the storyteller credentials as a superstitious man), replaced in WE the more prosaic explanation 'it was just as if the gudgeons wanted oiling'.

181 *Old Midsummer Eve*: 5 July.

Michaelmas: 29 September.

Andrey Satchel and the Parson and Clerk

In the MS this was titled 'The story of the Parson & Clerk'. The end of the story is missing and the MS shows signs of much detail being added during the writing; for example, the bride's suggestion that the clerk lock her and Andrey up in the tower is an addition written on a verso. The parson's name is given as Mr Matthew and the clerk's as Simeon. See the 1896 Preface for Hardy's comment on the model for Parson Toogood (Appendix A). A great number of changes for E1 concern the pronunciation and vocabulary of the master-thatcher who is telling the story.

Cf. Hardy's note: 'The honest Earl. Earl is accidentally shut up in a tower—the Hardy monument, say—with a blacksmith's daughter. Goes to parson next day & says he feels it his duty to marry her. Does so. Finds her not so good as she seemed, & . . .' (Memoranda I, November 1878, *Personal Notebooks of Thomas Hardy*, ed. R. Taylor, p. 19).

184 *owing to that young man*: this more explicit comment was added in WE.

November: MS has January deleted and replaced by December.

driving . . . Port Bredy: Port Bredy is Bridport. MS has 'by walking to C[asterbridge] & go on to B[udmouth]'.

the christening: in MS Andrey's brother's child had been christened the previous day (not his neighbour's).

185 *seeing the condition you are in*: added in WE.

Van Amburgh's horses: according to Pinion, Van Amburgh was an American circus manager and exhibitionist (1801–65) who travelled with his 'show' in England.

186 *In short, except o' Sundays . . .* : this paragraph describing Parson Billy's obsession with hunting was added for E1.

188 *Lippet Wood and Green's Copse*: MS has Yalbury Wood and Green's Wood.

Higher Jirton . . . Waterston Ridge . . . Yalbury Wood: MS is much less specific: 'up hill and down dale'. Waterston is WE revision of Climmerston.

189 *to everything there's a season*: Ecclesiastes 3: 1.

up the clock-case: cf. 'Lord Portsmouth made his whipper-in tell Emma the story of the hunted fox that ran up the old woman's clock-case' (*Life*, p. 183: concerning a visit made in October 1886).

190 *It is, sir; very . . . plain honest men.*): this extension to the conversation concerning the possible consequences of not having married the couple before going hunting was added for E1.

Does she look . . . know the worst!: this conversation as to the appearance of the bride-to-be was added to printer's copy for E1 and revised in the galleys.

Old Andrey's Experiences as a Musician

This short piece is not in the MS.

192 *the archdeacon, Lord and Lady Baxby*: this detailing of the visitors was added in the galleys for E1, as too was the other reference to the archdeacon below. The name Baxby appears also in *A Group of Noble Dames* and *The Woodlanders* and is associated with the Digby family.

193 *Giant o' Cernel*: the Cerne Abbas Giant, which is cut into the chalk on the hill above Cerne Abbas, Dorset.

194 *the organ*: MS has 'harmonium' deleted, with 'seraphina' written above and 'organ' below.

Absent-Mindedness in a Parish Choir

193 *Hornhead*: 'Muggeridge' in MS, where no oboe is mentioned.

The Tinker's Arms: MS has 'in the servants' hall', playing 'wi' united instruments'.

196 *Levi Limpet*: Levi Drummell in MS, where he deliberately misleads them into playing a dance rather than a church tune.

Sodom and Gomorrah: cities destroyed by fire from heaven because of their wickedness (Genesis 18: 20 and 19: 24–9).

The Winters and the Palmleys

The beginning of the story is missing in MS. An earlier title 'The history of Jack Winter' is deleted on fo. 28a (originally part of fo. 3) after a 'II' which shows that Hardy briefly considered placing the story as the second section of the collection. In MS Jack checks that the letters are in the box upon reaching home (and a deleted sentence shows Hardy's original intention was for him also to burn them at that point). No aunt is mentioned; instead it is Harriet's father who influences her not to speak up on Jack's behalf. Hardy's note to himself at the end of the MS fragment is: 'N. B. the person who tells this must be an old inhabitant.' (He uses the *aged* groceress.)

199 *Exonbury*: Exeter.

200 *Monksbury*: Abbotsbury.

205 *turnpike-road*: in MS, Holway lane.

206 *Longpuddle*: MS has Kings Hintock.

> *He was the only son . . . a widow*: Luke 7: 12.

> *a distant town*: MS has Lewgate.

Incident in the Life of Mr George Crookhill

MS is incomplete, the beginning of the story being missing (although a magazine reproduction survives of a later draft of the first page; which, to judge from the closeness of its text to the printed text, may well have been printer's copy). A sentence on the verso of a sheet shows that the story at one time was to have followed 'Absent-Mindedness in a Parish Choir'. Hardy writes a lengthy note to himself suggesting an alternative story-line, in which, instead of Georgy stealing the 'young farmer's' clothes, the young farmer claims to be not only rich but also given to benevolence towards the poor. When Georgy wakes up, the man has gone, taking Georgy's old clothes and horse and leaving his own clothes (labelled 'done in charity') and young horse. After Georgy leaves the inn, soldiers arrive looking for a deserter and are directed after Georgy by the landlord.

The germ of the story was a report in the *Dorset County Chronicle*, 2 April 1829, of an army deserter arrested in the clothes of the gentleman at whose house he had slept.

207 *Melchester*: Salisbury; in MS 'Shottsford' is deleted for the first appearance of the name in this story.

> *miserable screw*: a broken-down horse.

> *Bissett Hill*: on the Salisbury to Blandford road south of Coombe Bissett. MS also has the deleted form, 'Raceground Hill'.

Shottsford-Forum: Blandford Forum.

Woodyates Inn: a coach-inn, now demolished, 10 miles SW of Salisbury on the Dorchester road.

Trantridge: the name suggests Pentridge, but that was a mile off the highway and lacked an inn. Pinion and Kay-Robinson identify it with Tarrant Hinton. MS has Tranton.

211 *Dragoons at Cheltenham*: MS has 'the 151st D. G. at Budmouth'.

the remarkable . . . the ordinary: cf. Hardy's remarks, dated February 1893, in *Life* (p. 252): 'A story must be exceptional enough to justify its telling. We tale-tellers are all Ancient Mariners, and none of us is warranted in stopping Wedding Guests (in other words, the hurrying public) unless he has something more unusual to relate than the ordinary experience of every average man and woman.

'The whole secret of fiction and the drama—in the constructional part—lies in the adjustment of things unusual to things eternal and universal. The writer who knows exactly how exceptional, and how non-exceptional, his events should be made, possesses the key to the art.'

Netty Sargent's Copyhold

At one stage in the development of 'A Few Crusted Characters' Hardy had intended this to be the first story not the last (the first leaf of the story, now fo. 28a, has been cut away from the bottom of fo. 3, and deleted foliation on the story's other leaves follows on from that). In MS Netty is at first 'Susan', then 'Lucy', then 'Netty'; she lives with her father, but this changes to her uncle at the point where Netty is struck with her idea; her suitor is named James Cliffe; the story is told by Robert the Parish Clerk not by Mr Day the Painter; the title is 'The history of <Sus> Lucy Serjeant', with 'strange trick' written as an alternative above 'history'; and the very end of the story is not extant.

212 *copyhold—granted upon lives*: a similar arrangement attaches to the house of Marty South's father in *The Woodlanders*.

214 *opened his eyelids a bit*: this detail is added in E1 galleys.

216 *Every virtue . . . repented of her pains*: this little irony was added to the text for E1.

217 *head-stones . . . easily decipherable*: this section of MS is not extant, but most of the names listed as being on the head-stones are written on the verso of what is now the last sheet of the MS. According to Kay-Robinson (p. 126) 'they are not names in the registers of the real churches'.

DIALECT GLOSSARY

Excluded from the list are words whose non-standard pronunciations are indicated by Hardy, but whose meaning should be clear (such as 'pa'son', 've'se', ''scaped', 'oncontrollable', 'knowed', 'hosses', and 'half-chawed').

bain't   are not
busted   burst
chiel   child
Chok' it all   choke it all [an oath]
clane   clean
'ee   you
en   him [hear'n = hear him]
jineral   general
j'ined   joined, married
kick up a bit of a miff   quarrel, take offence
laylock   lilac
leery   hungry
linhay   a shed or open building, generally with a lean-to roof and an open front
mid   might
nunch   lunch
nunny-watch   a state of confusion, a quandary
nuss   nurse
oi   yes
oneyer   a rare one
'ooman   woman
raft   upset, rouse
seed   saw
sojers   soldiers
sparrer   sparrow
in too much of a taking   too agitated
tay   tea
tole   entice
totties   toes
wambling   wandering about aimlessly, tottering
whe'r   whether
winder   window

A SELECTION OF   **OXFORD WORLD'S CLASSICS**

HANS CHRISTIAN ANDERSEN	**Fairy Tales**
J. M. BARRIE	**Peter Pan in Kensington Gardens** and **Peter and Wendy**
L. FRANK BAUM	**The Wonderful Wizard of Oz**
FRANCES HODGSON BURNETT	**The Secret Garden**
LEWIS CARROLL	**Alice's Adventures in Wonderland** and **Through the Looking-Glass**
CARLO COLLODI	**The Adventures of Pinocchio**
KENNETH GRAHAME	**The Wind in the Willows**
THOMAS HUGHES	**Tom Brown's Schooldays**
CHARLES KINGSLEY	**The Water-Babies**
GEORGE MACDONALD	**The Princess and the Goblin** and **The Princess and Curdie**
EDITH NESBIT	**Five Children and It** **The Railway Children**
ANNA SEWELL	**Black Beauty**
JOHANN DAVID WYSS	**The Swiss Family Robinson**

THE OXFORD SHERLOCK HOLMES

ARTHUR CONAN DOYLE   **The Adventures of Sherlock Holmes**
The Case-Book of Sherlock Holmes
His Last Bow
The Hound of the Baskervilles
The Memoirs of Sherlock Holmes
The Return of Sherlock Holmes
The Valley of Fear
Sherlock Holmes Stories
The Sign of the Four
A Study in Scarlet

The Oxford World's Classics Website

www.worldsclassics.co.uk

- Information about new titles
- Explore the full range of Oxford World's Classics
- Links to other literary sites and the main OUP webpage
- Imaginative competitions, with bookish prizes
- Peruse *Compass*, the Oxford World's Classics magazine
- Articles by editors
- Extracts from Introductions
- A forum for discussion and feedback on the series
- Special information for teachers and lecturers

www.worldsclassics.co.uk

American Literature

British and Irish Literature

Children's Literature

Classics and Ancient Literature

Colonial Literature

Eastern Literature

European Literature

History

Medieval Literature

Oxford English Drama

Poetry

Philosophy

Politics

Religion

The Oxford Shakespeare

A complete list of Oxford Paperbacks, including Oxford World's Classics, OPUS, Past Masters, Oxford Authors, Oxford Shakespeare, Oxford Drama, and Oxford Paperback Reference, is available in the UK from the Academic Division Publicity Department, Oxford University Press, Great Clarendon Street, Oxford OX2 6DP.

In the USA, complete lists are available from the Paperbacks Marketing Manager, Oxford University Press, 198 Madison Avenue, New York, NY 10016.

Oxford Paperbacks are available from all good bookshops. In case of difficulty, customers in the UK can order direct from Oxford University Press Bookshop, Freepost, 116 High Street, Oxford OX1 4BR, enclosing full payment. Please add 10 per cent of published price for postage and packing.